MAY 1997

SLAVERY AND FREEDOM
IN THE RURAL NORTH

Published in cooperation with the
Friends of the Monmouth County Park System
with support from the
New Jersey Historical Commission

SLAVERY AND FREEDOM

in the Rural North

*African Americans in Monmouth
County, New Jersey, 1665–1865*

GRAHAM RUSSELL HODGES

MADISON HOUSE

Madison 1997

LIBRARY OF CONGRESS CATALOGING-IN-PUBLICATION DATA

Hodges, Graham Russell, 1946–
Slavery and freedom in the rural North : African Americans in Monmouth
County, New Jersey, 1665–1865 / Graham Russell Hodges. — 1st ed.
p.   cm.
Includes bibliographical references (p.   ) and index.
ISBN 0-945612-43-5 (alk. paper). — ISBN 0-945612-51-6 (pbk. : alk. paper)
1. Afro-Americans—New Jersey—Monmouth County—History.
2. Slavery—New Jersey—Monmouth County—History.
3. Free Afro-Americans—New Jersey—Monmouth County—History.
4. Monmouth County (N.J.)—History.   I. Title.
F142.M7H66   1996
974.9'4600496073—DC20   96–19334
CIP

Designed by Gregory M. Britton
Printed on acid free paper in the United States of America

Published by Madison House Publishers, Inc.
P.O. Box 3100, Madison, Wisconsin 53704

FIRST EDITION

CONTENTS

Dedicated to the memory of
James Creel
(September 2, 1975–June 18, 1994)
rasta scholar, spiritual traveler, beloved stepson

FOREWORD

While most historical writing originates in colleges and universities, the practice of history takes place in communities across the land, and reaches the public through local organizations and government agencies. This project was born of a desire to bridge academic scholarship and local public history objectives. Each year hundreds of people attend the exhibitions, lectures, and performances of Monmouth County Park System's African American History Celebration. Outside of this annual event, however, the long history of African Americans in this area is largely absent from historical publications and commemorations. Searching to expand available material on an unstudied area of our past, and cognizant that Monmouth County would provide fertile ground for exploring the larger subject of the African American experience in the rural North, Jane Clark and I commissioned Graham Hodges to deliver two lectures on the early history of African Americans in Monmouth County. The positive response to the resulting papers, originally presented at the African American History Celebration and distributed in booklet form, ultimately led to this larger study. Fortunately this project has had the generous financial support of the New Jersey Historical Commission from initial research to final publication, as well as the sponsorship of the Friends of the Monmouth County Park System. These partnerships have enabled author Graham Hodges, the Monmouth County Park System, and Madison House to collaborate on the making of this book. The result contributes to a greater understanding of our African American heritage.

Gail Hunton, Historian
Monmouth County Park System
Lincroft, New Jersey

ACKNOWLEDGMENTS

This book is a heavily revised and expanded version of two pamphlets originally published by the Monmouth County Park System. The park system sponsored the original lectures and publication of this material for its award-winning African American History Celebration. Chapter three includes material drawn from my article, "Black Revolt in New York and the Neutral Zone, 1775–1783," in Paul A. Gilje and William Pencak, eds., *New York in the Age of the Constitution* and is used by permission.

Numerous helping hands made this book possible. First I wish to thank the archivists at the New Jersey State Library and Archives in Trenton, the New Jersey Historical Society, the Monmouth County Archives, the Monmouth County Historical Association, Special Collections at the Alexander Library, Rutgers University, the rare book room at Olin Library, Cornell University, the William L. Clements Library at the University of Michigan, and the New-York Historical Society. Betty Epstein, Ronald Becker, Gary Saretsky, Mary Ann Kiernan, and Donald Sinclair were especially helpful. Several local historians were of great assistance including Joseph Hammond, Mauro Baldanza, Joseph Felcone, Ellen Morris, Phyllis Mount, Randall Gabrielan, and Pat Drummond.

I am deeply grateful to Douglas Egerton of Lemoyne College and Ira Berlin of the University of Maryland–College Park for their searching criticisms of full drafts of this manuscript. This work is decidedly better for their efforts. Thanks are due to David Hughes and Ann Ackerson of the interlibrary loan staff of Colgate's Case Library for patience and speedy delivery of important primary materials. Susan and Marshall Swartzburg of Princeton, New Jersey, offered warm hospitality on several of my visits. My students at Colgate deserve special applause. David Stradling, Jack Ruppert III, and Peter Shaw performed yeoman service with census manuscripts. Alan Brown did an outstanding job preparing the tables which consolidate much of the information in this book. Greg Britton of Madison House performed his editorial chores with cheer and encouragement. My parents, Graham and Elsie Hodges, assisted as only they can. At the Monmouth County Park System, Jane Clark and Gail Hunton gave unstintingly of time and effort. Gail's contribution to this book is enormous. She faithfully shepherded the project through many drafts, obtained a valuable publication grant from the New Jersey Historical Commission, and worked hard at finding illustrations for the book. This book, in my view, epitomizes the best kind of collaboration between public agencies and historians.

My wife, Margaret Washington, of Cornell University offered a complete critique of the book which was immensely helpful. My step-daughter, Celeste Creel, came to the talks at Monmouth and provided constant good cheer. My late stepson James Creel, also came to the presentations in Monmouth. When the four of us explored the cemetery at Clinton Chapel (A.M.E. Zion) in Middletown, Monmouth, he discovered a ceramic pipe adorning a grave. It was an exciting revelation for James, who, at fifteen, was an emerging student of history ever aware of the African heritage in America. Little did we know that James would soon join his ancestors. His spirit pervades this book.

INTRODUCTION

According to a recent survey, American historians overwhelmingly regard slavery as the darkest blot on America's past. The modern literature on slavery is correspondingly large, but the bulk of these studies concentrate on the plantation South, where most African Americans dwelled in the antebellum years. The saga of African Americans in the North has received only passing attention. A recent overview of slavery, for example, mentions New Jersey only twice.[1]

Slowly, long neglect is being superseded by interest, evident in innovative works by scholars such as Gary B. Nash, William Pierson, Jean Soderlund, Billy G. Smith, A. J. Williams-Meyers, Thelma Wills Foote, and Shane White. Their new studies broaden our understanding of the transition of urban slaves into freedom in the port cities of the North.[2] Meanwhile, the experiences of their rural counterparts remain largely hidden from history. This study attempts to address that gap, to enlarge our understanding of early rural black life in the North.[3]

Monmouth County, New Jersey, makes an excellent subject for such study because it had one of the largest rural black populations in the mid-Atlantic region. Its history offers insights into the conditions of rural black life in the North, from the first slave settlements in the seventeenth century to the final abolition of slavery under the Thirteenth Amendment in 1865. As the circumstances of agricultural laborers, both bonded and free, tell much about their material conditions and the society into which they were thrust, this history illustrates, more broadly, important themes about slavery and freedom in early America.

Slavery was, of course, no monolith, no mere abstraction whose particulars, regarding either place or time, may be readily inferred from andecdotal or analytical evidence of a single county. Yet slavery depended for its perpetuation on a core of assumptions and practices as solid as shackles themselves. Whether slavery is characterized as "mild," as by Nash for colonial Pennsylvania, or "harsh," as by White for post-revolutionary New York, the modern institution rests on economic and political assumptions that deny not merely the equality but indeed the humanity of the enslaved. Once one accepts the humanity of bondspeople, it matters little whether its denial is expressed through outright brutality (most famously on large plantations but also on small farms), through enforced isolation from family (commonly on Monmouth's farms), or through a dozen laws designed to render fruitless every effort to make a better world for one's children. Thus, while local recollections of slavery in Monmouth County refer to its mildness, the reality seems different.[4]

Monmouth County in colonial, Revolutionary, and antebellum times typifed the small-farm economy that prevailed then in the rural North. Few farms in the county exceeded 500 acres. On these farms masters, enslaved blacks, and free white and black laborers worked side by side. Such shared experiences might be expected to nurture feelings of solidarity. In practice, however, slavery in Monmouth's countryside fostered a fierce and rigid racial hierarchy. African Americans there lacked such mitigating urban influences as antislavery leaders and early access to schools. Instead, they found themselves vital to but bound by a monocultural economy regulated by whites generally more hostile than their city brethren. Slavery and freedom were experienced in ways vastly different from the cities. The hardscrabble achievements of Monmouth's blacks, though slower to accumulate than those of their city cousins, are therefore all the more striking.

Restrictive legislation, economic obstacles, and the self-interest of slaveholders insured that free blacks were rare in colonial Monmouth County. That changed with the American Revolution. In its aftermath the local free black class grew steadily, though under onerous conditions. Study of Monmouth's black life allows us to observe the full transition from enslavement through gradual emancipation, with its steady accretion of civil rights, to enfranchisement of black males under the Fifteenth Amendment in 1870. Within a durable architecture of oppression found in the North, Monmouth County's rural blacks slowly constructed an edifice of freedom based upon family, church, and land ownership.[5]

They did this in the most heterogeneous county of New Jersey, itself the most ethnically diverse American colony during the eighteenth century. There, beginning in the late 1660s, English, Huguenot, Dutch, and Scots-Irish immigrants vied for land with migrating Long Islanders and New Englanders. Africans' acculturation to the New World differed with each nationality they encountered.[6] Ethnicity was nowhere more clearly manifested than in religious preferences. The plethora of Protestant denominations in Monmouth included the established Anglican and Reformed Dutch churches and the dissident Society of Friends, Congregationalists, Huguenots, Presbyterians, Baptists, and Methodists.

The activities of these sects affected blacks in several ways. First, some declared slavery a grand Christian adventure, a boon to brutes and heathens who should be grateful for opportunities to study and practice saintly virtues. Second, slaves recognized many of Christianity's saintly virtues to be familiar African beliefs conveyed in European tongues; evangelical sects thus provided a beachhead from which blacks could claim cultural territory of their own.

The efforts of the proslavery sects were spearheaded by the Anglican Church, which lobbied for a 1704 law that carefully separated civil freedom from baptism, ostensibly removing any grounds for fearing that catechized bondspeople could demand emancipation as Christians. The effect of this law in Monmouth County was diluted later, when a dissident sect, the Society of Friends, found slavery to be in conflict with their basic tenets; Quakers became early and vocal abolitionists. While whites quarrelled over the proper place of slavery in Christian society, Monmouth became home to at least four distinct types of African American religious experience. These melded into an autonomous African American theology in the early nineteenth century.[7]

This study presents the African American experience in Monmouth County chronologically. Chapter 1 traces the establishment of small-farm slavery in the initial decades of settlement, from the legal institution of slavery by English rulers in 1665 to the full codification of slavery in the laws of 1704. To avoid repetition later, demographic data about blacks across the entire colonial era is merged in this chapter. Such information, I believe, helps define the parameters of local black experience.

Chapter 2 covers the latter half of the colonial era, from the final codification of slavery in New Jersey (1714) until the eve of the American Revolution (1775). This chapter examines work and home life, covering such topics as family size, relations with masters and mistresses, and an emerging black culture. Monmouth County was not the scene of major slave conspiracies or uprisings; its bond people resisted through flight and crime. Runaway notices for the county offer candid "snapshots" of the physical characteristics, clothing, personalities, and skills of at least an important portion of the county's enslaved people.[8]

The history of blacks in Monmouth County pivots on their role in the American Revolution, told in chapter 3. I first discovered Monmouth's fascinating black past through study of

Colonel Tye's guerrilla activities, which terrorized Monmouth residents in 1780. Many other local blacks, both enslaved and free, fled with the British army as it passed through, going behind British lines into New York City and thence to Nova Scotia, London, and Africa after the war. Of the African Americans who stayed behind, some were shuffled by the confiscation of Loyalist property after 1777; others were manumitted by slaveholders who, in increasing numbers, heeded Quaker antislavery appeals.

The second half of this study examines the gradual abolition of slavery in New Jersey and the growth of Monmouth's black community. As chapter 4 illustrates, the era between the close of the American Revolution in 1783 and the passage of gradual emancipation in 1804 was tumultuous. The Revolution did not end slavery in New Jersey. In fact, the number of humans in bondage increased throughout East New Jersey in the last decades of the eighteenth century.

Chapter 5 describes the continued strength of slavery in New Jersey in the years between 1804, when the gradual emancipation act was passed, and 1825, when its mandates were first effected. Recent scholars have demonstrated that slavery in New York and Pennsylvania was a vigorous institution well after the onset of gradual emancipation. In New Jersey slavery was abolished with even greater reluctance, persisting, as Simeon Moss showed many years ago, until the Civil War. During the years before 1825 relatively small numbers of blacks gained freedom within the state's conservative political and economic structure.[9]

Chapter 6 tells the story of Monmouth's African Americans between 1830 and the Civil War era, when they finally achieved citizenship and complete emancipation. The last decades before the war saw blacks shut out of civil society and barred from voting or holding office. In response, African Americans bonded together, creating churches, schools, newspapers, and benevolent societies. Their hard-won community culture, based on land ownership, church membership, and family formation, sustained

them for decades to come.[10] An epilogue to this study reveals
the legacies of freedom and slavery in Monmouth County.

Notes

1. For a survey, see *Journal of American History* 81 (1994): 1212.
For a synthetic history neglecting New Jersey, see Peter Kolchin, *American Slavery, 1619–1877* (New York, 1993).

2. For apposite studies, see Gary B. Nash, *Forging Freedom: The Formation of Philadelphia's Black Community, 1720–1840* (Cambridge, Mass., 1988); Gary B. Nash and Jean Soderlund, *Freedom by Degrees: Emancipation in Pennsylvania and Its Aftermath* (New York, 1991); Billy G. Smith, *The "Lower Sort": Philadelphia's Laboring People, 1750–1800* (Ithaca, N.Y., 1990); Shane White, *Somewhat More Independent: The End of Slavery in New York City, 1770–1810* (Athens, Ga., 1991); Thelma Wills Foote, "Black Life in Colonial Manhattan, 1664–1786" (Ph.D. diss., Harvard University, 1991); William D. Piersen, *Black Yankees: The Development of an Afro-American Subculture in Eighteenth-Century New England* (Amherst, Mass., 1988); A. J. Williams-Meyers, *Long Hammering: Essays on the Forging of an African American Presence in the Hudson River Valley to the Early Twentieth Century* (Trenton, 1994). For a seminal discussion of free black life in the North, see Ira Berlin, "The Structure of the Free Negro Caste in the Antebellum United States," *Journal of Social History* 9 (1976): 297–318.

3. Rural black life receives some attention in Nash and Soderlund, *Freedom by Degrees*, 33–37, 183–91; White, *Somewhat More Independent*, 51–53; Richard Shannon Moss, *Slavery on Long Island: A Study in Local Institutional and Early African-American Communal Life* (New York, 1993); Williams-Myers, *Long Hamering*; and in Vivienne L. Kruger, "Born to Run: The Slave Family in Early New York, 1626–1827" (Ph.D. diss., Columbia University, 1985).

4. Nash, *Forging Freedom*, 11–12; White, *Somewhat More Independent*, 80–113.

5. For the utility of this approach, see Ira Berlin, "Time, Space, and the Transformation of Afro-American Society in the United States," in *Autre temps, autre espace: Études sur l'Amérique préindustrielle*, ed. Elise Marienstras and Barbara Karsky (Nancy, 1986), 131–46.

6. For the importance of ethnicity in New Jersey, see most recently Peter O. Wacker and Paul G. E. Clemens, *Land Use in Early*

New Jersey: A Historical Geography (Newark, 1995), 44. For a call for study of interaction of blacks and Dutch, see Joyce D. Goodfriend, "The Historiography of the Dutch in Colonial America," in *Colonial Dutch Studies: An Interdisciplinary Approach*, ed. Eric Nooter and Patricia U. Bonomi (New York, 1988), 8.

7. Monmouth's black religious past is a good test of Jon Butler's contention that Africans suffered a religious holocaust in the early eighteenth century. See Jon Butler, *Awash in a Sea of Faith: Christianizing the American People* (Cambridge, Mass., 1990), 12–164.

8. See Graham Russell Hodges and Alan Edward Brown, eds., *"Pretends to be Free": Fugitive Slave Advertisements from Colonial and Revolutionary New York and New Jersey* (New York, 1994).

9. For New Jersey, see Simeon Moss, "The Persistence of Slavery in a Free State," *Journal of Negro History* 35 (1950): 289–314. For general study of emancipation in the North, see Arthur Zilversmit, *The First Emancipation: The Abolition of Slavery in the North* (Chicago, 1967). For a brief coverage of black life in Monmouth in this period, see Lenora Walker McKay, *The Blacks of Monmouth County: A Bicentennial Tribute* (n.p., 1976).

10. Here I am using the term *community culture* to emphasize the importance of religion in a slave society, as argued in Margaret Washington Creel, *"A Peculiar People": Slave Religion and Community-Culture Among the Gullahs* (New York, 1988), 1–3; see also Darrett Rutman, "Community Study," *Historical Methods* 13 (1980), 29–41.

1

The Creation of a
Slave Society
1664–1714

onmouth County, the shoulder of New Jersey's
coastal plain, reaches from Raritan Bay on its north-
eastern extremity, past the Navesink and Shrewsbury
rivers, to Metedeconk's Atlantic outlet at the southeast, and
inland as far west as Allentown. The county saddles the inner
and outer coastal plains of New Jersey. The fertile sandy clay-
and-marl soil of the inner plain, initially thought to be infertile,
proved capable of supporting a prosperous, slave-based agricultural society during the colonial and post-Revolutionary eras.
The outer coastal plain, located primarily in the county's southern portions, lacks clay and supports agriculture only along
higher elevations. During the colonial era the coast from Sandy
Hook southward, too marshy for good harbors, supported a
small maritime economy, including fishing and whaling. Behind
the sandy beaches and marshes lay the pine barrens, which originally covered much of southern Monmouth.

The Dutch claimed the region, from 1615, as part of New
Netherland. However, the ten thousand colonists who settled
New Netherland between 1623 and 1664 moved north and south

of Monmouth County, either to New Amsterdam (Manhattan), Long Island, or strategic waterways like the lower Hudson and Delaware rivers. Monmouth County's modern history stems from the English conquest of Dutch New Netherland in August 1664. On October 28 of that year a coalition of Quakers and Baptists from Long Island and Rhode Island purchased from the Leni Lenape Indians a tract of land reaching from Sandy Hook westward to the Raritan River and southward from that line for twelve miles. On April 8, 1665, Richard Nicholls, appointed by the Duke of York to be New York's first governor, gave legal recognition to this purchase by issuing the settlers a patent on the tract, the terms of which granted them a degree of autonomy within the larger political context of New York. The Quakers and Baptists immediately set to work establishing two towns, Middletown and Shrewsbury.[1]

The Long Islanders among them came from an area that had, over a period of four decades under Dutch rule, become increasingly dependent on slave labor. Now, under English rule, slavery was formally recognized in New York through the so-called Duke's Laws, promulgated on February 10, 1665 to govern the colony's English-speaking communities. If the Duke's Laws encouraged servitude, the Monmouth Patent virtually dictated it. Key among its features are clauses that required settlers to maintain "an able Man servant or two such weaker Servants" and that granted additional acreage to masters with more servants. Another clause permitted land grants only to "Christian Servants," hampering acquisitions by free blacks and Indians who had not converted.[2]

To those able to meet these requirements, the terms of the Monmouth Patent were intentionally liberal and tolerant. Settlers received farms averaging over 200 acres, a figure that compares favorably with, say, the modest patents of seventy-five acres allotted the Dutch settlers of Bergen County. Moreover, as the

Thomas Gordon, Map of the State of New Jersey, 1834 (detail showing Monmouth County). Courtesy of Monmouth County Historical Association.

original purchasers themselves represented more than one Protestant denomination, it was clear from the outset that Monmouth
would have sectarian sympathies as ecumenical as those of Rhode
Island.

In general, small agricultural communities characterized the
county's early development. Town centers were composed of
churches, mills, and taverns surrounded by dispersed, independent farms. Similar communities developed in the eighteenth
century. For instance, Upper Freehold, in the southwestern cor-
ner of the county, coalesced from a scattering of tiny villages
settled around 1700. These patterns of habitation broadly affected
black families. Divided among farmsteads spread across the landscape, blacks were close enough to retain ties yet inconveniently
distant from each other.

Ethnic Composition of Early Monmouth County

A diverse group of masters from other origins and denominations joined the Quakers and Baptists in developing the
Monmouth Patent. Among the first were Barbadians, often the
younger sons of planters, who could bring their African chattel
with them secure in the knowledge that the Duke's Laws recognized slavery. Immigrants from the West Indies were joined
by Huguenots and Presbyterians attracted by favorable land
grants and religious tolerance. The "servants" these settlers brought
were an equally diverse lot, some African, some Native American, some European. Whether by reason of race, language, country, or class, they were sure to differ from their masters in beliefs
and customs, thus further enriching the county's ethnic base.

After November 25, 1672, when the Duke of York annulled
the Monmouth Patent, this social diversity was increased. Until
then Monmouth residents had had a basis for claiming exemp-

tion from the laws of New Jersey, which required landowners to pay quitrents. To eliminate this basis was one of the annulment's intended effects. Another effect, perhaps unintended but no less important to the county's destiny, was to bring the Monmouth Patent under the more relaxed codes for immigration and residence found elsewhere in New Jersey (from 1684, East Jersey). Still, by the first decades of the eighteenth century only a minority of the county's freeholders were slaveholders.

The true ethnic multiplicity of Monmouth's earliest immigrants is partly disguised by conventional labels. While the Dutch, who migrated into Monmouth from Kings County (Brooklyn) in the 1690s were the most widely known ethnic group and well-represented among slave-owning families, other groups were present within the initial settlements. Thus, Spanish, Germans, and French were among the "Dutch" who emigrated from Holland, and Scots embarked from disparate clans and counties.[3] Blacks arriving in the middle colonies in the late seventeenth century similarly originated from a wide spectrum of societies along Africa's western coast or, after a brief "seasoning," from the West Indies.

Once in Monmouth County, whites and blacks melded into parallel charter societies even as they retained older cultural mores.[4] Part of this melding was achieved through intermarriage. It goes without saying that Africans, cast into this frontier in sparse and scattered lots, could scarcely expect easy access to partners from their own nations. Yet even among Dutch, English, and Huguenot families, intermarriage dissolved, generation by generation, ethnic dissimilarities. This was indicative of Monmouth's religious tolerance, for elsewhere the Dutch, at least, rarely intermarried. As white families expanded, intermarriage meant that slave owners throughout the county often were related. For example, family records indicate continual intermarriages between the (English) Holmeses and (Dutch)

Hendricksons, two of the largest slaveholding families in the county. Huguenot families also intermarried with other groups.

Socializing also crossed ethnic boundaries. Tavern licenses and account books for Monmouth show drinking and carousing across ethnic groups. Such relationships greatly enhanced social controls over slaves because bondpeoples could rarely circulate anonymously.[5] Not that they did not try. Among the early statutes of East Jersey was an act forbidding any person to buy, sell, or barter "with slaves" for any "rum, brandy, wine, or strong drink."[6] In this, as in many other things, African Americans were increasingly being defined as a caste apart.

Establishment of a Slave Economy in Monmouth

Of course, it is not surprising if *any* slave—regardless of color—be seen as something or someone other. In New Netherland, from which many of Monmouth's slaveholders came, slavery seems to have been predicated on the assumption that non-Christians, especially those taken in battle, could ethically be held in bondage. Such were the Native Americans taken as slaves and also, presumably, the Africans sold to Dutch slavers by rival nations.

The Dutch, who together with the Portuguese then dominated the world slave trade, used Africans from the outset to develop a viable infrastructure in New Netherland—clearing forests or building roads, fortifications, and public works.[7] But in a frontier where the cost of importing provisions was enormous, slaves performed no service more valuable than undertaking the arduous work of breaking new sod, tilling stony soil, and raising crops. Evidence of this value appears in a directive of March 1660 from the city council of Amsterdam to Peter Stuyvesant, director of New Amsterdam. The council, aware that the costs of provisions for New Amsterdam's growing garrison were becoming onerous, transferred some slaves from Curaçao to the colony, explaining to Stuyvesant that "agriculture would be beneficially promoted by Negroes, . . . and the prosperity of [New Netherland] is, for the most part, dependent thereon."[8] Four years later Stuyvesant requested more slaves, writing, "These Negroes have afforded a great relief in the purchase of provisions for the Garrison. . . . We [now] have a great need for a few slaves to truck the provisions."[9]

The "need" for slaves in developing Monmouth's first farms was no less evident to its purchasers. The terms of the Monmouth Patent required individual settlers to bring one or two slaves or indentured servants. Help was essential in every phase of settlement, beginning with the initial construction of homes. The first homes were not log cabins, but tents and dugouts. Richard Hartshorne, an early settler and slave owner, wrote that it was important to have three or four sons or servants to cut timber and plant corn quickly. Settlers and their slaves dug square pits in the ground, cellar fashion, six or seven feet deep, and as long and broad as feasible. Wooden foundations lined with bark kept out soil. Next the cellar was covered by a floor, followed by walls, and then a roof of spars insulated by bark and green sod. In this crude hut lived the master, his family and the slaves. Such homes served for several years until the sale of good harvests permitted larger dwellings.

The next task was clearing the land of dense foliage and trees. Settlers borrowed girdling and burning methods from Native Americans. Girdling was done by making an incision though the bark around the trunk, leaving the tree to die. Knowledgeable observers advised settlers to arrive in April in order to spend the summer clearing land and building homes. Hartshorne described the best crops as Indian corn and maize, rye, barley, oats and flax, all of which required extensive farm labor.[10]

Unfortunately, there are few records for assessing the purchase and use of slaves for agriculture in Monmouth County.

Farmers in Monmouth doubtless were important customers of the slave traders. But lists of purchasers survive infrequently and imports were spread over a wide region, so that the exact extent of Monmouth County's participation in the seventeenth-century slave trade cannot be precisely fixed.

Perhaps even less is known about the influx of indentured servants into the county. That they were present from an early stage is suggested by a 1683 East Jersey statute "against aiding runaway servants," occasioned specifically by cases in Shrewsbury.[11] The continued presence of indentured servants in Monmouth is suggested by the notices of white runaways from New Jersey, which began to appear with the establishment of newspapers in the early eighteenth century. Early colonists were also willing to pay contract workers from Europe, luring them with advertisements such as one aimed at prospective Scots-Irish immigrants which maintained that "ordinary servants" after laboring six or seven years could, with thrifty behavior, attain the "beginnings of a Comfortable Lively-hood." While indentured and hired labor continued to play a role throughout colonial times, in the end it was slavery that grew.[12]

Small farms meant small slave holdings. Of ten estate inventories listing slaves and recorded for Shrewsbury between 1680 and 1710, the average holding was less than two slaves per estate. Accordingly, while there were occasional deliveries of twenty or more slaves to the Monmouth region, most imports into eastern New Jersey arrived in small lots. The emphasis in single-slave transactions was on younger, healthy slaves, who probably had been in the West Indies only a few years, given the overwhelming human turnover in the islands. There was a reverse trade as well. New Jersey slaveholders occasionally shipped bondspeople back to the West Indies. For example, Daniel Hendrickson paid £10 to transport two young African men for sale in Martinique.[13]

Between 1718 and 1764, 480 slaves from the West Indies were imported into Perth Amboy, located in Middlesex County a few miles from Monmouth. This total averages about ten per year, and not all went to Monmouth. Similarly, slaves imported into Philadelphia, which supplied Upper Freehold, came in small parcels, with few exceptional years, until the Seven Years' War in the 1750s.[14]

In the early eighteenth century, mid-Atlantic masters began purchasing large contingents of slaves directly imported from Africa. Seven large shipments of Africans to New York and New Jersey arrived between 1715 and 1734, all from the "Coast of Guinea." The *Dragon, New York Postilion,* and the *Catherine and Mary* docked in New York City within three weeks of each other, the last two on the same day, September 12, 1717. The three vessels brought a total of 266 slaves. The next vessel arriving directly from Africa, the *Crown Galley* of London, docked on June 5, 1721. In 1725 fifty-nine slaves arrived from Africa in a Rhode Island slaver. The *Catherine,* owned by John Watts of New York City and Arnot Schuyler, a large slaveholder in Bergen County, arrived in Perth Amboy in the summer of 1731, and in New York a few weeks later. Two years later the *Catherine* returned with a second load of 100 slaves, docking at Perth Amboy and then New York City. Monmouth County farmers purchased many of these slaves in Perth Amboy just before the harvest.[15]

Ironically, the first real slave *community* in Monmouth was industrial rather than agricultural, being established at Lewis Morris's iron mine and forge at Tinton Falls, in Shrewsbury Township. There Morris brought about forty enslaved men and women in 1677. By the time of his death, in 1691, that number had increased to sixty-seven: his inventory of the plantation at Tinton Falls included "22 male Negroes, 11 women, 6 boys, 3 girls, and 25 children under ten years of unknown sex."

Because of its concentration of slaves, Tinton Falls was an

anomaly in Monmouth. Yet Morris's enterprise was important to Monmouth for two reasons (a third will be discussed later in this chapter). First, Morris employed both free white and enslaved African labor in his extensive operation, and he allotted the former special exemptions. Workmen, he decreed, were free from arrest for debt and from impressment into the militia. Morris also used white laborers as skilled labor and reserved hard physical labor for his Africans. Blacks and free white laborers lived in separate dormitories on the property. Naturally, these measures established unequal, race-based ranks among the laborers. In a society where the concept of servant implied bondage, such differentiation took on increasing weight as time passed.

The second reason for Tinton Falls' importance derives from the economic and political clout of the Morris family, several of whom became key ruling figures in colonial New Jersey. After the founder's death in 1691, his nephew, also named Lewis Morris, inherited the Tinton Falls plantation. A potent figure in the economy of New Jersey and its future governor, Morris's use of slavery set the tone for other Monmouth residents.[16]

The Character of Early Slaves

Enslaved Africans came into New York and New Jersey from Jamaica, Barbados, Curaçao, and Antigua, colonies characterized by intensive staple crop slave economies, heavy slave mortality, little cultural interaction between white and black beyond brutal management, and the retention of African culture. Each colony would experience powerful slave uprisings by the 1730s. Jamaica was unable to defeat or control its maroon population, and Barbados' and Antigua's slave revolts were repressed only by the savagery evident in New York City in 1712 and 1741. While Monmouth's slaveholders wanted healthy bondsmen, they had to accept and learn to control assertive young Africans.[17]

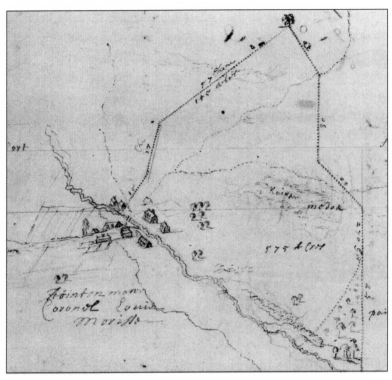

Map of Tinton Manor, Lewis Morris Plantation, c. 1695.
Courtesy of Monmouth County Historical Association.

Unquestionably Africans brought on the slave ships had a vast array of experiences. For many, brought directly from Africa in mass sales, the Middle Passage required immediate adaptation to new cultures. Part of this required unity among unrelated Africans. The diaspora created an Atlantic culture of many tongues.[18] The Middle Passage brutally married African identities with European and American cultures. Similarly, the West Indian slave trade, bringing blacks almost individually into New Jersey, propelled them into a polyglot society. Each person's reaction to this differed. Some found solace from their bondage in African mores; others mixed cultures, while a few doubtless followed the manners of their master's race.

Slave trading in small lots had unanticipated consequences. Blacks brought to New Jersey in small groups experienced very different passages from those imported by the hundreds. It can be presumed that ships bringing individual blacks from the West Indies used them as sailors or hands. Seafaring sometimes brought blacks into contact with sympathetic whites. Enslaved African men and white sailors, who were among the most notoriously egalitarian of early American workers, identified with each other's plight. As Orlando Patterson has reported, "Sailors and Negroes are ever on the most amicable terms." There was much "mutual confidence and familiarity between them . . . in the presence of the sailor, the Negro feels a man." Such experiences enabled a number of Monmouth slaves to hire out as seamen, or, if necessary, to escape by boat.[19]

Growth of Monmouth's Slave Population

By 1680 Shrewsbury and Middletown had a combined population of about 900, including about forty-eight slaves, accounting for 5.3 percent of the total county population, spread over a wide geographic area. This proportion is slightly smaller than the 5.9 percent slave population estimated for New Jersey generally and considerably smaller than the 12.2 percent slave population of Dutch-dominated New York. However, by 1691, there were sixty-seven slaves at Lewis Morris's Tinton Falls plantation south of Shrewsbury. Adding this number to the 1680 population brought the total number of enslaved blacks to at least 117. This increase raised the black percentage of East Jersey's population to 13 percent of the total, a figure which placed the colony fourth in British North American.[20]

Over the next hundred years the black population of colonial Monmouth grew steadily, as illustrated in Table 1. By 1726, the time of the first recorded census, Monmouth's black population had jumped to 433, the 258 male and 175 female blacks constituting almost 9 percent of the county's population. The next census, taken in 1737, showed a black population of 362 males and 293 females, accounting for nearly 10 percent of the local population. In 1745 the last surviving colonial census for East Jersey counted 513 enslaved males and 386 enslaved females, slightly more than 10 percent of the county's total population and the largest black population in East Jersey.

Assessors for the counties of East Jersey refused to complete a census in 1771, making impossible an accurate accounting of African Americans just before the Revolution. However, county constable Richard Stout did enumerate the adult slaves in Monmouth. Stout's total of 536 included 158 blacks in Freehold, 165 in Middletown, 97 in Shrewsbury, 9 in Dover, and 4 in Stafford. Stout counted only adult males and females, omitting slaves under the age of sixteen or those unable to work, which customarily meant anybody above forty years of age.[21] Demog-

Table 1
Population of Monmouth County, New Jersey, 1726–1784

	1726	1738	1745	1771	1784
White	4,446	5,431	7,728	9,840	11,576
Black	443	655	899	1,394	1,640
Total	4,879	6,086	8,627	11,234	13,216

All numbers except for those for 1771 come from the census of that year. The 1771 figures are estimates. See Evarts B. Greene and Virginia D. Harrington, *American Population before the Federal Census of 1790* (New York, 1932), 88–112; Peter O. Wacker, "Origins and Settlements," in *Land and People: A Cultural Geography of Preindustrial New Jersey* (New Brunswick, N.J., 1975), 189–205. For method used for the 1771 estimate, see Stella H. Sutherland, *Population Distribution in Colonial America* (New York, 1936), 98–99.

rapher Stella Sutherland estimated the white population of East Jersey for 1771 as 85 percent of the 1784 tax census. Applied to the black population, this method gives an estimate of 1,394 blacks in the county in 1771, a number in line with contemporary growth patterns in the colony.

By 1784, blacks in Monmouth numbered 1,640, or nearly four times the total of five decades earlier. During this span, the white population had only doubled. Although the white population remained larger, blacks remained important to rural society during the late colonial period.[22]

Factors in the Growth of the Slave Population

Two factors, the slave trade and natural reproduction, explain the growth of the black population of colonial Monmouth even as slave ownership was declining in northern cities. In the growth of its slave population, Monmouth County resembles the rural countryside around Philadelphia and New York City. However, Monmouth was more distinctly rural than those areas, and the steady growth of its slave society illustrates how valuable bonded labor was just before the Revolution.[23]

Some of the demand for new slaves was met, as has been seen, by the foreign slave trade. And in this New Jersey's colonial rulers helped by making the region a duty-free zone throughout most of the colonial period. Britain's governing bodies had two chief motivations for imposing no duty on slave imports. First, the Royal African Company wished to bolster imperial profits. Acceding to this wish, the English Privy Council regularly revoked any customs. For example, when in 1713 the assembly, more to raise revenues than to discourage slavery, ordered a £10 duty on any slave brought into New Jersey for purposes of sale, the Privy Council quickly disallowed the measure. In succeeding years New Jersey, like other colonies, resorted to temporary duties, but these lasted only until vetoed in London. Finally, the Privy Council, trying to halt such actions, ordered royal governors not to accept any legislation creating tariffs for slaves.[24]

Economic incentive worked with its usual efficacy. New Jersey and New York became attractive secondary markets for the African and West Indian slave trade in the early decades of the eighteen century. By the 1760s, New Jersey had also become an appealing market for Philadelphia slave traders.[25] Some of the trade was legitimate, but because New Jersey charged no duties on slaves, importers and masters from New York and Pennsylvania found it convenient to unload a small lot in Jersey, sell a few slaves locally, then smuggle the rest to the larger colonies.

The second motivation for eliminating tariffs on slaves was simply the demand of New Jersey's citizens for a ready supply of laborers. By the late 1720s the supply of free or contract laborers whom farmers could hire during harvests was quickly dwindling, as is suggested by the narrowing gap between numbers of white males and females. Some younger men were leaving Monmouth to seek cheaper, more accessible land elsewhere.[26] Others, according to members of New Jersey's assembly, had gone privateering in the West Indies, never to return. Those that remained charged exorbitant wages. Moreover, the success of the linen industry in Ireland and wars in Europe meant that traditional sources of white laborers had dried up.

Although the poorest of Europeans might still be willing to trade their freedom for passage to the New World, indentured servants had been tried and, in many instances, found wanting. Thus, Francis Harrison, a customs official and advocate of increased slavery in the mid-Atlantic colonies, found little interest among New Yorkers and East Jerseyans for indentured servants. The people, he wrote "(especially the Dutch who are ¾ of these colonies) are unwilling or rather in cases of necessity only take any white servants knowing by experience from their neighbors of Virginia & Maryland &ct that the worst in the world come out of Bridewell and Newgate."[27] Little wonder, then, that in 1744 members of New Jersey's assembly rejected Governor Lewis Morris's proposal for a duty on slaves, retorting that "it would be more for the Interest of the People of this Colony to encourage at this time the Importation of Slaves."[28]

For some the attractions of slave labor extended beyond the specifics of shifting demographics. One such advocate was Francis Harrison, who identified two further reasons why the slave trade could profitably expand in New Jersey. First, he contended, freeholders "manure no land but their own." Second, he noted that slaves were the key "portion which young men have from their parents or received with their wives when they set out in the world." Similar views were no doubt espoused by many Monmouth County immigrants who were purchasing Africans, perhaps for the first time.

Morris's plantation at Tinton Falls was perhaps the first place in Monmouth where natural reproduction significantly increased the number of enslaved African Americans. Perhaps Morris sought to encourage reproduction and not merely to economize when he chose not to provide separate housing for the sexes. In any event, and probably unbeknownst to Morris—seventeenth-century Europeans normally showed little interest in African customs—this compound style of living reinforced African cultural heritage and doubtless promoted the practice of polygamy. Present also at Morris's plantation was the first African cemetery in the county, creating a sacred space for the black community around Tinton Falls.[29]

Elsewhere in the county, an important obstacle to nuclear family development among blacks was the diffusion of related slaves between a number of farms. Just as Africans were not always imported in small groups, so did Monmouth slaveholders not always limit themselves to owning one or two slaves. The Monmouth Patent, after all, encouraged through the incentive of increased acreage larger aggregations of bondsmen on land grants. In practice, however, no farm in Monmouth County was large enough to support more than a dozen slaves. This contrasts with the West Indian and southern plantations, where masses of slaves toiled. In Monmouth, family ownership, a significant factor in the county's labor system, often split black families.

The most common condition for Monmouth's slaves was to live and work in ethnic isolation, remote from potential husbands or wives. Such living arrangements clearly could not support the development of black nuclear families. Accordingly, African Americans in Monmouth revived African traditions of extended, consanguinal families. Unlike the stem families that dominated white settlements in Monmouth, the core of slave families was a single adult, with closer relations to other adult blacks than to a single person.[30]

A master or mistress's death was a frequent cause for sales or distribution of slaves among several relatives. John Anderson of Freehold, for example, died in 1736 and ordered that the services of "Negro Judy" be divided between his son and daughter. Four other slaves were to be split among four children. Later John Pew of Middletown gave his wife "Negro Phillis," one daughter "Negro Dorcas," another daughter "Negro girl Effe," and a "Negro Man Ephraim." The hardships suffered by the black family through this commerce are obvious. Unlike the South, however, where enslaved blacks were often sold faraway, Monmouth allowed its Africans to remain in geographic proximity, preserving some family connections. The difficulty lay in the fact that the master, mistress, or overseer controlled access to black family members. Black families during slavery had to base family connection on emotional attachment more than proximity.[31]

Table 2
Slave Family Composition, 1680–1775

	1680–1726	1727–1746	1747–1775
Nuclear Family	2	2	9
Single Male	8	13	23
Single Female	6	2	11
Women and Children	4	4	17
Complex Groups	4	16	16
Couples	0	10	15
Total	24	47	91

Source: "Monmouth County Wills, 1680–1775," Archives Section, Division of Archives and Record Management, New Jersey Department of State, Trenton, N.J.

Evidence about family formation in census and probate records, shown in Table 2, indicates that Monmouth's blacks had mixed chances for family development and reproduction. Although single men and women were the most common configuration among slave holdings, women, children and complex groups of several generations accounted for the bulk of slaves in the county. In seventy-one estates inventoried with slaves between 1680 and 1746, there were only four black nuclear families. At the same time, increasing parity between numbers of males and females gradually supplanted earlier gender imbalances.

The black gender imbalance in seventeenth-century Monmouth is characteristic of a small agricultural society. During the eighteenth century it gradually shifted from 189 males for every 100 females, in 1726, to 132 males for every 100 females, in 1745, sustaining an annual growth rate for blacks of between 4 and 5 percent.[32] This was accomplished within a system of small-farm slavery in which the average size of slave holdings on ninety-five estates inventoried between 1743 and 1775 increased only by a factor of 2.83.[33]

. Children also appear in probate records with greater regularity, revealing the effects of natural reproduction. Gary Nash and Jean Soderlund have argued that for Philadelphia slaves to make the transition to a self-sustaining population, family units needed an average of at least one girl per adult woman.[34] In Monmouth County probate records, enumerated in Table 3, the number of slave girls for the entire colonial period was 79 for every 100 woman during a time of rising black population. Looked at more closely, one sees that the ratio improved substantially from 73 girls for every 100 women, in Monmouth's first fifty years, to over 83 girls for every 100 women, in the pre-Revolutionary period.

Other data suggest that Monmouth's blacks may have been numerically sufficient for sustaining their society. Across East Jersey and in Monmouth specifically, the black population tended to be a bit older than the white. In 1738, for example, almost 60

Table 3
Gender Distribution of Slaves in Estate Inventories and Wills, 1680–1775

	1680–1735	1736–1750	1751–1775
Wills Mentioning Slaves	25	34	37
Enslaved Men	23	37	46
Enslaved Women	15	24	40
Enslaved Boys	10	20	25
Enslaved Girls	11	20	33
Total Enslaved	59	101	144

Source: Monmouth County Wills and Inventories, New Jersey State Archives.

percent of East Jersey's black population was over sixteen years of age whereas among whites only 51 percent were over sixteen. In West Jersey, the percentage of blacks over sixteen dropped from 60 to 50 percent between 1737 and 1772, suggesting a large increase in the number of children. It seems reasonable that such patterns were even truer in East Jersey, with its heavier emphasis on slavery. This may also be seen in the number of black children per female in Monmouth, which rose steadily in the colonial period, reaching a peak in 1750 of 166 children for every 100 mothers. Finally, the number of children counted in wills after 1735 was five times greater than during the first half century of settlement.[35]

Slaves as Property

In the marginal, barter society of New Netherland's first decades, Africans could be exchanged for beaver skins or for provisions such as pork and peas.[36] As the colony progressed to a specie economy, slaves took on an additional value related to but partly independent of the value of their service.

Francis Harrison, the custom inspector, observed that slaves were the most important part of a young woman's dowry. In fact, slaves generally accounted for a significant portion of a white family's wealth.[37] Their numbers and monetary value can be ascertained through probate records. Bequeathals of slaves ran across all levels of society from Monmouth's earliest decades. Among the well-to-do, widow Elizabeth Brown of Shrewsbury bequeathed eight slaves to her daughter and five to her son. James Tallman's estate included twelve slaves.[38] Bondsmen accounted for much of a middling farmer's estate. Thomas Huitt of Shrewsbury left eight slaves worth £210 to his wife in 1712 in an estate worth £479. The majority of holdings were much smaller, the average slaveholder owning but two chattel.

Yet even poor men could own slaves. The most extreme example is Thomas Wobbly of Shrewsbury, whose one slave was worth £12 in an estate totaling only £29 in 1702.[39]

This pattern of small-family slaveholding was typical of the mid-Atlantic region. What is unique about colonial Monmouth County is the reliance of certain key families on slavery, as revealed once again through probate records. Of 294 estates that inventoried slaves between 1680 and 1800, fourteen families account for ninety-one, or 30 percent of all, slave masters. All fourteen were among the oldest Monmouth families and are represented in the records across several generations. One family alone, the Covenhovens, is represented twenty-four times, or 8 percent of the total. Clearly, slave ownership became a significant, permanent investment across the generations.[40]

Laws of Slavery in Colonial Monmouth County

Although ownership patterns intertwined the lives of generations of slaves and masters, and although slaves were often referred to as the "kitchen family," an ironclad slave code undergirded any sympathetic relations between white masters and black slaves. Through a bewildering succession of governments, New Jersey's proprietors, governing bodies, and legislators constructed, statute for statute, the most repressive legal system in the North.

During the first decades of Dutch New Netherland, slaves could (and did) successfully petition for manumission. In the beginning, then, the difference between slavery and indentured servitude there was less pronounced than it later became. But as the New World grew less new, and as the sense of possession became more entrenched, the Dutch became less inclined to part with their slaves.

English rule brought the aforementioned legal recognition of slavery through the Duke's Laws of 1665. Following the division of the colony into East and West Jersey in 1676, East Jersey's first assembly was convened to formalize its new government. A period of political complexities ensued, ending when East Jersey was sold to a group of twelve proprieters in February 1682. With stability came a new focus of legislative energy spent on supplementing, then supplanting the Duke's Laws. As part of these new laws, the assembly enacted, beginning in 1683, several statutes aimed at curtailing independent black activities in the colony.[41]

As slaves could not be citizens of East Jersey, the assembly could not regulate slaves directly. Instead it placed conditions on the actions of its freemen. As mentioned above, the act of May 1683 made it illegal to buy, sell, or barter with slaves for alcohol or commodities.[42] In theory, at least, this law had three major effects. First, it made it difficult for slaves to gather in licensed taverns and forced them to congregate at illicit groggeries. Second, it was devised to make it difficult for them to fence stolen items, but, in fact, sustained an underground economy. Third, it closed to slave entrepreneurs all markets for production (whether of home brew, garden produce, or handicraft), thereby forcing them to earn whatever cash they could through services alone. In short, it denied all but the most ambitious blacks any legal leverage with which to purchase freedom. County laws restricted slaves even further, barring them from hunting, using pistols, or even from tending hogs.

A black in Monmouth County had one owner but many masters. In John Locke's formulation of 1669, "Every Freeman . . . shall have absolute power and authority over Negro Slaves."[43] Although early New Jersey statutes did not make this declaration outright, legislators consistently emphasized the responsibility of citizens to assert their authority over servants and slaves.

For example, any white male who found a black more than five miles away from his master's home was required to whip and imprison the slave as a fugitive. In an act of February 28, 1683, harboring escaped servants also became a crime. Such laws suggest that masters had difficulty keeping slaves and servants at home—and that opinion was already divided as to whether masters had the right to do so.[44]

The law itself took a more liberal turn when a slave was charged with a capital crime, granting him the same right to justice as a freeman. This liberality was put to the test in October 1695 in Monmouth County when several blacks were accused of murdering their master, Lewis Morris of Passage Point. The attack may have been in revenge for Morris's earlier murder of a black woman, which New Jersey courts refused to investigate, despite pleas from the slaves. In any event, seven slaves in this case pleaded not guilty to a charge of shooting Morris with a handgun. At the end of the trial, five of them were acquitted; two others, Agebee and Jeremy, were convicted. Jeremy then escaped. After he was recaptured, his hand was cut off and burned before his eyes, after which he was hung until "dead, dead, dead." Agebee suffered a similar fate.[45]

Like all corporal punishments, this one was intended to intimidate; and intimidation required more extreme means in a society where tolerance for disfiguring punishments was higher than today. Still, in its violence the punishment of Jeremy and Agebee exceeded legal penalties applied to whites in East Jersey. The society of seventeenth-century Monmouth County was, of course, not the first or the last in which local authority, freed from direct oversight and restraint, exceeded its lawful mandate. Neither was rural society unique in its virulent admixtures of racism and cruelty, nor in the resulting and recurrent horrors that smoldered there.[46]

When the details of the case came to the attention of the

East Jersey assembly, the legislators realized that it did not make good economic sense to spend so much money to prosecute personal property. Accordingly, in February 1696 the East Jersey legislature passed a statute directing that enslaved felons should be summarily tried by a court consisting of one to three justices of the peace—retaining, however, the jury of "twelve lawful men of the neighborhood." Thereafter, capital trials of slaves were to be conducted much more swiftly.

In 1704 East Jersey legislators codified laws for blacks by either affirming earlier legislation or substituting stiffer penalties. What previously were county laws governing slaves now applied to the entire colony. The first clause, for example, forbade sales of "Rume, Wine, Beer, Syder, or other strong drink," to slaves. Additional clauses reaffirmed the duty of white persons to arrest wandering slaves and transport them to their masters for whipping, with fees set for rewards. Such requirements widened the gap between white and black. Jury trials were ordered for capital offenses, while petty thefts could be decided by only two justices of the peace. A controversial new clause mandated castration of blacks who raped white females or who ran away three times. The Privy Council in London quickly disallowed this law as contrary to nature—albeit without noting that the existence of slavery itself depended on law that had since the time of Justinian been considered contrary to nature. Further squeezing the rights of blacks, the lawmakers ruled that the children of free blacks could not inherit or purchase any land in the colony.[47]

In 1714, made anxious by the slave conspiracy in New York City two years earlier, New Jersey legislators strengthened the slave codes. They continued earlier injunctions forbidding black marketing and "frolicking," indications that the laws were difficult to enforce. A significant new law required that any master wanting to manumit his slave must post a £200 bond or instruct his estate to pay £20 annually for the slave's maintenance. This edict effectively curbed voluntary emancipation in New Jersey except by the most determined masters.[48]

By the second decade of the eighteenth century, African Americans in Monmouth County had been stripped of most civil rights by repressive legislation. White citizens feared that emancipated slaves would become a burden on the community, even as they labored to make it impossible for free blacks to survive economically. In fact, only one black received public assistance in Shrewsbury before the Revolution; three more were aided during it.[49] The laws did not foreclose black freedoms, but they clearly limited methods of gaining them.

The slave codes lasted throughout the colonial period. They were augmented by clauses tacked onto other legislation. Thus in a statute forbidding all New Jersey residents the use of large steel traps for muskrats or foxes, free persons were to be fined but slaves whipped for violations of the code. As time passed New Jersey's colonial government took increasing interest in the discipline of slaves, even offering slaveholders the option of having the state whip their chattel for them. Masters had only to bring unruly slaves to the workhouse, and seasoned professionals would whip thirty stripes into each of their backs.[50]

The Role of Religion

Laws alone could not create a peaceful slave society. European theologians and sympathetic slave masters accordingly attempted to inculcate religion into their servants in hopes of rendering them docile. When servants were bondsmen, this aim came into conflict with the common notion that it was permissible to enslave others so long as they were non-Christians. Dutch settlers were the first New Jerseyans to confront this issue by choosing possession over principle—though they did not do so without a struggle. Indeed, during the first decades of New Netherland, the Dutch Reformed Church welcomed blacks, and the Dutch West India Company of New Amsterdam set the tone for the region by obeying the 1618 Council of Dordrecht declaration that Christians could not remain enslaved. During the 1640s Africans working as servants of the Dutch West India Company routinely gained freedom through assimilation and by baptism into the Reformed Church. Subsequently, these Afro-Dutch became freeholders.

But by the 1650s, as the economic seductions of slavery grew more addictive and as theological reasons for manumissions accumulated, religious scruples and practical economics reached an impasse in New Netherland. In a lengthy treatise, *'t Geestelijk roer van 't coopmans schip* ("The Spiritual Rudder of the Merchants' Ship"), published in 1638, the Reformed minister Godefridus Cornelisz Udemans offered an answer. Addressing his thoughts to both the West and East India companies, Udemans argued that Christians could only be sold as slaves if they were captured in a just war or purchased for a fair price from their parents or other competent masters, practices common in Angola, a principal source for Dutch slaves. The merit of Dutch slavery, Udemans opined, was that it benefited Africans and kept them from "popish mischief."

Udemans's arguments were all the Dutch in the New World needed to rationalize slavery and the slave trade.[51] Reassured, Reformed clerics began espousing the belief that conversion to Christianity was a privilege Africans had abused. In the 1660s Dominie Selwyns advanced this view when, rejecting demands by the Classis of Amsterdam that he catechize slaves in rural Brooklyn, he noted that blacks "wanted nothing else than to deliver their children from bodily slavery, without striving for piety and Christian virtues." By the English conquest in 1664, Reformed ministers had virtually ceased catechizing or baptizing blacks.[52]

The Quakers and Baptists who founded Monmouth County, whatever their other doctrinal differences, agreed that it was permissible to enslave non-Christians. The same may be said of the second wave of settlers, which added Dutch Reformed, Huguenot, Methodist, and Scots-Presbyterian colonists to Monmouth's mix. Together with the Quakers and Baptists, these Christians would over the next few decades offer a plethora of dogmas and doctrines to African hearers. And if the invitation to join in eternal salvation was perhaps offered somewhat coolly, if at all (nudged, as shall be seen, by events beyond the pulpit or plantation), it was because so many of Monmouth's masters were willing to hold fellow Christians as slaves. The colonists knew where their priorities lay: in eighteenth-century Shrewsbury, for example, ownership of slaves was widespread across all these religious denominations.

Of the several developing relationships beween sects and slaves, two in particular merit closer study for what they show us about the earliest generations of African Americans in Monmouth County. The first concerns a denomination, the Church of England, that had the advantage—and disadvantage— of unique access to the source of political power in the colonies. As the state religion, the Church of England could hardly be viewed dispassionately by those who had left England to escape religious persecution. Nor could the church hope to make many converts among the Protestant disaffected in the New World. To do more than serve its existing flock, to significantly expand its minority congregation, Anglicans would have to recruit among those without strong Christian affiliations.

In the late seventeenth century, secret Crown instructions to royal governors ordered them to "facilitate and encourage the Conversion of Negroes and Indians to our Christian religion." The Reverend Alexander Innes, formerly chaplain to the fort in New York City, initiated Anglican services in Middletown in parishioners' homes in the late 1680s. Innes's lengthy tenure established the Church of England in Monmouth but did little to convert African slaves. Elsewhere, however, Anglicans became the denomination most visible in proselytizing Africans.[53]

To do this required, of course, the assent of owners. The initial barrier to Anglican success among slave owners was the controversy over baptism. English theologians dealt with this persistent issue by attempting an "invasion within" that reconciled sacred teachings with slavery. So construed, Christianity could be seen not as a threat to the peculiar institution but as the strongest bulwark against disloyalty and insurrection.[54] Saving a soul, pastors reassured anxious slaveholders, does not require one to relenquish a body. In London, Morgan Godwyn, an Anglican proponent of missions, insisted that baptism was no mandate for manumission. At the same time, he insisted that failure to teach Christianity to slaves invited a secular, licentious reading of the Bible and God's intentions.[55]

Amidst hostility from other denominations, principal support for proselytizing blacks came from wealthy colonists and crown officials, but from few other colonists.[56] To reconcile missionary efforts with their parishioners' determination to keep slaves, Anglicans turned to the legislature for support. In 1704 the New Jersey Assembly ruled that admission to the faith did not alter civil status. A clause in the black codes passed that year addressed baptism and slaves' rights to emancipation. The assembly noted, in terms Godwyn would have recognized, that the "Baptizing of Slaves is thought by some to be a sufficient Reason to set them at Liberty." Calling such a belief "groundless," the assembly decreed that baptism "shall not be the reason" for setting free any slave. Anglicans were, however, a minority in East Jersey, and despite their influence in the legislature, ethnic differences, as well as differences in faith, prevailed over the coastal plain. Law or no law, many slave owners still felt that church membership led to emancipation, a step few were willing to undertake.[57]

Enter the Society for the Propagation of the Gospel in Foreign Parts (S.P.G.), a newly instituted evangelical arm of the Church of England. For its inaugural mission to the colonies in 1695, the society chose South Carolina, the most populous slave colony. After successes there the S.P.G. spread to other colonies, arriving on Monmouth County's doorstep seventeen years later when, in 1712, George Ross carried the society's work into the Delaware Valley region.[58] By the third decade of the eighteenth century, the society had established branches in Shrewsbury and Freehold. Yet the initial efforts of S.P.G. missionaries faltered in northern rural counties such as Monmouth, and in the end the Anglicans could claim but few black adherents. At this point, the church's primary accomplishment seems to have been legitimating slavery. Anglican paternalism simply failed to reach the vast majority of Monmouth blacks.

In examining why, we cannot overlook the slaves' own African forms of spirituality. Blacks did not passively accept Christian messages. The relationship of seventeenth- and eighteenth- century Anglicans to their rite and faith may have seemed too constrained and abstract, too ready to deny people in bondage the possibility of earthly freedom. An African slave offered Christian fellowship had first to undergo catechism before he or she could be baptized into the faith. As the Anglican Church was centered in its rites, catechism entailed the study of liturgical texts and chant. This was a rather tall order for unlettered African farm hands. Rather than accept a faith that merely enforced deference, African Americans turned elsewhere and combined their own spiritual heritage with European religious practices to create a unique, blended belief system that could sustain their humanity. The primary importance of this amalgamation lies, of course, in the effect it had on generations of humans. It is also significant historiographically, insofar as discussions of slavery have typically emphasized the contrasting roles of paternalism, on the one hand, and economics, on the other.[59] Examination of the black religious experience in colonial America supports a third reading of history, in which black solidarity and group identity are forged out of the crucibles of race and slavery.[60]

The Anglican campaign no doubt stimulated some slaveholders belonging to other Protestant sects to reconsider the merits of Christian conversion. In any event, such conversions increased during the eighteenth century. The evangelical New Lights in the Presbyterian and Methodist faiths, who preached a version of salvation less hierarchical than that of the Anglicans, were heard by slaves and unintentionally inspired them to seek temporal grace. The best chance for legal manumission through religious affiliation came, ironically, through a sect that discouraged African membership, the Society of Friends; from the 1750s the Quaker church shifted toward gradual emancipation of all slaves owned by church members.

The Anglican goal of converting slaves met with particularly sharp resistance from Dutch Reformed slave masters, who moved into Monmouth County in increasing numbers from 1690 onwards. Deeply held animosities stemming from class inequities of the 1680s, the Leisler Revolt of 1689, the dislike of English governance, and dark suspicions that slave baptism inspired the revolt of 1712 in New York worsened Dutch attitudes toward English rule and church.[61]

As the Dutch population spread throughout East Jersey, the church split between anglicized clerics eager for government favor in New York City and more pietistic pastors in rural regions, who regarded Anglican efforts with suspicion. In a society, where one observer concluded, the Dutch "if opportueinity presents would Sacrifice the English," conversion of slaves was fraught with political consequences. Subsequently, members of the Reformed church regarded Anglican efforts as religious imperialism and expended much energy channeling the spiritual potentials of African slaves.[62]

Having lost the political contest with England for America, and lacking the Anglicans' leverage in the assembly, the Dutch avoided direct confrontation. They did so by using not weekly Sabbath services but the annual celebration of *Pinkster*, a celebration of Pentecost, as their primary religious interaction with Africans. Curiously, this nonintensive approach to conversion succeeded where the sustained, coordinated effort of the English had proven relatively ineffectual.

Widely observed as a sacred and folk holiday throughout Europe, Pentecost ranks among the great festivals of Christianity.[63] Pinkster was a major festival in the middle-Atlantic colonies, especially in rural pietistic churches. Pinkster functioned both as an agriculturally based community gathering and as a deeply private religious occasion. Its observance created a temporary community among Africans and Dutch and a safety valve for household tensions. The public face of Pinkster shall be examined in the next chapter. Here the focus is on the festival's spiritual dimensions.

Observance of Christ's sacrifice and resurrection occurred in Pinkster when the Holy Ghost rushed through the heart or home on a "Holy Wind" and provoked "speaking in tongues" among the participants. "Holy Wind" consisted of powerful preaching by males or females of any caste. Ecstasy happened when the participant, whether master or slave, became a "mouthpiece of God."[64] The ecstatic moments of Holy Wind and speaking in tongues served as replacements for church baptisms and acted as spiritual conversion. Dutch slaveholders could accept their slaves into the sanctity of the faith in the safety of their homes, without concern for the potentially emancipating effects of Anglican baptism. Among slaves, moreover, Pinkster ceremonies sustained promises of sacred equality.

Pinkster also differed from Anglican education in that its observance did not require perfect English, literacy, or command of scripture. Huguenots used similar pietist methods.

Pinkster's hallucinatory effects—its dreams, trances, visions—
prepared slaves for the enthusiastic equality found later in
Methodism.[65]

Summary

By 1714 slavery was firmly entrenched as the condition of
life for Monmouth County's black residents. Harsh, punitive
laws restricted personal and economic mobility. Present from
the beginnings of the county, Monmouth's black population
grew apace, reaching 9 percent of the total inhabitants by 1726.
The steady but small supplies of African and seasoned West Indian blacks changed in the 1720s to larger shipments arriving
directly from Africa. Christian influence on Monmouth's bonded
people led to occasional manumissions but was generally not
significant in these early years. The Anglican church mustered a
strong effort to dissociate Christianity from emancipation, while
Dutch Reformed slave masters preferred domestically based ritual
to church services. As the institutions of colonial society developed, legal, religious, economic, and social freedom became virtually inaccessible for Monmouth's blacks.

Notes

1. Unless otherwise identified, all towns and villages mentioned
in the text are located in Monmouth County.

2. The original patent may be found in Julian P. Boyd, *Fundamental Laws and Constitutions of New Jersey, 1664–1964* New Jersey
Historical Series 17 (Princeton, N.J., 1964), 51–67. For early settlement of Monmouth, see Peter O. Wacker, "Origins and Settlement
Patterns," in *Land and People: A Cultural Geography of Preindustrial
New Jersey Origins and Settlement Patterns* (New Brunswick, N.J.,
1975), 129–30, 168, 191–92; Peter O. Wacker and Paul G. E. Clemens,
Land Use in Early New Jersey: A Historical Geography (Newark, 1995),
90–91; John E. Pomfret, *Colonial New Jersey: A History* (New York,

1973), 26–38, 52–68; *idem, The Province of East New Jersey, 1609–1702: The Rebellious Proprietary* (Princeton, N.J., 1962), 42–47; Ned C. Landsman, *Scotland and Its First American Colony, 1683–1765* (Princeton, N.J., 1985), 99–195.

3. David Steven Cohen, *The Dutch-American Farm* (New York, 1992), 12–20; Landsman, *Scotland and Its First American Colony,* 100–140.

4. D. W. Meinig, *Atlantic America, 1492–1800,* vol. 1 of *The Shaping of America: A Geographic Perspective on 500 Years of History* (New Haven, 1986), 52–53.

5. For the complexity of family relations in Monmouth, see John E. Stilwell, *Historical and Genealogical Miscellany,* 5 vols. (1903; reprint, Baltimore, 1970). For comments on intermarriage, see Dennis C. Ryan, "Six Towns: Continuity and Change in Revolutionary New Jersey, 1770–1792" (Ph.D. diss., New York University, 1974), 39, 55, 58–59, 75. For the Conover family genealogy, which indicates frequent intermarriage with the Schenck, Van Voorhees, Wall, Hendrickson, and Van Dorn families, see Elizabeth Conover Kelly, *Conover Pioneers and Pilgrims: Celebration of a Family* (Detroit, 1982), 30–40. For Huguenots, see Jon Butler, *The Huguenots in America: A Refugee People in New World Society* (Cambridge, Mass., 1983) 158–59.

6. *Journal of the Courts of Common Right and Chancery of East New Jersey, 1683–1702,* ed. Preston W. Edsall (Philadelphia, 1937), 125.

7. On early importations of slaves, see Morton Wagman, "Corporate Slavery in New Netherland," *Journal of Negro History* 66 (Winter 1980): 34. On kinds of work done, see George Fishman, "The Struggle for Freedom and Equality: African-Americans in New Jersey, 1624–1849/50" (Ph.D. diss., Temple University, 1990), 20.

8. David Hackett Fischer, *Albion's Seed: Four British Folkways in America* (New York, 1989), 10.

9. Directors of Amsterdam to Peter Stuyvesant, 9 March 1660, *New York Colonial Tracts* 3, 168; cited in Fishman, "Struggle for Freedom," 10. Peter Stuyvesant to the directors of Amsterdam, in E. B. O'Callaghan, trans., *Voyage of the Slaves of St. John and the Arms of Amsterdam* [1663] (New York, 1869); cited in Fishman, "Struggle for Freedom," 8.

10. Percy Wells Bidwell and John I. Falconer, *History of Agriculture in the Northern States, 1620–1860* (Washington, 1925), 6–10, 105–13; and Harry S. Carman, *American Husbandry* (reprint, New York, 1939), 99; [Richard Hartshorne], *A Further Account of New Jersey in*

an *Abstract of Letters Lately Writ from Thence, by Several Inhabitants There Resident. Printed in the Year 1676* (Trenton, n.d.).

11. Act of 28 February 1683, in *Journal of the Courts of Common Right and Chancery of East New Jersey,* 125.

12. For many examples see Daniel Meaders, *Eighteenth-Century White Slaves Fugitive Notices,* Vol. 1 (Pennsylvania, 1729–1760), (Westport, Conn., 1993), *passim.* For advertisement to imigrants, see *A Brief Account of the Province of East New Jersey in America. Published by the Scots Proprietor* (Edinburgh, 1683), 5.

13. For smuggling, see Elizabeth Donnan, ed., *Documents Illustrative of the History of the Slave Trade to America,* 5 vols. (Washington, D.C., 1932), 3:456. For discussion of heavy mortality, see Richard S. Dunn, "Servants and Slaves: The Recruitment and Employment of Labor," in Jack P. Greene and J. R. Pole, eds., *Colonial British America: Essays in the New History of the Early Modern Era* (Baltimore, 1984), 174–75; Richard B. Sheridan, *Sugar and Slavery: An Economic History of the British West Indies, 1623–1775* (Baltimore, 1973); Elsa V. Goveia, *Slave Society in the British Leeward Islands at the End of the Eighteenth Century* (New Haven, Conn., 1965). For discussion of youthfulness of New Jersey slave imports, see James A. Rawley, *The Transatlantic Slave Trade: A History* (New York, 1981), 390–91. For sale to Martinique, see Hendrickson Family Papers, box 1, folder 8, Special Collections, Alexander Library, Rutgers University.

14. Donnan, *Documents,* 3:510–12, and "Naval Shipping Lists for New Jersey, 1722–1764," PRO CO 5/1035–36.

15. Donnan, *Documents,* 3:464, 472, 479, 492. James Lydon, "New York and the Slave Trade, 1700–1774," *William and Mary Quarterly,* 3d ser., vol. 35 (1978), 375–95, expands upon Donnan, finding additional voyages from Africa but none of over a hundred slaves. *The Dragon* arrived on August 23 with 106 slaves, the *Postillion* on September 12 with one hundred, and the *Catherine and Mary* the same day with sixty. For purchases at Perth Amboy, see James H. Levitt, *For Want of Trade: Shipping and the New Jersey Ports, 1680–1783* (Newark, 1981), 96, 106, 117–18.

16. For Morris, see "Inventory of Lewis Morris," Miscellaneous Manuscripts, no. 14577, New York State Library, Albany, and Dean Freiday, "Tinton Manor: The Iron Works," *Proceedings of the New Jersey Historical Society* 74 (1952): 250–61. For the number of slaves at Morris's arrival in 1677, see John Robert Strassburger, "The Origins

and Establishment of the Morris Family in the Society and Politics of New York and New Jersey, 1630–1746" (Ph.D. diss., Princeton University, 1976), 67. For exemptions, see Lewis Morris Papers, box 1, folder 3, Special Collections, Alexander Library, Rutgers University. For servants, see Robert J. Steinfeld, *The Invention of Free Labor: The Employment Relation in English and American Law and Culture, 1350–1870* (Chapel Hill, N.C., 1991), 44–52.

17. The literature on Jamaica and Barbados is vast. For recent important studies on slave economy, conditions, race relations, and resistance, see Hilary Beckles, *The Black Rebellion in Barbados: The Struggle Against Slavery, 1627–1838* (Bridgetown, Barbados, 1984); idem, *White Servitude and Black Slavery in Barbados, 1627–1715* (Knoxville, Tenn. 1989); Dunn, "Servants and Slaves," 173–75. For Africanity, see Mervyn Alleyne, *Roots of Jamaican Culture* (London, 1988), and Orlando Patterson, *The Sociology of Slavery: An Analysis of the Origins, Development, and Structure of Negro Slave Society in Jamaica* (Rutherford, N.J., 1967), 113–32, 160–99. For rebellions see *A Genuine Narrative of the Intended Conspiracy of the Negroes at Antigua* (Dublin, 1737); Michael Craton, *Testing the Chains: Resistance to Slavery in the British West Indies* (Ithaca, N.Y., 1982), 67–81, 105–40; David Barry Gaspar, *Bondmen & Rebels: A Study of Master-Slave Relations in Antigua, with Implications for Colonial British America* (Baltimore, 1985).

18. Peter Linebaugh, "All the Atlantic Islands Shook," *Labour/Le Travailleur* 10 (1982): 87-121.

19. Patterson, *Sociology of Slavery*, 50. For sailors, see Marcus Rediker, *Between the Devil and the Deep Blue Sea: Merchant Seamen, Pirates, and the Anglo-American Maritime World, 1700–1750* (New York, 1987).

20. For percentages of slave populations, estimated by colony for 1680, see Peter Kolchin, *American Slavery, 1619–1877,* (New York, 1993), 240.

21. See "Lists of Negroes in Monmouth, 1771," Monmouth County Archives, Manalapan, N.J.

22. Stella Sutherland, *Population Distribution in Colonial America* (New York, 1936), 98, and Ryan, "Six Towns," 66.

23. Gary B. Nash and Jean Soderlund, *Freedom by Degrees: Emancipation in Pennsylvania and Its Aftermath* (New York, 1991). For similar evidence about New York City and its surrounding counties,

see Shane White, *Somewhat More Independent: The End of Slavery in New York City, 1770–1810* (Athens, Ga., 1991).

24. For attempts at duties, see *The Laws of the Royal Colony of New Jersey*, comp. Bernard Bush, 5 vols. (Trenton, 1977–1989), 2:163–64; 4:171–75, 435–36, 510.

25. Darold D. Wax, "The Negro Slave Trade in Colonial Pennsylvania" (Ph.D. diss., University of Washington, 1962), 42–46, 48, 127.

26. Wacker, "Origins and Settlement Patterns," 146.

27. [Francis Harrison], "Observations Humbly Offered to His Grace the Duke of Chandos Sharing the Advantages Which the Royal African Company May Receive by Settling an Agency at New York in Order to Supply that Province, the Colonies at East and West New Jersey, Connecticut, Rhode Island, Narragansett and the Southwest Parts of New England with Slaves," Ms. Gough Somersetshire 7 (S.C. 18217), Bodleian Library, Oxford University. See Lewis Morris's comments on this plan in Eugene R. Sheridan, ed., *The Papers of Lewis Morris*, 3 vols. (Newark, 1991), 2:265.

28. For quote, see Donnan, *Documents,* 3:50–51.

29. African-American cemeteries dot the Monmouth landscape, as they do in every American county where slavery thrived.

30. For concepts of consanguinal families, see Niara Sudarkasa, "Interpreting the African Heritage in Afro-American Family Organization," in Harriet Pipes McAdoo, *Black Families* (Beverly Hills, Calif., 1981), 37–54. For comments on size of farms, see Jackson Turner Main, *The Social Structure of Revolutionary America* (Princeton, N.J., 1965), 25–26.

31. See Monmouth Wills, no. 657 (Anderson), no. 2221 (Pew). For other good examples, see nos. 2571, 2771, 2745. Archives Section, Division of Archives and Records Management, Department of State, Trenton, N.J. (hereafter New Jersey State Archives). See also the Conover Family Papers, box 13, folder 2, Monmouth County Historical Association. For other sales, see James Mott Papers, Cherry Hall Papers, box 10, folder 3, Monmouth County Historical Association, Freehold, N.J., and Indenture of Jonathan Webb, December 3, 1729, Slavery File, Monmouth County Historical Association.

32. For this data, see Wacker, "Origins and Settlement Patterns," 189–202; Edgar McManus, *Black Bondage in the North* (Syracuse, N.Y., 1973), 212–13; Jim Potter, "The Growth of Population in America,

1700–1860," in D. V. Glass and D. E. C. Eversley, eds., *Population in History: Essays in Historical Demography* (Chicago, 1965), 656–57. For similar developments in Flatbush, see William John McLaughlin, "Dutch Rural New York: Community, Economy and Family in Colonial Flatbush" (Ph.D. diss., Columbia University, 1981), 195–97. East Jersey generally had a low mortality rate as well. See Ryan, "Six Towns," 70–72, and "Inquisitions on the Dead, 1688–1798," 4 vols., New Jersey State Archives.

33. Figures taken from Monmouth County Wills, 1744–1775. For value of property, see "Unrecorded Wills," 12 vols., New Jersey State Archives, 1:165 (Thomas White) and 12:43 (Elizabeth Brown).

34. Nash and Soderlund, *Freedom by Degrees*, 23–24.

35. For discussion, see Robert V. Wells, *The Population of the British Colonies in America before 1776: A Survey of Census Data* (Princeton, N.J., 1975), 137–40. On southern counties of New Jersey, see Alice Hanson Jones, *Wealth of a Nation to Be: The American Colonies on the Eve of the Revolution* (New York, 1980), 60.

36. Adrian Van der Donck et al., "Of the Persons and Causes, Why and How New Netherland Is So Decayed," in John Franklin Jameson, *Narratives of New Netherland, 1609–1664* (New York, 1909), 320–32.

37. Soderlund, *Quakers & Slaves*, 76, 119, 125.

38. Monmouth County Wills, no. 63 (Brown), no. 747 (Tallman), New Jersey State Archives. For comments on labor, see Ryan, "Six Towns," 91.

39. For Wobbly, see "Unrecorded Wills," 12 vols., New Jersey State Archives, 11: 269; for others, see Morris's Will above and "Unrecorded Wills," 1:165; 10:379; 11:239, 311, 373–74; 12:11–12, 355 in John E. Stillwell, ed., *Unrecorded Wills and Inventories, Monnmouth County, New Jersey* (New Orleans, 1975), 16. For similar findings in a nearby settlement, see McLaughlin, "Dutch Rural New York," 141, 152–55, 180–97, 200–205.

40. "Monmouth County Wills, 1680–1775," New Jersey State Archives. The families and slave holdings are Covenhoven/Conover, 24; Holmes, 8; Lawrence, 6; Lippencott,6; Schenck, 6; Forman, 6; Van Mater, 5; Tallman, 5; Taylor, 5; Smock, 4; Throckmorton, 4; Bowne, 4; Cooke, 4; Hendrickson, 4.

41. Marion Thompson Wright, "New Jersey Laws and the Ne-

gro," *Journal of Negro History* 28 (April 1943): 156–200. For comment about "kitchen family," see Cohen, *The Dutch-American Farm*, 132–36.

42. Act of May 1683, in *Journal of the Courts of Common Right and Chancery of East New Jersey*, 125.

43. John Locke and the Earl of Shaftesbury, Fundamental Consitutions of South Carolina, sec. 110, in *The Law of Freedom and Bondage: A Casebook*, ed. Paul Finkelman (New York, 1986), 20 n.6.

44. John E. Pomfret, *The Province of East New Jersey, 1609–1702: The Rebellious Proprietary* (Princeton, N.J., 1962), 292.

45. For this case, see *Journal of the Courts of Common Right and Chancery of East New Jersey*, 131, 282–85; Franklin Ellis, *History of Monmouth County, New Jersey* (Philadelphia, 1885), 399–400; and Henry Clay Reed, "Chapters in a History of Crime and Punishment in New Jersey" (Ph.D. diss., Princeton University, 1939), 126. See also Wright, "New Jersey Laws," 164.

46. J. M. Beattie, *Crime and the Courts in England, 1660–1800* (Princeton, N.J., 1986), 75–77; Pieter Spirenburg, *The Spectacle of Suffering: Executions and the Evolution of Repression: From a Preindustrial Metropolis to the European Experience* (New York, 1984), 44–45, 56–58, and Michel Foucault, *Discipline and Punish: The Birth of the Prison* (New York, 1977), 3–32.

47. *Acts of the General Assembly of the Province of New-Jersey from the Surrender of the Government to Queen Anne, on the 17th day of April in the Year of Our Lord, 1702 to the 14th Day of January 1776*, ed. Samuel Allinson (Burlington, N.J., 1776) [hereafter *1702–76 New Jersey Acts*], 5, and *Journal and Votes of the House of Representatives of the Province of Nova Caesaria or New Jersey, in the First Sessions of Assembly, Began at Perth Amboy, the 10th Day of November, 1703* (Jersey City, N.J., 1872), 32. For discussion, see Wright, "New Jersey Laws," 166–67. On the European reception of Roman law regarding slavery, see Alan Watson, "Seventeenth-Century Jurists, Roman Law, and the Law of Slavery," in *Slavery & the Law*, ed. Paul Finkelman (Madison, Wis., 1997).

48. For the laws, see *1702–76 New Jersey Acts*, 18–22; Wright, "New Jersey Laws," 167.

49. For relief records, see Shrewsbury, New Jersey, Town Poor Book, 1743–1848, New-York Historical Society, 34, 91, 93, 95, 97–98, 101.

50. For traps, see Bush, *Laws of the Royal Colony of New Jersey*, 4:52, 583; 5:70. For workhouse, see *ibid.*, 3:135, 291.

51. For Council of Dordrecht declaration, see Orlando Patterson, *Slavery and Social Death: A Comparative Study* (Cambridge, Mass., 1982), 276. For assurance on slave trade, see Godefridus Cornelisz Udemans, '*t Geetstelijk roer van't coopmans schip* (Dordrecht, 1638).

52. I have looked at over fifty Reformed baptismal records from 1680 to 1776 and found only scattered black baptisms.

53. James Axtell, *The Invasion Within: The Contest of Cultures in Colonial North America* (New York, 1985).

54. For Innes and early church history in Monmouth, see Nelson R. Burr, *The Anglican Church in New Jersey* (Philadelphia, 1954), 58–59, 614–15.

55. Morgan Godwyn, *The Negro's and Indians Advocate, Suing for their Admission into the Church; or, A Persuasive to the Instructing and Baptizing of the Negro's and Indians in Our Plantations. Shewing, That as Compliance Therewith Can Prejudice No Mans Just Interest: So the Wilful Neglecting and Opposing It Is No Less a Manifest Apostasy from the Christian Faith* (London, 1680). For the classic discussion of this text, see David Brion Davis, *The Problem of Slavery in Western Culture* (Ithaca, N.Y., 1966), 204–10, 339–40.

56. Lords Commissioners of Trade and Plantation to Archbishop of Canterbury, 25 October 1700, Society for the Propogation of the Gospel in Foreign Parts [hereafter S.P.G.] Papers 13, 3–4; "Extract from the Instructions to the Earl of Clarendon when Lord Cornbury and Governor of New York, January 1, 1702/3," S.P.G. Letter Book B:1 (Appendix). For discussion, see John Calam, *Parsons and Pedagogues: The S.P.G. Adventure in American Education* (New York, 1971), 12–17.

57. For law, see Nicholas Trott, ed., *The Laws of the British Plantations in America, Relating to the Church, and the Clergy, Religion, and Learning* (London, 1725), 257. Two years later New York's legislature passed a similar law. See *Colonial Laws of New York from 1664 to the Revolution*, 5 vols. (Albany, 1894), 1:597–98. See relevant discussion of the problem of baptism in Arthur Zilversmit, *The First Emancipation: The Abolition of Slavery in the North* (Chicago, 1967), 7–10.

58. Denzel T. Clifton, "Anglicanism and Negro Slavery in Colonial America," *Historical Magazine of the Protestant Episcopal Church* 43 (1974): 63–64.

59. A good survey of the conflicting visions of economics and paternalism is Peter J. Parish, *Slavery: History and Historians* (New

York, 1989), 2–6, 37–51. The classic text on paternalism is Eugene D. Genovese, *Roll, Jordan, Roll: The World the Slaves Made* (New York, 1974), 3–7. For growth of black nationalism, see Sterling A. Stuckey, *Slave Culture: Nationalist Theory and the Foundations of Black America* (New York, 1987).

60. Historians have tended to explain the origins of black religion in North America by using single models of acculturation. Jon Butler, for one, has framed the African colonial religious experience by tracing the rise of Anglican hegemony. Butler found few traces of African belief-systems in colonial North America and has argued that a holocaust of African religion occurred in the early eighteenth century. Other relevant studies vary only slightly from this model. In his study of the formation of Philadelphia's free black community, Gary B. Nash touches briefly on the influence of the S.P.G. and George Whitefield on colonial African American Christianity, but he reserves the bulk of his analysis of religion for the post-Revolutionary period. Joyce Goodfriend's analysis of ethnicity in colonial New York highlights African conversion to the Church of England. William D. Piersen, examining the development of an African American subculture in New England, emphasizes the Congregational church's overwhelming powers of acculturation. All of these studies focus on the urban context of the black religious experience. See Jon Butler, *Awash in a Sea of Faith: Christianizing the American People* (Cambridge, Mass., 1990), 129–64; Gary B. Nash, *Forging Freedom: The Formation of Philadelphia's Black Community, 1720–1840* (Cambridge, Mass., 1988), 16–24; Joyce D. Goodfriend, *Before the Melting Pot: Society and Culture in Colonial New York City, 1664–1730* (Princeton, N.J., 1992), 125–32; William D. Piersen, *Black Yankees: The Development of an Afro-American Subculture in Eighteenth-Century New England* (Amherst, Mass., 1988), 49–87, and Patricia U. Bonomi, *Under the Cope of Heaven: Religion, Society, and Politics in Colonial America* (New York, 1986), 35.

61. Richard Pointer, *Protestant Pluralism and the New York Experience: A Study of Eighteenth-Century Diversity* (Bloomington, Ind., 1988), 15–27; Randall H. Balmer, *A Perfect Babel of Confusion: Dutch Religion and English Culture in the Middle Colonies* (New York, 1989), 72–99; Bonomi, *Under the Cope of Heaven,* 73–74; John Pershing Luidens, "The Americanization of the Dutch Reformed Church" (Ph.D. diss., University of Oklahoma, 1969), 86–94.

62. For Dutch willingness to overthrow the English, see Margaret Kincaid, "John Usher's Report on the Northern Colonies, 1698," *William and Mary Quarterly,* 3d ser., vol. 7 (1950): 101.

63. For a general discussion of Pentecost, see William Hurd, *A New Universal History of the Rites, Ceremonies, and Customs and the Whole World,* new ed. (Newcastle upon Tyne, 1811), 154. For Pinkster's presence in New Netherland and New York, see Donna Merwick, *Possessing Albany, 1630–1710: The Dutch and English Experiences* (New York, 1990); Cohen, *The Dutch-American Farm,* 161–63; and, for a later period, White, *Somewhat More Independent,* 95–106.

64. A. C. Barnard, "Die Pinksterfees in die Kerklike Jaar" (Ph.D. diss., University of Amsterdam, 1954), 14–22, 24–25, 32, 40, 45–46, 48, 54, 57. For Dutch traditions, see A. G. Roeber, "'The Origin of Whatever Is Not English among Us': The Dutch-Speaking and German-Speaking Peoples of Colonial British America," in *Strangers within the Realm: Cultural Margins of the First British Empire,* ed. Bernard Bailyn and Philip D. Morgan (Chapel Hill, N.C., 1991), 220–84.

65. Barnard, "Die Pinksterfees," 106. For safety valve, see White, *Somewhat More Independent,* 99–100. For Huguenots, see Butler, *Huguenots in America,* 161–66. For link with Methodism, see Hurd, *A New Universal History,* 700.

2

Small-Farm Slavery
1714–1775

At work, at play, and at worship, blacks in Monmouth County claimed an ever stronger purchase on the colony's culture during the eighteenth century. Even while denying them the fruits of their labors, whites took notice of their amusements and increasingly sought to win their allegiance through faith. Blacks responded in many ways. In this time of taxes, tithes, and self-evident truths, they found themselves, like the white culture enslaving them, caught in a contest between authority from without and knowledge from within. Some dared to emancipate themselves. Others, perhaps, dared to die for disobediance. None, we may easily imagine, so sublimated the natural impulse to liberty that they measured happiness by fidelity to another's ideals.

Yet in this third generation of Monmouth County, many of its blacks were now New Jersey born. Their native tongue was English, their first horizon Monmouth's fields, their father, sometimes, their master. Inevitably, enslaved blacks came to share some key values and beliefs of colonial culture. At the same time, the continued importation of seasoned Africans to Monmouth

County ensured that black Americans would maintain a strong identity with traditional folkways.

Unable to return to the continent of their original heritage and denied humanity in their nominal homeland, African Americans in the eighteenth century faced a cultural landscape no less strange and uncharted than the bleakest of New Jersey's pine barrens. In this crisis they did what people with gumption always do—the best they could. Using the same industry, perseverance, and resourcefulness that enabled them to transform Monmouth's wilds into European countryside, blacks turned slavery's imposed limitations into facets of a richly melded African and American culture.

This could only have been accomplished mind by mind. Yet we know all too little about these minds. Where stories do attach to names, it is usually because the individuals challenged authority from without. Less frequently, we are able to learn when and how blacks heeded their inner voices. Thus the history, like the legacy, of African Americans in eighteenth-century Monmouth County is collective, known through its effects more than its agents. With rare exceptions, the lives of black men and women must be inferred from a few specific instances.

Types of Black Labor

Above all, the lives of enslaved people were spent at work. As new settlers entered the county, moving to the south and southwest of the original settlements, male slaves and servants toiled as bondsmen had during the initial phase of settlement: building shelters, clearing forests, breaking sod. Among the established farms of the eighteenth century, the duties of slaves did not lessen, but became more varied. These farms ranged in size from fifty to four hundred acres, with the arable land usually divided into four fields with a four-year planting cycle. The first year's crop was Indian corn, oats, flax, and buckwheat; the second year the plot lay fallow; the third and fourth years winter grain and pasture grass were grown on it.

Manuring was extremely important to avoid soil exhaustion. But the scarcity of cattle meant manure was often in short supply, which led to poor crops. Most farms included areas devoted to orchards and to timber as well as a meadow for grazing. Farmers in Monmouth County, on average, kept twenty to forty sheep, three to ten cows, besides young stock, and three to eight horses.[1]

The primary duties of the preponderately male black workers on county farms were the production and carting of corn, grain, fruit, and garden produce. Additional chores included tending cattle, hogs, and sheep.[2] A good hand performed a range of tasks. "Mr. Low's Cato," who ran away from Raritan Landing in October 1763, was "an exstream handy fellow at any common work, especially with horses, and carriages of almost any sort, having been bred to it from a little boy, and to the loading and unloading of boats, a good deal used to a farm, can do all sorts of house work and very fit to wait on a gentleman." Sales advertisements for male slaves in Monmouth County also suggest that versatility was wanted in a good hand. Men "understood all kinds of husbandry"; they were skilled as blacksmiths, coopers, carpenters, and farriers; some could also work on privateers and fishing boats.[3]

Work followed the seasons. From the eighteenth-century diary of James Parker, a mid-Jersey farmer in nearby Hunterdon County, we can glean the pace and seasonal cycles of agricultural life in Monmouth. (Though situated west of Monmouth County proper, Parker's freehold approximates many there.) January was a time for slaughtering animals and curing meat, cutting and hauling cordwood, threshing oats, breaking flax, and hauling buckwheat straw. Similar tasks were performed in

February and March along with rail splitting, hauling limestone (for conversion to lime), and working with livestock.

Work began in earnest in the early spring. In addition to the chores just enumerated, Parker's workers brought up hay stored in the meadow, sowed some vegetables, and started grafting apples trees in the orchard. They also prepared the potato fields by harrowing and sowing flax in them. With April came the time for planting potatoes and plowing cornfields. In May Parker's men castrated ram lambs, washed sheep, spread lime, mended fences, and planted seed corn. During spare moments they cleared trees, stones, roots, and other materials from land intended for future planting.

Summertime brought new chores. In mid-June Parker's men planted pumpkins, harrowed and dressed the corn, and sharpened scythes for the coming mowing season. In July they harrowed buckwheat. There was also an occasional change of pace, a trip to town to buy clams and oysters. More typical were monotonous tasks repeated whenever a spare moment was available. For example, the laborers put in "New Wheat," dressed pumpkins, and raked clover throughout the late summer and early fall.

The beginning of harvest overlapped with summer's other chores. July was time for pulling flax from potato fields, for harvesting the hay, then the rye. Workers harvested wheat and corn in August and early September, pumpkins in October. Apple season also began in October and included collection and cartage to a nearby cider mill. James Parker visited town during November. Leaving his laborers in charge of his farm, he warned them especially against thievery by passing troops. In late November Parker had his hogs slaughtered.

After the Christmas holidays the year's cycle of tasks began anew. Winter, far from offering a respite from hard work, simply renewed agriculture's demand for the broadly varied skills of bondspeople. Clearly, any enslaved black on a reasonably large farm had to perform a vast array of chores efficiently and well.

The ceaseless demands of agriculture's seasons belie any notion that northern farmers lacked sufficient work to make slave ownership profitable. To the contrary, slaves in East Jersey were not so numerous that they could meet a farm's demands alone. On Parker's farm, for example, slave labor was supplemented by contract labor throughout the growing and harvest seasons. Parker began taking on additional workers in April. He dismissed a few hands in July, after the spring and summer's planting, and a number more in November, after harvest.[4]

Winter, apparently, was the only season when Parker did not hire temporary labor. And if his reliance on contract labor was greater than that of some other farmers, it nevertheless conformed generally to the practice seen elsewhere. Even at Tinton Falls, with its sizeable slave population, Lewis Morris hired wage laborers for his plantation at harvest time, as in 1728, when he paid three black and several white workers ten shillings each for haying. Records of another farmer, Gersham Mott, indicate that he too brought in free blacks and white laborers to work with slaves on his estate.[5]

Though temporary contract workers made larger-scale farming possible, African American slaves were the core labor force in the critical operations of farms. The importance of slaves is borne out by Monmouth County's tax rolls. Across the county, enslaved laborers outnumbered free white workers. The county tax ratables for 1751 list 262 male slaves and 194 single white males without property. This ratio was more balanced than in neighboring Middlesex County, which assessed 281 male slaves and only 81 free wage laborers. In Dutch-dominated Bergen County the 306 slaves far outnumbered the eight free wage laborers. Another surviving tax roll, recorded seventeen years later, shows the same disparities.[6] These figures show the demand for slave labor increased over the eighteenth century as taxes, soil exhaustion, natural increase, and diminishing supplies of land led to emigration of poorer farmers and white laborers, making the ownership of slaves all the more important.[7]

Within the boundaries of home, yard, and field, then, masters were not the only whites that slaves knew. Their companions in labor were mixed. Some were whites, including former servants, still struggling to gain an economic foothold in the colony. Others were indentured servants, hired out by their masters. Some contract laborers were free blacks. Among them the threat of poverty was common enough that Toby, a slave escaped from John Coward of Freehold in 1764, was expected to pose as a free black and plausibly "pretend to want a new Master for himself."[8] For the most part the indentured servants were not related to the great wave imported into Virginia and the Chesapeake colonies during the seventeenth century. Those had hailed from the English midlands, the same general area that produced the Quakers and Baptists who settled Monmouth County (as names like Shrewsbury and Monmouth attest). Eighteenth-century indentured servants to the mid-Atlantic colonies were far more likely to be Scots or Irish Protestants.[9] Although New Jersey was not a popular mid-Atlantic destination for indentured servants compared to Pennsylvania and Maryland, account books and surving personal documents reveal their presence on farms, toiling side by side with African Americans. One such servant was William Moraley, who cleared land with several slaves for a New Jersey Quaker.[10]

Notably absent from the pool of supplementary labor were the convict workers that England was shipping to the colonies during the first half of the eighteenth century. Despite the need for a steady supply of labor, and despite mounting fears of black conspiracy (particularly after New York's scare in 1741), officials in the mid-Atlantic colonies avoided the lively traffic in felons.

Rubbing shoulders with free black laborers and contracted white servants, Monmouth's agricultural slaves developed conceptions of work relations that were broader than would have been possible on southern plantations. Different but no less varied interactions developed for African Americans who worked in the heart of the white world, the master's home. At a time when nearly twenty thousand blacks worked as servants in London, the more prosperous of New Jersey's colonists, particularly the Anglicans, displayed their wealth partly through well-dressed and educated servants.[11] William Dunlap, in his recollections of childhood in Revolutionary Perth Amboy in Middlesex County, said that "every house in my native place where any servants were to be seen, swarmed with black slaves."[12]

In Monmouth County, as elsewhere, most African American domestics were women. As the term *domestic* subsumed a great variety of skills, statuses and degrees of experience,[13] black women, too, had to be resourceful in many different areas. Perhaps the most fortunate black women lived in Anglican houses, where they could ascend to positions of remarkable responsibility. In such homes chosen females learned the rudiments of literacy, wore clothing as expensive and well made as their owners, and were well fed and housed.

On Monmouth farms the boundaries between house, yard, and field often blurred. James Parker's diary points out that domestic women, for instance, joined the men in such agricultural chores as pulling flax. Over the course of the eighteenth century, as sources of temporary contract labor became scarcer, the range and number of tasks expected of black women expanded and multiplied.[14] A black woman advertised for sale in 1734 "does all sorts of housework, she can brew, bake, boyle soft soap, wash iron and starch and is a good darey woman she can card and spin at the great wheel cotton linnen and wollen. She has another good property she neither drinks rum nor smoaks tobacco and she is a strong hale healthy wench, she can cook pretty well for royst and boyl, she can speak no other language than English; she has had the small pox when a childe in Barbados."[15] African women arrived in the colonies well prepared. Versatility had been the hallmark of women in most African societies, where they typically performed the greater proportion of tasks, including most forms of agricultural labor and all types of domestic work.

Slaves and Masters

Given the circumscribed roles of women generally in eighteenth-century society, it was inevitable that the experiences of black and white women would become inextricable. On small farms they labored together in producing food and clothing, rearing children, and plowing. In some homes, however, mistresses were also heads of household. Though white female control within families gradually diminished in the second half of the eighteenth century, over half of Monmouth's widows retained property rights over their slaves. Among Dutch and English families, bondspeople were considered common property within marriage. Widows often received slaves without any condition and retained them even after remarriage. Enslaved people were a form of dower or property automatically awarded to the wife. Slaves could ease a widow's life or be sold to protect her against debt. Enslaved people were often bequeathed to daughters, enhancing their marital prospects. At the same time, the presence of young adult bondspeople in homes supervised by aged widows or unmarried, younger women required heightened community surveillance and quickened reaction to any domestic turmoil.[16]

Bondswomen owned by widows may well have considered themselves fortunate. When black girls worked and lived in close proximity to white masters, the result was frequently exploitative sexual relations. Such is the evidence of the Shrewsbury Scrapbook of the Society of Friends, which lists numerous mulattos with no explanation of the race of the father. Although occasions for sexual relations were uncommonly limited among Friends, one has only to look at the burgeoning mulatto populations of all slave colonies to see the generality of interracial breeding. In the absence of evidence documenting a sense of responsibility or mutually tender feelings, such relationships must be seen as fundamentally unequal. The children of these sexual liaisons followed the enslaved status of their mother. Hence sexual interaction did not loosen the chains of bondage in Monmouth County. In Dutch-dominated Bergen County to the north, there is evidence that some interracial marriages existed. In Monmouth itself a Dutch-named magistrate, Justice Vandervear, was accused, according to the county's public record, of "lying with a negro wench." Given the number of adulterous Quaker masters who remain cloaked in anonymity, this public charge may simply veil a more nuanced breach of social etiquette: perhaps the magistrate was lying with a "wench" he did not own.[17]

Coerced breeding forces the unwilling (or unwitting) mother to perpetuate her state of bondage beyond herself. It thus represents the ultimate transgression of a slave's individuality. And in dashing the hopes that any mother has for her child, it also denies her humanity. To understand the stubborn tolerance of colonial society for such consequences, one has only to look across the Atlantic. The culture that English settlers brought with them included both a powerful rhetoric of freedom and social conventions often rigidly hierarchical and sometimes savagely so. The political and social instruments of class division in England—codes, customs, cruelty, complicity, complacency—were imported to New Jersey, where they daily strengthened the edifice of slavery.

West Africans numbed by the cruelties of slave ships could

still encounter these aspects of English culture with a measure of shock. Olaudah Equiano, as a slave en route to Virginia in the 1730s, "had never seen among any people such instances of brutal cruelty. . . . One white man in particular I saw . . . flogged so unmercifully . . . that he died in consequence of it; and they tossed him over the side as they would have done a brute."[18] Knowing England at first hand, Virginia Governor William Byrd II felt sanguine about forced labor in his colony, asserting that "our poor negroes are freemen in comparison with the slaves who till [England's] ungenerous soil; at least, if slavery consists in scarcity and hard work."[19] But of course it doesn't, as the former slave Ottobah Cugoano was aware when he wrote that while "some of the poor [in Great Britain and Ireland] suffer greater hardships than many of the slaves, . . . bad as it is, the poorest in England would not change their situation for that of slaves."[20]

The Baptist and Quaker slaveholders who originally settled Monmouth County were, as a group, perhaps the most benign of New World masters. The willingness of both the Baptist Roger Williams and the Quaker William Penn to study the tongue of local Indians (so as to speak with them—in the most literal sense—on their own terms) stands in marked contrast to the attitude of, say, New Jersey's original coproprietor, Sir George Berkeley, who had scarcely arrived in the colonies before he ventured to establish a slave trade in Native Americans. Nevertheless, it would be naive to suppose that slavery under Quakers and Baptists was benign. William Byrd merely touched on a general and indeed predictable human fallibility when he deplored both the inflated pride of masters (who "ruin the industry of our white people") and "the necessity of being severe" with slaves.[21]

Descriptions of scars and deformities in notices of runaway servants provide evidence that some Monmouth County masters "corrected" their slaves in brutal fashions. William Moraley, an English indentured servant in Monmouth County, observed that "the Condition of the Negroes is very bad, by reason of the severity of the laws." Moraley commented that, after capture, fugitive slaves were "unmercifully whipped," and that "if they die under the Discipline, their Masters suffer no punishment, there being no Law against murdering them."[22]

Reports from the time also picture masters who became abusive without resorting to corporal punishment. While staying in a tavern in rural New Jersey in 1744, Dr. Alexander Hamilton was "waked this morning before sunrise with a strange bawling and hollowing without doors. It was the landlord ordering his negroes with an imperious and exalted voice. In his order the known term or epithet, son of a bitch, was often repeated." Other contemporary documents indicate that Lewis Morris also become exasperated with slave performances and developed antagonistic relationships with some of his bondsmen.[23]

Optimally, masters considered bondspeople part of their *kitchen family*, people with whom they worked and lived comfortably. Homes in the earlier eighteenth century were usually a story and one-half, heavy timber framed and wood-sided, with sharp, steep roofs and small windows. Servants lived in the dark and airless upper stories or, as oral tradition has it, in barns and outbuildings. A few real estate advertisements mention "Negro-Houses." When the houses combined living and cooking areas, they were "Negro Kitchens."

Later accounts of the architecture of colonial homes suggest that as homes became larger and living space more specialized, masters and their kitchen families lived further apart, with the whites and the bondspeople divided in separate wings. The Holmes-Hendrickson house in Holmdel typifies this architecture. Mixing English and Dutch framing with a hybrid floor plan, the house consists of two large rooms in the front, two smaller rooms in the rear, and a kitchen wing where slaves lived.[24]

Some northern households went to considerable lengths to create an extended, paternalistic family within the home. An early-nineteenth-century volume, Anne Grant's survey of domestic life in pre-Revolutionary rural New York (a society approximate to Monmouth's) describes a striking ritual designed to bond master and slave for life. When a slave child reached three years of age, the first New Year's Day thereafter it was formally given to a son, daughter, or other young relative of the same sex. At that time the white child gave the black some money and a pair of shoes, creating a powerful emotional tie between the two. The slave mother then taught her child the skills of a servant, believing, according to Grant, that servanthood was the best life-expectancy. In return the mother could expect the child would never be sold without her consent.[25]

In the wealthiest Anglican homes, likewise, familiarity between masters and servants was common. Alexander Graydon, an English officer quartered in a New Jersey home noticed that the black servant was treated, "not as a waiter, but as a kind of *enfant maison*, who walked about, or took a post in the chimney-corner with his hat on and occasionally joined in the conversation." Graydon sensed that had he not been there, the servant probably would have joined the group at the table.[26]

Slaves on Their Own

When enslaved blacks forged strong ties of trust with their masters, they could be allowed considerable autonomy. Lewis Morris's slave, Watty, for instance, regularly escorted his master's daughters from Tinton Falls to Morrisania in New York. Entrusted with large sums of money, Watty bought goods and on at least one occasion paid off a hired white man with whom

Morris had a dispute. In this case, Watty took the man to New York City, paid him, withheld luggage until a minor tangle was resolved, and reported back to Morris. Morris also negotiated fees with Watty for extra work such as digging ditches at Tinton Falls.[27]

Simply on its own terms, travel provided trusted blacks a kind of temporary freedom, a relief from the monotony of slavery. Slaves traveled most often to pick up commodities for their masters at general stores. Armed with a pass or the trust of white familiars—masters were expected to furnish passes, but over time few probably bothered—slaves obtained easy passage within a particular region. General stores frequently serviced large areas. Thus delivery work in Monmouth County enabled rural blacks to travel freely into New York City and village blacks to gather without suspicious gazes from whites. As Dell Upton has remarked about Virginia's enslaved, once past the all-important boundary of the master's property, they could go almost anywhere without question.[28]

Inevitably, purchasing commodities for their masters allowed enslaved men to exploit the privilege to buy their own items at stores or spend money earned selling skins and extra vegetables. Examples may be found in the ledgers of various grocers and merchants. In Shrewsbury, despite the laws, free and enslaved blacks bought rum, molasses, tobacco, and cloth from local merchants as early as 1729. On weekends, slaves took such family produce as eggs, pork, and beef, or their own foodstuffs, skins, and firewood into the towns.[29]

The money garnered from the sale of these goods was sometimes spent on Sundays and such annual holidays as Easter, Christmas, or Whitsunday—for slaves especially anticipated moments of liberty.[30] Custom gave the Sabbath to bondspeople for themselves, and wise masters permitted their chattel to travel on holidays. On long holidays slaves from Monmouth County even journeyed into New York and Philadelphia.

Holiday activities represent some of the clearest examples of African and European syncretism. Pinkster, a four-day secular observance of Pentecost, provided a chance to gather during warm weather. Like other major Christian holidays, Pinkster was both an intimate family affair (as seen in the last chapter) and an expansive public festival. Although Pinkster originated among the Dutch, variations of it were also observed in New York and New Jersey by members of Lutheran, Huguenot, and Anglican churches, together with their slaves and other laborers.[31] Monmouth's African American slaves routinely ventured into Manhattan for Pinkster.

A remarkable satire on the secular face of Pinkster by "a Spy," printed in the *New-York Weekly Journal* in 1737, offers a rare representation of a holiday celebrated in both town and country, and provides evidence of African selective adaptation before the Revolution. The Spy begins his description of Pinkster with a household bondsman: "This morning I heard my Landlord's black Fellow very busy at tuning of his Banger [banjo] . . . and playing some of his Tunes." Intrigued, the author wandered into the kitchen and asked about the occasion. The slave's response was, "Massa, to-day Holiday: Backera not work; Ninegar no Work; me so savvy play Banger; go yonder, you see Ninegar play Banger for true; dance too; You see Sport today for true." He directed the narrator to the festival. "You savvy the Field, little way out of town, no Houses there, grandy Room for Dance there."

Upon reaching the area, which doubtless was the Fields, the Spy found "the Plain partly covered with Booths and well crowded with Whites." He observed the "Negroes divided into Companies, I suppose according to their different Nations." He listened as enslaved and free blacks danced to "the Hollow Sound of a Drum" and to "the grating, rattling noise of Pebles or Shells in a small Basket." Others plied the banjo, and "some knew how to joyn the Voice." "Companies of the Blacks" were using cudgels and small sticks to act out military dances. With disgust, the Spy noted that some blacks were "unlucky enough to get a Dram too much, and I suppose were got to Loggerheads, all cursing and swearing, and that in a Christian Dialect, enough to raise one's Hair on end."

Seeking refreshment, the narrator went into a booth and called for a tankard of beer. Before he could sip it, he found himself "in a Place little better (if anything at all) than a brothel." He observed the mixed multitude, "some with their Dexies on their laps, others in close Hugg." Shocked, the visitor saw "a grave Person, not unknown to me, slyly hiding himself behind a seemingly sanctified Beast, both professing our Religion." The man he "considered as a Master and Father of a Numerous Family and yet [here would] go astray with a Thing that in my opinion almost deserved the name of Hagg." Fleeing the importunities of a "Jade who seemed to have a Months Mind more for me than I had for her," the Spy rushed into another booth. There he "found my Hopes were vain," for his companions were drunken "Gentlemen with Mechanics, some Maudlin, and some so far intoxicated that they were passed making any noise." Others greeted the visitor with "Oaths, Curses and Blasphemies, [which] soon sent me hence. . . . One was so kind as to Send a Curse after me."

Outside, his black guide—who evidently had stopped short of entering the booths—took him to cockfights, boxing matches, and wrestling. Tired of the noise, the Spy reflected on the way home about such religious holidays, particularly this one, "set apart to commemorate the Resurrection of the Blessed Savior." He concluded drolly that "Holidays thus Spent could be of very little service if they were not pernicious."[32]

The Spy's satire reveals much about the African and European interpenetrations of culture in an American ambiance. At festival time blacks and whites frolicked together. Pinkster was a manifestation of syncretism possible only around East Jersey and New York City, with the integration of English, Dutch, German, French, and African cultures.

At such gatherings blacks found one of the few available public venues for African cultural expression. Colonial legislators had banned celebrations of African holidays, reasoning that they led to riots. In response, Africans adapted European rituals, interlarding them with vital African belief systems that blended with white American polycultural modes of behavior.

But blacks also used Christian holidays with different intent: as disguised performances of their own rituals. Pinkster was similar to African celebrations such as a Gold Coast festival, observed by Willem Boseman, held in early June to banish the devil.[33] The Spy's account documents the presence at Pinkster of another important element of African ritual—its music. Africans from the Guinea Coast in particular were adept at drums and stringed instruments. The use of several instruments at Pinkster created an ensemble style akin to that heard at a West African festival.[34] Banjos, rattles, drums, and fiddles, common at slave festivals, were carryovers from African rituals, which often merged the sacred and secular. Pinkster songs, as well, with their emphasis on role reversal, were close cousins to African songs and dances of derision.

Flight from Slavery

For the most assertive slaves, autonomous moments afforded by holidays and frolics were not enough to ease the ache for freedom. Colonial newspapers printed at least thirty-five advertisements for runaway slaves from Monmouth County. While this number, extended over sixty years, may seem low, one should consider that masters in rural areas often failed to advertise a short-lived escape or gave up without attempting to recapture their lost property. Actual instances of flight probably outnumbered runaway notices by a significant margin.[35]

The reasons for fleeing varied. Some sought to escape mistreatment, others the threat of sale. Still others were trying to join distant relatives. Once a slave determined to run away, a master's strongest efforts could not dissuade him. Slaves disappeared at the first moment of opportunity. Prince fled Joseph Allen of Metedeconk with an iron collar around his neck. Quaco fled in 1761 wearing an "iron collar with two hooks to it, round his neck, a pair of Handcuffs with a chain to them, six feet long." Jacob, of Upper Freehold, New Jersey, "went from work at his plough and was without shoe or stocking and no other clothes but an Oznabrig Shirt and Trowsers, an Old ragged waistcoat and an old hat."[36]

As the notice for Jacob illustrates, masters who took out advertisements often hoped that precise description of their slaves' attire would facilitate identification and recapture. However the same parsimony that helped slaveholders turn a tidy profit on their farms worked against them here. In Monmouth County slave dress—excepting the wardrobes of a very few privileged servants—was distinctly ordinary and usually homemade. Undaunted, however, by the uniformity of their descriptions, masters recalled in extraordinary detail a procession of towcloth shirts and trousers, buckskin breeches, and used beaver hats. A description somewhat more extended than usual was the sartorial inventory of escaped Jack by Shrewsbury slaveholder Gabriel Stelle. Stelle said the bondsman left with the requisite towcloth shirt, leather breeches, and old beaver hat, but also wearing a woolen shirt, a homespun jacket, a "fashionable" coat, and a brown greatcoat, together with a pair of square-toed shoes with wooden heels. If Jack ran away during the winter, he was bundled up well enough to move through New Jersey wilds without risking hypothermia. In any season he was carrying a convertable currency on his back: good coats could be sold at one of the used clothing markets in the cities, places visited by slaves doubt-less hungry for the variety of attire available there.[37]

The enslaved might swap clothing, of course, but they could not hide body types, scars, disfigurements, or birthmarks. Ac-cordingly, notices paid considerable attention to physical de-tails, some of which testify to the brutal conditions in which northern slaves worked. James, who fled from Thomas White of Shrewsbury in 1740, had "his Right Shoulder out . . . which by lifting up his Arm may soon be discovered." York of Middletown had one "of his foreteeth broken off at the gum." Robin, who fled from Joseph Taylor of Freehold in 1744, had a "small Wart upon his neck; large Hands and Feet." In Monmouth's increasingly creole population, a fugitive's skin pigmentation was important; one escapee might be "yellow-ish," another "of a very black Color"; yet another, like Jacob, "passes himself as an Indian."[38] Smallpox often pitted a slave's face.

Newspaper advertisements for self-emancipated Africans sometimes went beyond physical description to reveal charac-teristic personalities. Ben, for example, was known to talk "too much when a little elevated with liquor."[39] Not infrequently such notices allow us glimpses of black versatility, talent, and quick wittedness. Ishmael was "a great fiddler, and often shewing sleight of hand tricks." The reluctant bondsman and would-be Indian Jacob had "several times changed his name, calling him-self James Start, and James Pratt, &ct." Joe was a "smooth-tongued fellow, and will likely change his name." Toby, who escaped from John Coward of Freehold in 1764, could "write and read. . . . It is likely he will forge a pass and pretend to want a new Master for himself." The African Cato, alias Toby, was described by his erstwhile master, Richard Stillwell of Middle-town, in 1756 as being "a sly, artful fellow" who "deceives the credulous by pretending to tell fortunes, and pretends to be free, speaks English as if country born, and plays on the fiddle."[40]

The 1764 notice for Toby shows the leverage that literacy could provide in a society where whites themselves were often unable to read and write. Making a great show of obsequiousness and earnestly proferring their counterfeit passes or out-of-date indenture papers to suspicious but illiterate whites, African Americans like Toby could transmute worthless paper into passports to liberty. Cato's notice of 1756 shows, further, that the power of the pen could also be harnessed by slaves who had never held one—Stillwell, according to his advertisement, believed Cato to be armed with a fake pass given him by some "Base person." Eighteen months later, with Cato still at liberty, Stillwell intimated in a revised and updated advertisement that the resourceful dodger had fled bondage to join with a woman and that he had "since his elopement changed his name several times," managing to stay one step ahead of his pursuers.[41]

Though most fugitives journeyed alone, some traveled in pairs or groups. Stoffels left his master Judith Vincent accompanied by two other men, "one being half Indian and half Negro and the other a Mollatto about thirty years of age & plays upon the violin." Abraham fled John Coward along with Toby in 1764; he too could play the fiddle and also read and write, making it "likely that he will forge a pass."[42] Pompey and Nero, "new negroes from the River Gambia," escaped John Gartner of North Carolina and, despite minimal English, journeyed together through Appalachian wilderness, Pennsylvania plateau, and New Jersey coastal plain to Shrewsbury. Even sly, artful escapees need a place to collect their wits and catch their breath. Monmouth County was that stopping point for some slaves on the run. But there were dangers; legislation empowered—indeed, required—Monmouth's white citizens to seize and jail suspect blacks.[43] Pompey and Nero were snared by an alert John Morris in November 1765. Their saga, however, did not end there. Eight months later they escaped Morris "in a small boat, 16 feet keel, a black bottom and her wales painted brown, had 4 oars on

board." Another southern slave, Arnold, formerly Harry, relo-
cated from South Carolina and was "supposed to be in this province." There is no record of his capture.[44]

The best hope of support, sustenance, and eventual employment for escaped slaves was to mingle with free blacks where
they were most numerous, in and around the larger cities. The
versatility required of enslaved farmhands no doubt stood them
in good stead wherever there was a need for teamsters or general laborers. Some slaves from Monmouth County fled to re-
gional ports such as Perth Amboy, where they worked along the
wharves or shipped on privateers. In times of war some joined
the army. Urban employment was probably most risky for runaway house servants; while their skills suited them for domestic
service in large cities, prospective white employers there would
be among the first to read notices of runaways. Accordingly,
where blacks were numerous enough to sustain a sudsidiary
economy, the safest course for escaped servants (and laborers as
well) was to make their way within it. The frequent mention of
fiddling in newspaper advertisements by Monmouth slave masters shows one way escapees were likely to do this. A talented
fiddler—in African American terminology of the late eighteenth
century, a *songster* or *music physicianer*—could survive by singing and playing for fellow blacks. Another advantage surely not
lost upon those most hotly pursued: the professional life of the
musician typically involves extensive travel.[45]

The Mirage of Manumission

Even with the major black population centers of the urban
North only a day's hard ride from Monmouth's fields, the liberty of runaways must have seemed precarious at best. The most
durable freedom, slaves knew, came with legal emancipation.
Yet the codes of colonial New Jersey virtually eliminated oppor-

tunities to obtain freedom by legal means. And the rare instances of emancipation reveal how, even then, liberty came burdened by conditions.

The first known emancipation in Monmouth County occurred in 1698, when Mary Silverhood of Freehold manumitted her "negro Man Sambo" with the proviso that he "should serve my son Samuel Hopmore for five years and then my son-in-law for two more." Only "then he shall go free and dispose of himself as he pleases."[46]

With the augmented slave code of 1714, masters were required to post a £200 bond for each emancipated slave—enough to effectively stifle further emancipations at a slaveholder's death. Even the most generous master had to demand promises of self-support as a condition of freedom. In 1731 Elias Mestayer, a Shrewsbury Huguenot, provided his two slaves with freedom five years after his death and after payment of £100 to his executors. Although he demanded financial independence of his former slaves, Mestayer awarded them "use of my farm with the utensils, husbandry tools, conveniences and stock of all sorts and the Eastern Room of my house with all out houses, barne, garden and orchardes." A similar arrangement was reached with "my Negro girl Nan." In conjunction with the others, Mestayer granted her freedom "when they have paid £100 at the rate of £20 per annum. I give and bequeath them 2 horses two cows and 2 heifers, four sheep and a goat." Liberty for his former bondspeople arrived only when they had amassed the small fortune needed to ransom themselves.[47]

Some masters treated slavery like an extended period of indenture, as did Quaker John Lippincott of Shrewsbury when he gave his "negro woman Hester her freedom and my five negroes, children of said Hester, if they behave themselves, shall be free at their several ages of 35 years." Lippincott's inventory listed the value of the five at £200 and noted that for the children to attain their freedoms, Ishmael had to work six years, Primis eleven, Hagar thirteen, Buss seventeen, and Oliver nineteen. Thomas White of Shrewsbury found terms considerably more generous when he ordered that "my negro man James serve my son Thomas for one year and after that time if he thinks he can pay the sum of £5 per year to Thomas, the said Negro is free; if he cannot Thomas is to maintain him at no expense to other children." Occasionally masters went so far as to require that relatives care for former bondsmen unable to support themselves. John Hulet of Shrewsbury gave his slave Oliver liberty to work for himself and "if sick or unable his son Joseph Hulet is to take him in."[48]

Free Blacks

By the American Revolution an estimated forty Monmouth County African Americans were free, about 3 percent of the black population of 1,394. The most prosperous were John Portland, Sr., and Obadiah, both of Shrewsbury, who had fifty acres each.[49] Few of the others owned much property. Nevertheless, as the Revolution approached, the gathering numbers of free blacks had to hearten their compatriots trapped in the pressure cooker of slavery.

Free blacks could avoid the worst excesses of Monmouth's slave society but not the inequities fostered by a ubiquitous racism. Frustration sometimes broke into open defiance. In 1755 Ben Moore, identified as a free black, was presented at the Court of General Sessions in Monmouth, accused of menacing words. A young man, Robert James, had been on an errand when he stopped by a neighbor's kitchen, where several blacks were sitting. Among them was Moore, who asked James to "treat him" to a drink. James gave the withering retort, "Who do you think will treat Negroes?" to which Moore responded, "When the

French come and take you, you will be Negroes and we will be Gentlemen and Masters over you."[50]

Moore's attitudes and words were not atypical of assertive slaves in the North. They indicate that seditious feelings circulated among northern blacks in the period between the failed insurrection in New York City in 1741 and the revolutionary tumult three decades later. The group portrait of Monmouth's African population suggests that a restive, skillful, and unhappy black population refused to accept slavery as a permanent condition. Like many of their white counterparts, black bondspeople would be ripe for revolution when the opportunity arose.

Slave Subterfuge

As slaves returned from Pinkster festivities to Monmouth's newer, larger homes, with their separate wings for whites and blacks, they entered a world designed to demonstrate white prosperity and authority. Yet the increased architectural distance also hampered control over slaves and their movements. Dispersed singly or in small groups over the county, blacks no doubt had frequent occasion to slip away in search of companionship or trysts.

Sometimes this had grave consequences. A sensational incident occurred in 1760 "a few days before Christmas [when] a very valuable Negro named Caesar, belonging to the Widow Forman of Colt's Neck . . . was found dead." After a neighbor reported having heard cries of murder, Caesar was disinterred and found to have suffered two broken legs and a dislocated neck. Investigation showed that he had been hanged from a tree by a jealous rival suitor. It appeared that Caesar and an enslaved black woman were to be married on Christmas Day, but a "Jealous fellow used an 'Old Wench' to tell Caesar that if he continued to visit [the woman] "he would not live to see

Christmas."[51] In the end it was the uncontrolled black rival and not Widow Forman who determined Caesar's destiny.

Such incidents were rare in Monmouth County. But not, of course, attempts to evade, or at least to limit, control; there are no slaves in nature. Freedom was always a desired, if elusive, goal for African Americans in Monmouth. And as subservience requires invention and fantasy as well as imposed power, its denial, whether for an hour or forever, invites ingenuity—in the parlance of the day, *conceit*.

The Lockean equation of liberty and property, which fueled so much political rhetoric in pre-Revolutionary America, forced the issue. Being property themselves, bondspeople were well defined under the law as having rights to nothing, least of all their time. In practice, slaves owned little more than the clothes on their backs and the "slave bedding" commonly mentioned in wills. In this environment, long on hard labor and short on luxury, it is not surprising that some slaves resorted to subterfuge to gain their small pleasures. In time they established an alternative economy based on petty crime.

In a typical case from Monmouth County, Ash, a slave of Johannes Smock of Middletown, was accused of stealing "rum & tobacco and a pewter quart and ten and half gallons of cyder." Lewis Morris believed petty theft to be common on his plantation. When his nephew John Morris, hired to manage the estate at Tinton Falls, reported an unusually bad harvest of grain, the owner blamed slave embezzlement, exclaiming that "you must not trust to the negroes measure, for they are both Stupid & conceited [i.e., ingenious], & will follow their own way if not carefully looked to. . . . [They] will steale." Later, Morris complained that a slave picked his pocket on a trip to New York City.[52]

Any economy requires commerce, and any community contact. But opportunities for either were limited in Monmouth

County for blacks, who usually lived in closer proximity to their masters than to each other. Accordingly, they used any pretense available to mingle as they labored. The common-pasturage method of tending livestock permitted slaves from different farms to group together and communicate. Similarly, fishing and hunting provided blacks with legitimate reasons to gather.[53] One of the best opportunities for slaves to get together was provided by frolics. Designed to help poorer farmers construct buildings or harvest crops, these occasions were used by slaves not only to party but to scheme and sometimes to plan for insurrections. In nearby Somerset County cases of petty theft are recorded as having occurred during frolics.

Among petty thieves race mattered little. There was no shortage of whites willing to fence stolen goods from blacks. In one year alone, 1753, two Shrewsbury men, Henry Cooper and Vincent White, were indicted separately for trading with slaves.[54] White indentured servants and slaves also banded together to rob their masters. Johan Jeremiah Myer, a white servant of Josiah Halsted of Shrewsbury, ran away with Tom, a slave of John Shepard of Shrewsbury, in 1756. To finance their new freedom, they absconded with both money and a large amount of clothing to sell at the used market in New York City.[55]

Blacks and Religion

If fear of the master was not sufficient to curb persistent petty theft, there were but a few options available. One could curse, as Hamilton's innkeeper did. One could pass acts to undergird the fragile slave economy, as New Jersey's assemblymen did—to little avail since such laws were ignored by black and white alike in Monmouth County. Or one could escalate the matter to a righteous, wrathful God.

Protestant slaveholders knew, of course, that the latter option could motivate only baptized slaves; the rest would be enjoying eternal damnation regardless of their conduct on earth. So the old question persisted: to baptize or not to baptize? Since the New Jersey assembly had already removed any legal obstacle to the ownership of Christians, arguments for and against had to be religious, political, or practical.

Reenter the Society for the Propagation of the Gospel in Foreign Parts. The S.P.G.'s pastoral clerics could make the religious argument, as Morgan Godwyn had in the 1680s, that baptizing slaves is a Christian duty. As members of a sect whose titular head was the king, they could make the political argument that a heathen baptized by an Anglican was an ally of England—a point of no small importance in a period of wars between England and France in North America.[56] And Anglicans could make the practical argument that a slave at church is under better control than a slave at liberty on Sunday. As an S.P.G. missionary explained in 1709, "One of the conditions of baptism . . . was that slaves were required to promise that they would not spend the Lord's Day in feasts, dances, and merry meetings."[57]

For Anglican missionaries baptism was not a mere formality to be accomplished with a few drops of water. The Church of England is a church of rites and texts, and membership in the church entails catechism, through which nonmembers may come to understand and engage with those rites and texts. Catechism for a black slave was, then, a lengthy process that included learning to read and write, and in the first decades of the eighteenth century the society was assiduous in its efforts towards black literacy.[58]

The issue of literacy shifted the grounds of debate over baptism beyond those considered by the law of 1704. Many slaveholders were convinced that catechism caused trouble among slaves and linked it to the rebellion of 1712 and conspiracy of 1741 in New York. And in this slaveholders judged aright, since literacy generally amplifies ambition by enlarging one's sense of the possible. The same conclusion seems to have been reached by William Knox, Anglican missionary to Virginia and West Indies. Knox argued that catechized blacks were more likely to "teach each other mischief than to profit by the catechist's instruction." These apprehensions prompted S.P.G. missionaries to screen carefully applicants for admission to their catechismal classes. Increasingly, Anglican priests in the North gave preference to enslaved or free black domestics from wealthier families. Inadvertently, Knox's racist message reveals that blacks looked to spiritual egalitarianism as a mechanism to freedom—a view they spread among themselves.[59]

In Monmouth County the S.P.G. effort bore little fruit until 1745, when Thomas Thompson was appointed missionary there. Thompson, after a brilliant career as student, professor, and dean at Cambridge, resigned his comfortable position to accept a mission in America. Whites and blacks in Monmouth flocked to the distinguished cleric's church, St. Peter's, in Freehold. Within three months Thompson baptized forty-nine white people. Although anxious about rumors that Monmouth County blacks practiced poisoning, Thompson especially yearned to baptize them, too, and during his five-year tenure in Freehold, Thompson welcomed them into the church.[60] He also reformed Christ Church in Shrewsbury, which had never before baptized a black.

Thompson preferred catechizing well-recommended domestic slaves, but he also baptized a slave named John, who was sentenced to be burned alive for a rape. Although custom demanded immediate execution, Thompson convinced the authorities to "allow the Space of a fortnight to be prepared in for death . . . and at length bring him to a true repentance." The priest found that the condemned man knew something of Christian principles, which made it easy to give him further knowledge. In order to speed the man's conversion, Thompson read psalms to him, asking that he repeat "verse after verse after me; every now and then bidding him raise up his Mind and Thoughts to Heaven, and Consider that he was speaking to the Almighty God." After receiving the slave's confession, Thompson baptized him three days before he was burned and on the fateful day gave him Communion.[61]

During his five years in Monmouth, Thompson baptized thirteen enslaved people, including "Phoebe, a wench in my service," and five free blacks, among them an interracial child, named Zebulon, son of Black Robin and Elizabeth Holland.[62] Thompson resigned his Monmouth post in 1750 to travel to S.P.G. missions in Africa, where he wrote a famous essay on slavery and conversion.[63] His successor in Monmouth County, Samuel Cooke, baptized at least twenty-two enslaved and eleven free blacks. Usually these were servants of the elite. For example, in 1753 Cooke baptized seven slaves of the widow Thorne of Shrewsbury.[64]

What were the effects of decades of Anglican efforts in Monmouth County? Were the S.P.G. missionaries agents of the slave masters intent only upon inculcating docile attitudes among slaves? In their zeal to anglicize slaves, did missionaries blot out all traces of an African past in a black religious holocaust?[65] Or did an African use of European religion sustain traditional values in an otherwise oppressive context?

Anglican churches provided a selective acculturation to European values. In rural areas like Monmouth, Anglican divines paid careful attention to local anxieties over urban insurrections carried out by educated slaves, and to the unending controversy over baptism, and so did not generally evangelize the enslaved. Black catechismal students came principally from the classes of servants of elite merchants and farmers. Anglican clerics put their enslaved students through a rigorous education emphasizing literacy, prayers, biblical devotion, and secular docility. For committed African students intent on accepting Christian conversion, Anglicanism presented the most clear-cut and receptive channel of communication. Students were primarily female, and acceptance of Anglican education and hierarchy offered the best, if limited hopes for emancipation. The missionaries' informal Sunday afternoon schools created a tiny class of literate and highly acculturated African Americans, but left the majority untouched.

Politically, despite the small numbers of converts, Anglican missionary efforts had four important consequences, undermining the authoritarian power of the master in important ways. As a transatlantic faith, Anglicanism stressed the importance of international and imperial bonds over local governance. Anglican instructors accentuated the importance of sacred power over the temporal authority. Although Anglicans vigorously denied that baptism mandated emancipation, folk customs held that refusal of this rite placed slave masters in opposition to God, instilling among blacks a critique of slavery. Finally, Anglican educational efforts constructed genuine English establishment ties to blacks, which made African American choices in the American Revolution very easy.[66]

Unlike Anglicans, who failed to question slavery directly, members of one denomination, the Society of Friends, debated its morality. Constituting over 40 percent of Monmouth's colonial population, Friends enjoyed a position among the economic elite throughout the Revolutionary period. Quakers were important slaveholders and traders themselves, with one-half of the Shrewsbury monthly meeting who died before 1741 bequeathing slaves.[67]

In Monmouth County, Quaker slaveholding first caught the critical eye of John Hepburn, a Scot living near Freehold. His abolitionist tract of 1715 argued that slavery is inconsistent with Christianity and violates the Golden Rule. He maintained that slaveholders violated each of the Ten Commandments, especially the Seventh, by forcing husband and wives apart and promoting adultery—the master's own, surely, but also perhaps African American polygamy. Hepburn initially found few followers in Freehold. Slavery did not become an important issue for the New Jersey Quakers until the 1750s.[68]

Monmouth's Quaker geography divided the county into an eastern portion, including Shrewsbury and Middletown, where, despite Hepburn, Friends were influenced by the conservative New York Meeting, and a western portion included in the Philadelphia Meeting, whose Friends took the lead on the issue of slavery. This split demonstrates that even among Quakers there was little unanimity about manumission.

As early as 1758, in a remarkable move, the Philadelphia Meeting voted to act against slavery. Once committed to manumission, these Friends were unquestionably energetic about cleansing the souls of members and washing away the sin of slavery. To encourage compliance, church leaders visited member slave owners, admonishing them to manumit their slaves and end any involvement with the slave trade. John Woolman, the leading Quaker advocate for emancipation, visited Shrewsbury Friends in 1761 with such intentions. Another leading Friend, Daniel Stanton, spoke out against slavery in large meetings in New Jersey and New York in the early 1760s. Such meetings were more open than regular services, and it is likely that slaves attended and heard the debate, though the record is silent on any black participation in Quaker meetings. Aside from an altruistic concern for blacks and for the purity of members' souls, Quakers feared for white safety. Quakers worried greatly that such discussion might encourage slave revolts. Anthony Benezet, anxious about a possible revolt, asked a London merchant to ensure that blacks could not obtain his pamphlets because "this was thought to be of too tender a nature to be exposed to view, in places where it might fall into the hands of the negroes."[69]

Despite the prominence being given to the issue of emanci-

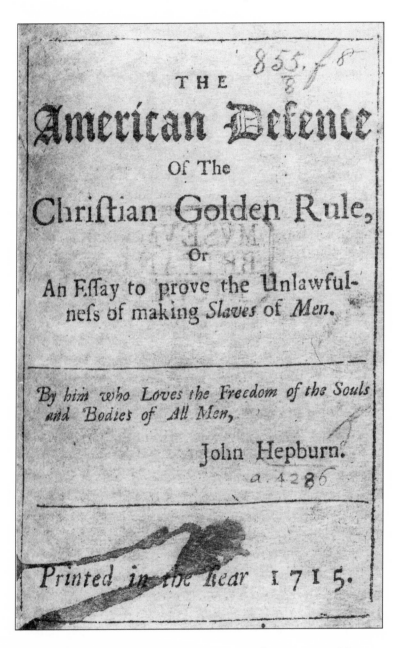

Title page of John Hepburn's anti-slavery pamphlet,
The American Defense of the Christian Golden Rule, 1715.
Courtesy of the British Library, London.

pation, Quakers in eastern Monmouth remained unenthusiastic about freeing their own slaves. Manumissions did not become common among Shrewsbury Quakers until the American Revolution, when sixteen African Americans gained freedom through gradual emancipation.

When more liberal Quakers began freeing their slaves in the 1760s, they typically encumbered manumission with weighty conditions such as deferring emancipation until the slave's thirtieth or thirty-fifth birthday. In part, these restrictions were attempts to satisfy the 1714 laws requiring masters to furnish £200 sureties to prevent freedmen from becoming public charges. But there were other motivations as well, seen in the fact that the terms of deferred emancipations often were set in a will. In this way, Quakers could comply with the policy of their Meeting and at the same time retain the benefits of their bondspeoples' labors, the responsibility for emancipation being shifted to their own descendants.[70]

When manumissions were not deferred, Friends consistently required cash payments from blacks as compensation for emancipation. Evidently, Quakers could favor emancipation and still see their servants as property. Friends in eastern and western New Jersey were agreed on this: a grant of emancipation should require either a term of years or a payment of money. Quakers' practices in this regard became deeply influential in New Jersey society, becoming the social standard for granting freedom.[71]

Once freedom was obtained, Quakers expressed little interest in African Americans. The Meeting instructed Friends who emancipated their bondspeople to insure their livelihood and provide for their education. Memoranda in the Shrewsbury Scrapbook reveal, however, that several members had failed to do either. The Society of Friends was also extremely reluctant to admit any blacks into its fellowship.[72] The example of William Boen is instructive. Boen was born in New Jersey in 1735 and taught himself to read and write. Shortly after purchasing his own freedom at twenty-eight, he applied to the Mount Holly Meeting for membership. He was refused, as the "way was not opening in the Friend's minds." Only in 1814, at the age of 79, was he finally admitted because of his "humility."[73] This indicates Quaker unwillingness to accept African Americans in spiritual fellowship and supports the view that their interest in manumission had more to do with their own souls than the souls or human conditions of black folk. Nevertheless, the Society of Friends set the standard for gradual manumission in Monmouth County.

Aside from their early liberation efforts, the importance of the Quakers lies in their equation of slavery and immorality. The question of Christians enslaving fellow believers had arisen before, but the Anglicans, Dutch Reformed, and Huguenot churches had dodged the issue. The Quakers met it head on, determining to erase slavery from their fellowship. Blacks apparently listened with great interest to public and private Quaker debates in which proponents of manumission sought to convince recalcitrant Friends. Blacks' awareness of this split among masters would have powerful consequences during the Revolution.[74]

If the Quakers refused to view blacks as spiritual equals, the nascent, evangelical sects were less distant. At the love feasts and mass rallies of the Great Awakening they embraced Africans. The first salvos of the evangelicals came in 1740 in George Whitefield's resounding attacks on slave masters in a letter: "I think God has a quarrel with you for your abuse and cruelty to the poor negroes," he challenged. He castigated owners for refusing baptism to their bondspeople.[75] Like the Anglicans, Whitefield did not intend to undermine slavery but rather to open the way to religious instruction. He taught that "servants . . . are required to be subject, in all lawful things to their master." Indeed, Whitefield himself became a slave owner. Yet the faith that Whitefield preached appealed to his audiences' hearts as much as their intellects. Rejected by staid Anglican clerics in New York and New Jersey, Whitefield nonetheless attracted thousands of hearers in these colonies. Among the attentive listeners was a black woman with whom Whitefield conversed in rural New Jersey. She told him "she was filled with a love of Christ & being too fond of the instrument would fair have gone with me. Her master assented but I bid her go home & with a thankful heart serve her present master."[76] Despite Whitefield's emphasis on docility and obedience, blacks interpreted his words by distinguishing between good Christians, who opened Christianity to them, and false Christians, who enslaved them.

The Great Awakening, which democratized the ideal of personal salvation, galvanized Monmouth County Presbyterians. Although the Presbyterians differed from Anglicans in many ways, they copied their approach to blacks. In Freehold the Tennent brothers, a family of ministers and religious leaders in New Jersey, welcomed Whitefield with open arms. In response to his messages, they began baptizing slaves in 1741 and continued to attract a trickle of converts until the Revolution. On July 5, 1741, Mink, "the Negro Man of Arent Schenck," became the first black baptized in Freehold's Old Tennent Church. He would remain but one of few. Over the next thirty-five years the Presbyterians baptized only nine slaves and no free blacks.[77]

Despite the Great Awakening, Presbyterians did not open doors to the general population of African Americans, preferring to limit black participation to public rituals. The "Sacramental Season," which occurred in late fall, included fasting, lengthy family orations, and prayers. Like Pinkster in the Dutch Reformed Church, the Presbyterian sacramental season was uncharacteristically egalitarian. Love feasts, open to all, instilled a temporary sense of equality before God. At the same time, colonial Presbyterians held a cautious and uncritical position regarding slavery.[78] Enslaved peoples remained outside the spiritual family. Such was not the case with Methodism.

Introduced to Monmouth County late in the colonial period, the new religious wave of Methodism attracted adherents of all races. Unlike older European faiths, Methodism did not require catechism before baptism, making it very attractive to the great masses of unlettered whites and blacks. Emphasizing universal salvation, experiential religion, and sanctification, Methodism made its greatest impact in the 1760s and 1770s. As Nathan Hatch has argued, blacks flocked to Methodism in its formative years because it was openly opposed to slavery, focused on immediate salvation, and willing to sponsor a nascent black ministry.[79] African Americans created within Methodism a space from spiritual elements of their traditional African heritage, however unrecognizable to whites and something that whites disallowed. Methodists did not respect African spirituality as much as fail to recognize it. A striking example of mutual black and white spirituality is found in the memoirs of Benjamin Abbott, an itinerant minister traveling in New York and New Jersey in the early 1770s. In early 1773 Abbott held a love feast at Lord Stirling's home in Basking Ridge, Somerset County, west of Monmouth.

> At the time of family worship, an abundance of black people assembled in the kitchen, and the door was set open so that they could enjoy without coming into the parlour. I gave out a hymn, brother Stirling went to prayer and after him myself. The power of the Lord came down in a wonderful manner among the black people some cried aloud and others fell to the floor, some praising God, some crying for mercy; after we had concluded, brother S went among them, where he continued upwards of an hour, exhorting them to fly to Jesus the ark of safety.[80]

But even Methodism could not satisfy all the spiritual needs of Africans in Monmouth County. And so blacks constructed their own fusion of Christianity and African cosmology. Evidence of African religious traditions are harder to trace in the colonial North than they are in the South.[81] Here and there, however, surviving records allow us early glimpses of a black ministry that arose like a phoenix after the American Revolution. Runaway notices provide evidence of black preachers like Simon, who ran away from Middlesex County in 1740. Simon was "a great Doctor . . . and says he is a Churchman." In 1775 Major Prevost of Bergen County advertised for Mark and Jenney. Mark was "a preacher, short, black, and well set and speaks slow; the woman is rather lusty, has a cast in one eye, bad teeth, smooth tongued and very artful." Other fugitive blacks passing through eastern New Jersey were described as being "professors of religion"; one, the notice tells us, "preaches to his color" and "makes a great show of religion, on which he has much to say."[82]

Black preachers and their audiences kept alive the sparks of old ways through spiritual communion. Their transforming religious influences emboldened them to hold to their former traditions while embracing the progressive aspects of Christianity where they occurred. A good example is the conversion narrative of Katy Schenck, a onetime slave of Gerrit Vanderveer of Monmouth County. Interviewed at age 97 in the Colored Home of New York City in 1851, she recalled vividly her early "sins" and subsequent conversion. Her words offer a rare view into the heart and mind of one slave who, doubtless like others, prepared for freedom and sought a larger meaning of life.

> About 12 years of age, I had strong convictions of sin, but resisted them and strove to get freed of them by carelessness and endeavoured to drive religion from my thoughts . . . I fought against the Lord and the Devil seemed determined I should serve him . . . One day when my mind was dreadfully distressed, I was going a milking but felt so wretched, I did not know what to do; it seemed that hell was ready to receive me. It was evening. I fell upon my knees. I prayed Lord Have

Mercy on Me and Help Me! All at once I looked up and I thought I saw heaven Open and it appeared to Me that the Lord was Stooping Down and Lifted Me up! And the Words came to me 'Thy people shall be willing in the day of thy power!' I stood still. I hardly knew what I was doing! I could not milk, I could only rejoice—I shouted aloud and ran home, telling all my folks how happy I was. They did not know what to think. I went to bed, but I could not sleep for my happiness. I felt now that the Lord had fast hold of me and I was safe. I was willing and desirous to serve God and I went on my way rejoicing.[83]

Schenck's testimony lays out the pathways and reveals the promises of black religious conversion. Her acceptance of sinfulness, her depression over her fate, and her appeal to a natural God followed by redemption are elements found in virtually every contemporary black religious narrative. Through her salvation Schenck found her own black voice and vision in a hostile world. Her newfound spirituality undoubtedly imbued her, as an enslaved female, with a dignity and self-worth absent in her previous "sinful" state. She heard the Lord's promise, "Thy people shall be willing in the day of thy power" This potent covenant between the Lord and an enslaved woman reveals the extraordinary and liberating fusion of spirituality and emerging African American identity. Bestowed upon a simple milkmaid, these words empowered Schenck to go "on my way rejoicing," a clear indication of a calling to preach. The place of her salvation was a pasture, a place as common and sweet as a baby's smile in the "Negro Kitchen"—and as unknown to white congregations. Despite the restrictions of European denominations, Schenck's salvation released her from the emotional shackles of slavery, pledged her to an authority higher than her master or the colonial government.[84]

Summary

Schenck's inner liberation was one of many small acts that foretold the experiences of African Americans in the American Revolution. Monmouth's enslaved population was ready for any opportunity which offered freedom. Over the course of the eighteenth century, Monmouth consistently ranked among the top three slaveholding counties in the colony. Composed of creolized bondspersons augmented by recent arrivals from Africa, the county's black population remained distant culturally and economically from its white farm populace. The slave owners self-serving paternalism offered little amelioration for slaves, but served to heighten the contradictions of slavery and freedom. Weekends and holidays brought fleeting glimpses of freedom; close proximity in the household created a mockery of ostensible bonds between master, mistress, and slave; familiarity could breed hatred and desires to attack or flee. Religious institutions in Monmouth were unsuccessful at inculcating docility among slaves or destroying completely their ties to an African past. Anglican missionaries were too limited in their appeal; use of ritual by the Dutch Reformed, Presbyterians and the spiritual equality of Methodists only prompted greater African zeal for liberty. Only the Society of Friends, however divided, openly opposed slavery by mid century, and offered a clear alternative to other denominational support for bondage.

Notes

1. Peter Wacker and Paul G. E. Clemens, *Land Use in Early New Jersey: A Historical Geography* (Newark, N.J., 1995), 140–65.

2. David Steven Cohen, *The Dutch-American Farm* (New York, 1992), 112–21, 145.

3. For Cato, see the *New-York Gazette; or, The Weekly Post-Boy*, 8 August 1757. For other versatile blacks, see the *New-York Gazette*, June

1, 1734, May 10, 1736, October 8, 1738, April 7, 1739. See also the *Pennsylvania Journal* (Philadelphia), October 13, 1763; *New-York Gazette; or, The Weekly Post-Boy*, September 6, 1764; *New York Weekly Mercury*, June 8, 1771.

4. This partial list of chores and seasonal work is reconstructed from a longer section in Wacker and Clemens, *Land Use*, 244–49.

5. See Eugene R. Sheridan, ed., *The Papers of Lewis Morris*, 3 vols., (Newark, 1991), 1:377; Obadiah Holmes, "Account Book, 1746–1756," and Gersham Mott, "Account Books, 1725–1769," Gersham Mott Papers, Monmouth County Historical Association, Freehold, N.J.; William Watson Papers, Yale University Archives.

6. Peter Wacker, "The New Jersey Tax-Ratable List of 1751," *New Jersey History* 107 (1989): 23–49; Wacker and Clemens, *Land Use*, 101.

7. "Notes on the State of New Jersey, Written August, 1776, by John Rutherford," *Proceedings of the New Jersey Historical Society*, 2d ser., vol. 1 (1867): 79–90. For agreement on growing scarcity of land in colonial Monmouth, see Wacker and Clemens, *Land Use*, 97.

8. For Toby's escape from Coward, see *Pennsylvania Gazette* (Philadelphia), May 31, 1764.

9. On the destinations of midland servants, see appendix 1 in David W. Galenson, *White Servitude in Colonial America: An Economic Analysis* (Cambridge, 1981). On Scots and Irish indentured servants, see tables 6.1 and 6.2 in Richard S. Dunn, "Servants and Slaves: The Recruitment and Employment of Labor," in *Colonial British America: Essays in the New History of the Early Modern Era*, ed. Jack P. Greene and J. R. Pole (Baltimore, 1984), 165, 170.

10. *The Infortunate: The Voyage and Adventures of William Moraley, an Indentured Servant*, ed. Susan E. Klepp and Billy G. Smith (University Park, Pa., 1992), 94–95 (hereafter cited as Moraley, *The Infortunate*). For a fuller discussion of indentured servants, see Sharon V. Salinger, *"To Serve Well and Faithfully": Labor and Indentured Servants in Pennsylvania, 1682–1800* (New York, 1987).

11. See, for example, Charles Nicoll Day Book, 1758–1768, New-York Historical Society. For blacks in England, see J. Jean Hecht, *Continental and Colonial Servants in Eighteenth-Century England* (Northampton, Mass., 1954), 33–52.

12. William Dunlap, *A History of the Rise and Progress of the Arts of Design in the United States*, 3 vols. (Boston, 1918), 1:288.

13. For a useful typology of domestics, see Whittington Bernard

Johnson, *The Promising Years, 1750–1830: The Emergence of Black Labor and Business* (New York, 1993), 149–59.

14. For roles of enslaved women, see Lois Green Carr and Lorena S. Walsh, "Economic Diversification and Labor Organization in the Chesapeake, 1650–1820," in *Work and Labor in Early America*, ed. Stephen Innes (Chapel Hill, N.C., 1988), 144–89; Johnson, *The Promising Years*, 150–51. See also Barbara Bush, *Slave Women in Caribbean Society, 1650–1838* (Bloomington, Ind., 1990), 33–46; Marietta Morrissey, *Slave Women in the New World: Gender Stratification in the Caribbean* (Lawrence, Kans., 1989), 62–81; Hilary M. Beckles, *Natural Rebels: A Social History of Enslaved Black Women in Barbados* (New Brunswick, N.J., 1989), 24–50.

15. For woman being sold, see *Zenger's Weekly Journal* (New York), April 15, 1734.

16. For patterns of wills, see David Narrett, "Men's Wills and Women's Property Rights in Colonial New York," in *Women in the Age of the American Revolution*, ed. Ronald Hoffman and Peter J. Albert (Charlottesville, Va., 1989), 118, 124–26; Dennis P. Ryan, "Six Towns: Continuity and Change in Revolutionary New Jersey, 1770–1792" (Ph.D. diss., New York University, 1974), 84; Cohen, *The Dutch-American Farm*, 139–42.

17. Shrewsbury Scrapbook, Haviland Record Center, New York; Holmes Papers, folder 3, Special Collections, Alexander Library, Rutgers University; Steen Collection, box 2, Monmouth County Historical Association, Freehold, N.J. Examples of genuine affection are evident in the marriages performed between whites and blacks in Bergen County, N.J., a rural county even more dedicated to slavery than Monmouth. See "Baptisms and Marriages of the Lutheran Church from 1725," *New York Genealogical and Biographical Record* 97–99 (1966–68): 97:95–105, 163–70, 223–32; 98:17–23, 92–95, 150–53, 222–24; 99:105-12, 134-40, 227–31.

18. *Interesting Narrative of the Life of Olaudah Equiano or Gustavus Vassa, the African, Written by Himself* [1789], in *Three Black Writers in Eighteenth Century England* (hereafter cited as *Three Black Writers*), ed. Francis D. Adams and Barry Sanders (Belmont, Calif., 1971), 130.

19. William Byrd II to the Earl of Egmont, 1736, in Elizabeth Donnan, ed., *Documents Illustrative of the History of the Slave Trade to America*, 4 vols. (1930–35; New York, 1969), 2:35.

20. Ottobah Cugoano, *Thoughts and Sentiments of the Evil and Wicked Traffic of the Slavery and Commerce of the Human Species* [1787], in *Three Black Writers*, 54.

21. William Byrd II, diary entry, cited in David Hackett Fischer, *Albion's Seed: Four British Folkways in America* (New York, 1989), 389.

22. Moraley, *The Infortunate*, 94.

23. *Gentleman's Progress: The Itinararium of Dr. Alexander Hamilton, 1744*, ed. Carl Bridenbaugh (Chapel Hill, N.C., 1948), 186. *The Papers of Lewis Morris*, 1:148, 2:17.

24. For Dutch architecture, see Cohen, *The Dutch-American Farm*, 51–53; Rosalie Fellows Bailey, *Pre-revolutionary Dutch Houses and Families in Northern New Jersey and Southern New York* (New York, 1936), 269–381, esp. 272–75, 288, 306, 314, 326–27, 370, 377; Helen Wilkinson Reynolds, *Dutch Houses in the Hudson Valley before 1776* (1929, reprint New York, 1965), 14; Inventory and Administration of the Estate of Adolph Phillipse, 1749–1763, New York Public Library.

25. [Anne Grant], *Memoirs of an American Lady, with Sketches of Manners and Scenery in America as They Existed Previous to the Revolution* (New York, 1809), 25–28.

26. Alexander Graydon, *Memoirs of His Own Time with Reminiscences of the Men and Events of the Revolution*, ed. John Stockton Littell, (Philadelphia, 1846), 247–49. See also *The Journal of Madam Knight*, ed. Malcolm Freiburg (Boston, 1972), 20–21.

27. See *The Papers of Lewis Morris*, 2:13–17, 30–31. For other trusted slaves at Tinton Falls, see *ibid.*, 126, 265; Lewis Morris Papers, "relating to Tinton Falls," folder 3, Lewis Morris Papers, Special Collections, Alexander Library, Rutgers University.

28. For examples of blacks picking up commodities at stores, see Kenneth Scott, "John Evert Van Allen's Account Book, 1771–1774," *New York Genealogical and Biographical Record* 108 (1977): 10–16; Samuel Deall Account Book, 1756–1778, cited in Robert W. Arthur, "The Deall Account Books," *New York Genealogical and Biographical Record* 116 (1985): 36–46, 105–10, 146–52, 216–20; Van Neste and Van Liew General Store Ledger, 1774–1775, Special Collections, Alexander Library, Rutgers University, Claire M. Lamers, "The Ledger of Doctor Elias Cornelius," *New York Genealogical and Biographical Record* 111/112 (1980–81): 111:79-89, 134–42, 230–32; 112:25–30, 117–76; Dorothy A. Stratford, "Nathaniel Holmes' Day Book," *Genealogical Magazine of New Jersey* 54 (1979): 35–40; Charles Nicoll

Day Book, 1758–1768; Kenn Stryker-Rodda, "The Janeway Account Books, 1735–1746," *Genealogical Magazine of New Jersey* 33 (1958): 1–10, 73–82. For a study of the colonial New Jersey general store, see Rebecca Yamin, "The Raritan Landing Traders: Local Trade in Pre-Revolutionary New Jersey" (Ph.D. diss., New York University, 1988). For ease of movement, see Dell Upton, *Holy Things and Profane: Anglican Parish Churches in Colonial Virginia* (Cambridge, Mass., 1986), 218.

29. For evidence of slaves selling their goods, see the following manuscript collections in the New-York Historical Society: Account Book of a Shrewsbury, New Jersey Merchant, 1750; William Townsend, The Negro Ledger, 1761–1762, Oyster Bay, New York, Thomas Holmes, General Merchant Day Book, 1729–1754 (2 vols.). For a discussion of importance of the rural markets and trips to New York City, see Wacker and Clemens, *Land Use*, 24–26, 229–30.

30. Moraley, *The Infortunate*, 94–95.

31. For a recent discussion of Pinkster, see Cohen, *The Dutch-American Farm*, 161–63. Anglicans celebrated Pinkster as Whitsuntide.

32. For a serial article on Pinkster, see the *New-York Weekly Journal*, March 7, 14, 21, and 28, 1737. The Spy's comment about the resurrection indicates that the holiday was Pentecost, rather than General Training Day, as argued in Shane White, "'It Was a Proud Day': African Americans, Festivals, and Parades in the North, 1741–1834," *Journal of American History* 81 (1994): 13–50.

33. Sterling A. Stuckey, *Slave Culture: Nationalist Theory and the Foundations of Black America* (New York, 1987), 80–83.

34. *Ibid.* For African styles of music, see Robert Farris Thompson, "An Aesthetic of the Cool: West African Dance," in *The Theater of Black Americans: A Collection of Critical Essays*, ed. Errol Hill (New York, 1987), 99–112; Peter Van Der Merwe, *Origins of the Popular Style: The Antecedents of Twentieth-Century Popular Music* (Oxford, 1989), 30–39.

35. The notices cited in this chapter are drawn from Graham Russell Hodges and Alan Edward Brown, eds., *"Pretends to be Free": Runaway Slave Advertisements from Colonial and Revolutionary New York and New Jersey* (New York, 1994).

36. For Prince, see *New-York Gazette; or, The Weekly Post-Boy*, August 9, 1756. For Quaco, see *Pennsylvania Journal* (Philadelphia), August 20, 1761. For other uses of iron collars, see notices for Harry,

New-York Gazette; or, The Weekly Post-Boy, December 31, 1759, and Cyrus, *New-York Gazette; or, The Weekly Post-Boy,* October 15, 1761. For Jacob, see *New York Mercury,* September 10, 1764.

37. For Jack escaped from Stelle, see *American Weekly Mercury* (Philadelphia), August 1, 1723.

38. For James escaped from White, see *New-York Weekly Journal,* June 23, 1740. For York, see *New-York Journal; or, The General Advertiser,* May 19, 1768. For Robin escaped from Taylor, see *Pennsylvania Gazette* (Philadelphia), April 5, 1744. For yellowish pigmentation, see notice for Toney, *New-York Gazette; or, The Weekly Post-Boy,* November 17, 1755. For very black pigmentation, see notice for Abraham, *Pennsylvania Gazette* (Philadelphia), June 26, 1760. For passing as an Indian, see notice for Jacob, *New-York Gazette; or, The Weekly Post-Boy,* September 13, 1764.

39. For Ben, see *Rivington's New-York Gazetteer,* July 8, 1773. For Ishmael, see *New-York Gazette and The Weekly Mercury,* August 22, 1768. For Joe, see *Pennsylvania Gazette* (Philadelphia), May 18, 1767.

40. For Toby escaped from Coward, see *Pennsylvania Gazette* (Philadelphia), May 31, 1764.

41. For Cato escaped from Stillwell, see *Pennsylvania Gazette* (Philadelphia), April 15, 1756, and *New-York Gazette: or, The Weekly Post-Boy,* August 29, 1757.

42. For Stoffels escaped from Vincent, see *New-York Gazette,* June 24, 1734; for Toby and Abraham escaped from Coward, see *Pennsylvania Gazette* (Philadelphia), June 14, 1764.

43. These statutes turned many young white men into slave hunters.

44. For Nero and Pompey escaped from Gartner, see *Pennsylvania Gazette* (Philadelphia), November 8, 21, 1765; escaped from Morris, see *New-York Gazette; or, The Weekly Post-Boy,* June 5, 1766. For Arnold, see *New-York Gazette; or the Weekly Post-Boy,* November 20, 1760.

45. Traveling black musicians were significant catalysts in the synthesis of new African American cultural amalgams. Just as professional musicians in Africa, touring up and down the west coast, took inspiration from polycultural sources, so black traveling musicians in America drew from Scots, Irish, and English as well as African vernacular genres. For discussion of songsters, see Paul Oliver, *Songsters and Saints: Vocal Traditions on Race Records* (New York, 1984), 22–25. The frequency of fiddlers in a black population was not unusual. In the South, Ster-

ling Stuckey argues, fiddlers constituted one out of every ten slaves and were essential to black music and dance traditions. See Stuckey, *Slave Culture*, 18, 21, 107, 370 n.159. For advertisements of fiddlers, see *New-York Gazette; or, The Weekly Post-Boy*, July 11, 1748, June 12, 1752, January 31, 1757, June 6, 1757, October 10, 1757, July 24, 1758, December 11, 1758, April 29, 1762, August 26, 1762; *Pennsylvania Gazette* (Philadelphia), May 9, 1751, April 15, 1756; *New York Mercury*, May 14, 1764.

46. Will of Mary Silverhood, "Unrecorded Wills," 12 vols., Archives Section, Division of Archives and Records Management, Department of State, Trenton, N.J., 10:379.

47. Will of Elias Mestayer, "Monmouth County Wills, 1680–1775," New Jersey State Archives, item 457.

48. Wills of John Hulet, John Lippincott, and Thomas White, "Monmouth County Wills, 1680–1775," New Jersey State Archives, items 685, 1161, 1413, 1459, 1537; see also items 1671, 2087, 3753, 3881.

49. As no census of free blacks was taken, the figure for free blacks is an estimate based on various business, tax, and church records. Christ Church, Shrewsbury, baptized fifteen free people in the late 1740s and 1750s. Business and tax records offer other free black identities. The Dover Township tax ratables of 1773 mention Joseph Cromwell and Negro Thomas. Norrice and Elizabeth Negro were members of the Baptist Church and labored as farm hand and domestic. Shrewsbury Quakers manumitted sixteen enslaved blacks during the American Revolution. Tax ratables levied during the Revolution list twelve more free blacks scattered across the county. See David J. Fowler, "Dover Township 1773 Rateables," *Genealogical Magazine of New Jersey* 59 (1984): 115–18; Shrewsbury Scrapbook, 1–21; "New Jersey Tax Ratables, 1778–1780," New Jersey State Archives; Samuel Holmes His Book of Accounts, Cherry Hall Papers, box 4, Monmouth County Historical Association, Freehold, N.J.

50. For Ben Moore's words, see *King* v. *Ben Moore*, 1755, Monmouth County Archives, Manalapan, N.J. Ten years later, Moore, now forty and by some misfortune slipped into servitude, ran away from Henry and John Robins of Freehold. Moore was identified as "formerly an indented servant and . . . has taken those old passes, pretending to be a free Negro." For notices, see *New-York Gazette; or, The Weekly Post-Boy*, February 6, 1766.

51. For Caesar's murder, see *New York Mercury*, February 2, 1761.

52. For Ash, see Monmouth Country Court of Oyer and Terminer, "February and April Sessions, 1753," Monmouth County Archives, Manalapan, N.J. For Morris quotes see *The Papers of Lewis Morris*, 1:148, 2:17. For similar comments, see *The Journal of Esther Edward Burr, 1754–1757*, ed. Carol F. Karlsen and Laurie Crumpacker (New Haven, Conn., 1984), 104, and Robert G. Livingston to Henry J. Livingston, June 18, 1752, in *Dutchess County Historical Society Annual* 6 (1921): 54–58.

53. Wacker and Clemens, *Land Use*, 26.

54. For cases of Henry Cooper and Vincent White, see Monmouth County, Court of Oyer and Terminer, "February and April Sessions, 1753," Monmouth County Archives, Manalapan, N.J.

55. For Meyer fugitive from Halsted and Tom escaped from Shepard, see *New-York Gazette; or, The Weekly Post-Boy*, March 1, 1756, June 5, 1756. The history of interracial gangs is little understood. For their presence among independent but associated ethnic groups, see Florike Egmond, *Underworlds: Organized Crime in The Netherlands, 1650–1800* (Cambridge, Eng., 1993), 134; and J. M. Beattie, *Crime and the Courts in England, 1660–1800* (Princeton, N.J., 1986).

56. The Anglicans persisted in viewing not only blacks and Indians but also other Protestants as heathens. David Hackett Fischer mentions the establishment of an S.P.G. mission across from Harvard in *Albion's Seed*, 824–25.

57. *Communications of the Society for the Propagation of the Gospel*, ser. A, vol. 5, no. 49 (20 October 1709), quoted in Edgar E. Pennington, *Thomas Bray's Associates and Their Work among the Negroes* (Worcester, Mass., 1939), 25.

58. Letters from missionaries testify to this effort. For example, a missionary in South Carolina wrote the society on December 3, 1726 requesting "Bibles, primers, spelling books, horn books, testaments, and psalters." And in a letter dated September 30, 1745, an S.P.G. clergyman in New York reported that "the singing of a psalm had produced a good effect: it had engaged many of the Negroes to a closer application in learning to read." See Pennington, *Thomas Bray's Associates*, 63–64, 78.

59. William Knox, *Three Tracts Respecting the Conversion and Instruction of Free Indians and Negro Slaves in the Colonies, Addressed to the Venerable Society for the Propagation of the Gospel in Foreign Parts*, 2d ed. (London, 1789), 16, 19, 27, 36–39.

60. For Thompson's career in New Jersey and concerns about poisoning, see [Thomas Thompson], *A Letter from New Jersey in America, Giving Some Account and Description of That Province, by a Gentleman, Late of Christ's Church, Cambridge* (London, 1746).

61. Thomas Thompson, *An Account of Two Missionary Voyages by the Appointment of the Society for the Propagation of the Gospel in Foreign Parts. The One to New Jersey in North America, the Other from America to the Coast of Guinea* (London, 1758), 13–14, and "The Parish Register of Christ Church, Shrewsbury, New Jersey," in *Historical and Genealogical Miscellany: Data Relating to the Settlement and Settlers of New York and New Jersey,* ed. John E. Stillwell, 4 vols. (New York, 1903; reprint Baltimore, 1970), 1:166. For a similar account of a baptism of a black executed for infanticide, see Theodore Tappert and John W. Doberstein, eds., *The Journals of Henry Melchior Muhlenberg,* 3 vols. (Philadelphia, 1942–58), 2:7, 11–12.

62. Parish Register of Christ Church, Shrewsbury, Monmouth County Historical Association, Freehold, N.J., 1:166–71.

63. An early proponent of the "fortunate fall," Thompson argued that the slave trade worked positively for Africans by bringing them into contact with Christianity. Thus, while he believed strongly in religious instruction, he viewed slavery as an enlightened condition for people of African descent. See Thompson, *An Account,* 14–15. In this way, Thompson's ideas reaffirmed the contentions of Godefridus Udemans which influenced seventeenth-century masters.

64. Nelson R. Burr, *The Anglican Church in New Jersey* (Philadelphia, 1954), 225–27; Parish Register of Christ Church, Shrewsbury, Monmouth County Historical Association, Freehold, N.J., 1:176–78, 182, 185–89, 191–96, 201, 204.

65. For these views, see Albert J. Raboteau, *Slave Religion: The "Invisible Institution" in the Antebellum South* (New York, 1978), 43–95, and Jon Butler, *Awash in a Sea of Faith: Christianizing the American People* (Cambridge, Mass., 1990), 129–64.

66. For Anglican attitudes toward the Revolution, see John Calam, *Parsons and Pedagogues: The S.P.G. Adventure in American Education* (New York, 1971), 158–78; for African American choices, see Graham Hodges, "Black Revolt in New York City and the Neutral Zone: 1775–83," in *New York in the Age of the Constitution, 1775–1800* ed. Paul A. Gilje and William Pencak (Rutherford, N.J., 1992), 20–47.

67. Jean Soderlund, *Quakers & Slavery: A Divided Spirit* (Prince-

ton, N.J., 1985), 54–86, 112–47 (discussing the Shrewsbury Meeting and its evolving views on slavery).

68. [John Hepburn], *The American Defence of the Christian Golden Rule; or, An Essay to Prove the Unlawfulness of Making Slaves of Men. By Him Who Loves of the Freedom of the Souls and Bodies of All Men.* (New York, 1715), 1–2, 12–25. See also Ralph Sandiford, *An Examination of the Practice of the Times* (Philadelphia, 1729).

69. See Soderlund, *Quakers & Slavery*, 112–48, for Shrewsbury. For Benezet quote, see Betty Fladeland, *Men and Brothers: Anglo-American Antislavery Cooperation* (Urbana, Ill., 1972), 15–16. For Woolman, see Phillips P. Moulton, *The Journal and Major Essays of John Woolman* (New York, 1971), 18, 52, 95–99, 107–8, 117. See also Daniel Stanton, *A Journal of the Life, Travels, and Gospel Labours of a Faithful Minister of Jesus Christ* (Philadelphia, 1772), 111, 145–48, 152–55.

70. Soderlund, *Quakers & Slavery*, 121–23; Shrewsbury Scrapbook, 1, 5, 9–13, 15, 17–23.

71. For the influence of the Society of Friends in New Jersey, see Wacker, *Land and People*, 178–83. For the conservatism of New York Meeting, see "Oblong (Pawling) Monthly Meeting, 1757–1781," Haviland Record Center, New York, N.Y., 126, 141–45. For visits to slave owners and subsequent gradual emancipations, see Shrewsbury Scrapbook, 1, 5, 7, 9, 11, 13, 15, 17, 19, 21, 23, 45, 47, 50.

72. For memoranda, see Shrewsbury Scrapbook, 45–48. For memberships, see Henry J. Cadbury, "Negro Membership in the Society of Friends," *Journal of Negro History* 21 (1936): 151–213; Soderlund, *Quakers & Slavery*, 177.

73. *Anecdotes and Memoirs of William Boen, A Coloured Man, Who Lived and Died near Mount Holly, New Jersey* (Philadelphia, 1834), 3–8; *Memorial of the Mount Holly Monthly Meeting of Friends Concerning William Boen, A Coloured Man, Received in the Yearly Meeting of Friends, Held in Philadelphia, 1829* (Philadelphia, 1831), 3–6. See also Charles F. Gren, *Pleasant Hills, New Jersey, Lake Nescochoque, a Place of Older Days: An Historical Sketch* (n.p., n.d.), 27, for account of David Mapps, a black Quaker without a meeting who traded regularly along the Jersey Coast but refused to carry the "devil's pills" (cannon balls).

74. See, for example, Hodges, "Black Revolt," 21–23.

75. Whitefield's missive was published in the North by Benjamin Franklin in *Three Letters from the Reverend G. Whitefield* (Philadel-

phia, 1740), 13. See Margaret Washington Creel, *"A Peculiar People"*: *Slave Religion and Community-Culture among the Gullahs* (New York, 1988), 87–88, 90–91, and Patricia U. Bonomi, *Under the Cope of Heaven: Religion, Society, and Politics in Colonial America* (New York, 1986), 119.

76. *George Whitefield's Journals* (London, 1960), 490; see also 345–60, 415–17, 483, 486–91.

77. "Old Tennent Church Records, 1730–1800," 5 vols., Monmouth County Historical Association, Freehold, N.J., 1:19, 25, 40, 44, 48, 56, 58.

78. For Presbyterian festive practices in colonial America, see Leigh Eric Schmidt, *Holy Fairs: Scottish Communions and American Revivals in the Early Modern Period* (Princeton, N.J., 1989), 69–85, 196. For slavery, see Irving S. Kull, "Presbyterian Attitudes toward Slavery," *Church History* 7 (1938): 101–15.

79. *Journal and Letters of Francis Asbury*, 3 vols., ed. Elmer E. Clark (London, 1958), 1:9, 25, 43; *The Journal of Joseph Pilmore, Methodist Itinerant*, ed. Frederick E. Maser and Howard T. Maag (Philadelphia, 1969), 74, 96, 131; Nathan O. Hatch, *The Democratization of American Christianity* (New Haven, Conn., 1989), 102–13; Graham Russell Hodges, ed., *Black Itinerants of the Gospel: The Narratives of John Jea & George White* (Madison, Wis., 1993), 10–39.

80. *The Experiences and Gospel Labours of the Reverend Benjamin Abbott, to Which Is Annexed a Narrative of His Life and Death* (Philadelphia, 1801), 102–3.

81. Stuckey, *Slave Culture*, 41–53; Creel, *"A Peculiar People,"* 47–52.

82. For Simon, see *Pennsylvania Gazette* (Philadelphia), September 11, 1740. For Mark and Jenney escaped from Prevost, see *Rivington's New-York Gazetteer*, June 8, 1775. For other black ministers, see Billy G. Smith and Richard Wojtowicz, comps., *Blacks Who Stole Themselves: Advertisements for Runaways in the Pennsylvania Gazette, 1728–1790* (Philadelphia, 1989), 97, 110, 120, 124, 125, 152.

83. Narrative of Katy Schenck, in Mary W. Thompson, *Sketches of the History, Character, and Dying Testimony of Beneficiaries of the Colored Home, in the City of New York* (New York, 1851), 40–44.

84. For commentary, see *Interpreter's Bible*, 12 vols. (Nashville, Tenn., 1955), 4: 587–90. For a similar conversion and rejection of slavery, see John Jea's account in Hodges, *Black Itinerants*, 89–159.

3

Black Revolution
in Monmouth
1775–1783

In late 1775 a delegation from the Shrewsbury Meeting of
the Society of Friends visited member John Corlies about
his slaves. Corlies and the local meetings had quarreled several times in the past about his drinking, cursing, and fighting,
but this visit was much more serious. The Shrewsbury Meeting,
after years of delay, was finally heeding the 1758 Quaker edict to
end slavery among Friends. Monmouth County Quakers gradually reduced the number of slaveholders in their meeting down
to a very few. Corlies and his mother, Zilpha, were the most
intransigent. Zilpha owned two slaves, and her son owned four
more, aged 14 to 25. As the meeting sadly noted, "They have no
learning and he is not inclined to give them any." Corlies, known
for his quick temper, told his fellow Friends that "he has not
seen it his duty to give [the slaves] their freedom."

Corlies's stubborn refusal to emancipate his bondspeople
eventually cost him his membership in the Society of Friends.
The meeting concluded in 1778 that "after a considerable Deal
of Labour bestowed on him Respecting his keeping Negroes in
Slavery, [Corlies] still continues to decline complying with the

yearly meeting. . . . Therefore, there is the necessity to disown him."[1]

While the Shrewsbury Meeting was warning its slaveholding members to free their chattel or face expulsion, other Americans were worried about slave uprisings encouraged by the British leadership. On November 7, 1775, five months after declaring martial law and moving his government to an offshore man-of-war, John Murray, Earl of Dunmore and governor of Virginia, proclaimed freedom to all "indent[ur]ed servants, negroes . . . willing to serve His Majesty's forces to end the present rebellion."[2] Coincidentally, the following day, Titus, the second eldest of John Corlies's bondsmen, fled his master and headed for Virginia to fight with Dunmore's Ethiopian Regiment.

In a runaway advertisement Corlies described Titus as "about 21 years of age, not very black near 6 foot high, had on a gray homespun coat, brown breeches, blue and white stockings and took with him a wallet drawn up at one end with a string in which was a quantity of clothes." The reward was "three pounds proclamation money."[3] Titus's decision to flee hinged on a combination of local factors. He surely had observed the Quakers' unsuccessful visits to convince the irascible Corlies to free his slaves. He no doubt was also aware that his recent twenty-first birthday marked the age at which nearby Quakers freed their slaves.[4] He may also have been alienated by Corlies's refusal to educate his slaves at a time when Quakers were encouraging such programs. Unlike other Friends, Corlies was not a pacifist, and he did not inculcate that important aspect of the Quaker creed in his bondspeople.

Although word of Dunmore's promises flew quickly northward from Virginia, Titus could not have known of the proclamation just one day after its promulgation. Nevertheless, blacks along the Atlantic seaboard had for months been following reports and rumors from Virginia with the keenest interest, and at least some of them were, like Titus, clearly anticipating the nature and general timing of Dunmore's bold action. The Virginia governor succeeded, as he hoped, in inciting conspiracy among slaves, in Monmouth County no less than the region generally.[5]

While Patriots were debating independence, African Americans made plain their own rebellious attitudes. In New England, blacks listening to the Patriot revolutionary demands countered with petitions designed to end slavery. Free and enslaved blacks in Massachusetts petitioned the colonial and later the state assembly to end slavery and include the voice of African Americans in the constitutional debate.[6] In eastern New Jersey poor racial relations prohibited such discussion. Patriot whites there cautioned against any encouragement of black freedom and considered alternate means of dealing with the problem of slavery. In county after county slave owners worried about slave uprisings.

Titus made his escape during a decade of festering local tension. During the tumultuous years just before the Revolutionary War, New Jersey's African Americans left no doubt just how anxious they were for freedom. Instances of subterfuge and insolence multiplied. In Somerset County, northwest of Monmouth, masters found themselves unable to keep their bondspeople in after nine o'clock. Some slaves "borrowed" their masters' horses to ride to late-night meetings. George Van Nest charged his enslaved man, Tom, with theft and "riding horses three nights after midnight." Masters complained that their slaves stole liquor, "fowls," and other food. Other slaves shocked masters by arguing that "it was not necessary to please their masters, for they should not have their masters long." Residents fretted over reports of mass meetings of slaves and as early as 1772 seriously debated proposals for an African colonization scheme. One Somerset County Patriot wrote in 1775, "The story of the Negroes may be depended upon, so far at least to them arming or attempting to form themselves. Our militia are gone off in such numbers that we have hardly Men in Arms left in those Parts which are least affected to the cause."[7]

Monmouth County residents were alarmed by the possibility and consequences of black freedom. In 1772 Chief Justice Lord Mansfield rendered a decisive judgment that legally emancipated slaves in Britain. Would slaves in the colonies be next? In Shrewsbury and Middletown slaveholders responded to rumors of abolition in 1774 by firing off remonstrances to Governor William Franklin and the New Jersey Assembly. The signers of the petition described blacks in the county as "Increasing in Number and Impudence." They worried that blacks were "running about in all times of the Night Stealing and Taking and Riding Peoples Horses." Whites in the two towns placed the blame for problems on free blacks and warned against "any Law that may Enlarge the Liberty" of slaves. The two petitions were signed by ninety-two residents of Middletown and Shrewsbury; signatures were fairly evenly divided between future Loyalists and Patriots, indicating unanimity over the issue of manumission.

As war approached, Monmouth County slaveholders noted nightly meetings of blacks with increasing apprehension. Fears of rebellion in Shrewsbury prompted "a Mechanic" to complain that "a deluded King and a corrupted and venal ministry have endeavoured to rise up our own Domestics to cut the throats of their Masters." Anguished by reports from near and far, the Committee of Safety in Shrewsbury ordered search parties to stop "meetings of servants Negroes and other disorderly persons as they are attended to with great mischief." On October 11 and 16, 1775, the committee ordered "Colonel Breeze to secure the Negroes" and stop "Riotous and numerous meetings of Negroes at unlicensed houses." The committee demanded that all guns and ammunition be taken from blacks "until the present troubles are settled." Shortly afterwards, the Shrewsbury committee exhorted citizens and constabulary to arrest all "Slaves, Mulattos and Negroes found off their masters premises."[8] In February 1776 Shrewsbury magistrates passed an ordinance requiring that "all slaves either negroes mollatos or others that shall be found off their masters' premises any time of the night after the daylight is done shall be Taken up [and] delivered to the Minute Men to be kept under Guard until he shall receive fifteen stripes on the Bare Back."[9]

The slaveholders' fears were well founded; their bondsmen were preparing a move. As war approached, blacks fled to the British. In July 1776 Colonel Daniel Hendricksen of Monmouth appeared before the New Jersey Council of Safety and "reported that several of his slaves had run off and were on board the enemy's fleet."[10] By the end of the war, at least thirty-one Monmouth County slaves had chosen freedom in British-held New York City over enslavement at home.[11]

Monmouth County was not alone in its losses. When British infantry stationed on Staten Island swept through eastern New Jersey in the late summer and fall of 1776 in search of supplies, blacks flocked to join as soldiers, laborers, sailors, or domestics. Encouraged, Monmouth County Tories flocked to the British lines in December 1776.[12] The British parade through Bergen, Essex, Somerset, and Middlesex counties also resulted in the flight of over fifty slaves in December 1776 alone.[13] The events of 1775–76 were part of a "wave of revolt" sweeping the general African American population, seeking, as the black Loyalist leader Boston King put it, "the happiness of liberty, of which I knew nothing before."[14] In Monmouth County these waves occurred throughout the Revolution and deeply affected the African American experience in slavery and, later, in freedom.

In early 1777 the British retreated unexpectedly. However, wartime conditions continued to afford blacks opportunities to flee their masters and find refuge with and military service for the British. Within the first few months of 1777, at least eight local slaves, including Samuel Smith, a slave owned by Colonel Breeze, fled to freedom behind British lines. In Monmouth County James and Catherine Van Sayl left their masters early in 1777. In February 1777 the Black Pioneers and Guides, a regiment of Black Loyalists specializing in reconnaissance for the British, made their first local appearance in the Battle of Navesink.[15] Other Monmouth County blacks sought to join the British. The New Jersey Council of Safety reported the arrest of two slaves from Shrewsbury "suspected of having been in arms & aiding to the enemy" in May 1777. Others were more successful. Aaron and Sarah Jones and Oliver Vinson left their masters in Middletown in 1777 to join the British. Thomas Drake joined them the following year.[16]

In 1777 New Jersey Patriots began confiscating and selling Tory property. Those actions, together with Patriot raids on suspected Tories, scattered more slaves. In claims made to the British government after the war, slaveholding Tories described the loss of fifteen males, five females, and nine children. Christian Van Mater of Middletown alone lost ten slaves. Samuel Cooke, pastor at Christ Church and missionary of the S.P.G. at Shrewsbury from 1751 to 1775, lost "a negro man worth £100 and a Negro wench worth £56."[17]

A Black Leader for the Loyalists

The British concentrated their military efforts on small but effective raids into New Jersey from Staten Island and Powles Hook at the beginning of 1778. British strongholds protected raiders and offered safe refuge to escaping blacks. Colonel Asher Holmes noted that "Depredations have been committed by the Refugees (Either Black or White)." More is known about the African Americans who fought for the colonies in the Battle of Monmouth. None of them, however, hailed from Monmouth. All told, nearly eight hundred black men took up arms in the colonial army, chiefly from New England regiments but also from New Jersey, including six teamsters—none from Monmouth—and an assortment of others who had volunteered to support their masters' cause.

Fought near Freehold on June 28, 1778, the Battle of Monmouth proved indecisive militarily but pivotal for New Jersey's black Loyalists in that it marked the first known appearance of an African American who would become one of the war's most feared Loyalists, white or black—Colonel Tye, formerly known in Monmouth County as John Corlies's slave Titus. Colonel Tye comported himself gallantly in his first known military venture, capturing Elisha Shepard, a captain in the Monmouth militia, and removing him to imprisonment at the Sugar House in New York City. Tye's title is noteworthy. Although the British army did not formally commission black officers, it often granted such titles out of respect, particularly in Jamaica and other West Indian islands. The transformation of the servant Titus into the warrior Tye was evidently overseen by soldiers who had served in the Caribbean.[18]

Tye's successes at the Battle of Monmouth led to his involvement the next year in the military arm of a plan sponsored by William Franklin, son of Benjamin and governor of New Jersey from 1763 until his arrest by Patriots in 1776. During Franklin's internment, British commanders chose the cream of New Jersey's Tories as officers, enlisted a few others, but largely ignored the rest. By 1778, when the former governor was returned to the British in an exchange of prisoners, many Tories had seen their property confiscated and sold, and some were desparate for ways to vent their rage. Anger turned to fury in early 1779 when Monmouth Patriots began summarily hanging captured Tories under the vigilante law that then governed the county. "A Loyal Refugee," writing in the *Royal Gazette* of June 5, 1779, demanded immediate retaliation.[19] Franklin and the British became convinced that the time was now ripe to turn the bitter anger of loyalists against Monmouth's Patriots.

On July 15, 1779, accompanied by the fierce Tory John Moody, Colonel Tye and "about fifty negroes and refugees landed at Shrewsbury and plundered the inhabitants of near 80 head of horned cattle, about 20 horses and a quantity of wearing apparel and household furniture. They also took off William Brindley and Elisha Cook, two of the inhabitants."[20]

This action established a pattern that was to be repeated over the next year. Combining banditry, reprisal, and commissioned assistance to the British army, these raids served the aims of local black rebellion quite intentionally, often being aimed directly at former masters and their friends. In Monmouth County, where slavery was a family affair and owners were not distant patricians, enmities between slaves and masters could understandably become prolonged and intense. Moreover, as will be seen in subsequent chapters, the family names of many of Tye's especial targets appear disproportionately in notices of runaways from later generations, suggesting tendencies to especially unjust or brutal treatment of slaves passed from fathers to sons.

The effects of Tye's incursions upon the general population of Monmouth County were exacerbated by reports during these months that blacks were planning massacres of whites in Elizabethtown and in Somerset County. To some, no doubt, the muted threats of incautious blacks before the Revolution now loomed large in recollection.

In a typical raid Tye and his men, at times aided by white refugees known as "cow-boys," would surprise Patriots in their homes, kidnap soldiers and officers, and carry off silver, clothing, and badly needed cattle for British troops in Staten Island and New York City. For these accomplishments Tye and his men were paid handsomely, sometimes receiving five gold guineas. Tye's familiarity with Monmouth's swamps, rivers, and inlets allowed him to move undetected until it was too late. After a raid, Tye and his interracial band, known to Patriots as a "motley crew," would disappear again into nearby swamps, later returning to Refugeetown at Sandy Hook, headquarters for maroon activity.

But British and Tories in their New York stronghold had their share of problems as well that year. The planting season of 1779 proved unfavorable to crops, and although New Jersey farmers preferred British gold to American paper money, food, hay, and firewood were scarce. One Loyalist in New York City had to make do with green twigs for firewood. The winter of 1779–80 was unusually harsh, and the icebound Hudson River made the British apprehensive about protecting New York City. The Black Brigade—an elite group of twenty-four black Loyalists that included Tye—joined with the Queen's Rangers, a British guerrilla unit employed for reconnaissance and quick, debilitat-

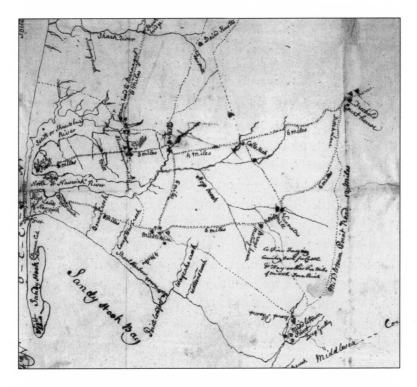

General Henry Clinton's Reconaissance Map of Eastern Monmouth County, 1780, showing area of Colonel Tye's incursions. Courtesy of William L. Clements Library, University of Michigan, Ann Arbor.

ing raids. Together they were used to protect British-held New York City and to raid the countryside for food and fuel.[21]

In a raid on March 30, 1780, Tye and his men captured a Captain Warner, who purchased his freedom for "two half joes." Less lucky were Captain James Green and Ensign John Morris, whom Tye took to Refugeetown en route to internment at the Sugar House in New York City. In the same raid Tye and his men looted and burned the home of John Russell, a fierce Patriot associated with raids on Staten Island, before killing him and wounding his young son. Three weeks later a band of refugees and blacks captured Matthias Halsted at his home near New Ark, plundering "bed, bedding, family wearing apparel and 7–8 head of creature [cattle]."[22]

During the second week of June 1780, Colonel Tye conducted three actions in Monmouth County, on the eighth, ninth, and twelfth. During the second raid Tye and his men murdered Private Joseph Murray of the Monmouth militia at his home in Colt's Neck. Murray, a foe detested by local Tories, had been personally responsible for several of their summary executions.[23] Three days later Tye led a large band of self-emancipated blacks and refugee whites in a daring attack on the home of Barnes Smock, a leader of the Monmouth militia, while the main body of British troops was attacking Washington's forces. Using a six-pound cannon to warn residents of the raid, Smock summoned a number of men around his house to fight Tye. After a stiff battle Tye and his men captured Smock and twelve other Patriots, depriving Monmouth's militia of many leaders and Washington's troops of their effective aid. The Loyalist victors captured valuable livestock and looted Smock's home. Tye himself spiked Smock's cannon—a symbolically disheartening action for the Patriots—before spiriting the prisoners back to the Loyalist stronghold at Refugeetown, from which they were sent to imprisonment at the Sugar House.

Tye's June incursions inspired great fear among New

This letter from David Forman to William Livingston, 1780,
describes Tye's attacks in Monmouth County. Courtesy of
Monmouth County Historical Association.

Jerseyans. In the space of one week he and his men carried off
much of the officer corps of the Monmouth militia, destroyed
their cannon, and flaunted an ability to strike at will against a
weakened Patriot population. If before Tye had been seen in
Monmouth County as a bandit in service to the British, he now
had to be reckoned an important military force. Local Patriots
wrote anguished letters to Governor William Livingston, beg-
ging for help against the ravages of Colonel Tye and his raiders.

In response the governor invoked martial law in the county. But a law is only as effective as its enforcement, and there were few able-bodied men to police. Many farmers ordinarily warm to the Patriot cause were in the middle of the planting season. Livingston openly despaired of supplying even George Washington with a full complement of troops from Monmouth County. While the New Jersey Patriots were distracted by Tye and his men, other blacks were quick to take advantage. The *New Jersey Journal* noted that "twenty-nine Negroes of both sexes deserted from Bergen County in early June 1780."[24]

These attacks came during a period of rising concern about Patriot prospects in New Jersey. Governor Livingston, who two years before had attempted to abolish slavery in New Jersey, now wrote fearfully of Lord Dunmore's effect upon local blacks. The borders between New York and New Jersey were flooded with black refugees bound for sanctuary with the British. Tories in New York, eager to organize against Livingston's government, were encouraged by reports that Washington's army was reduced to 1,600 men. As part of the concern over black runaways to New York City, Monmouth slaveholders were urged to remove their slaves "to some more remote or interior parts of the state."[25]

There were more attacks to come. On June 22, 1780, "Tye with thirty blacks, thirty-six Queen's Rangers and thirty refugees landed at Conascung, New Jersey." The invaders slipped stealthily past Patriot scouts and captured James Mott, second major in the Monmouth militia's second regiment. Tye's men sacked and destroyed the houses of Mott and "several Neighbors." Tye's troops also captured Captain James Johnson of the Hunterdon militia as well as several privates: Joseph Dorsett, James Walling, Philip Walling, Matthew Griggs of Monmouth County, William Blair of Hunterdon County, and James Hall of Middlesex County.[26] It was a stunning blow to the Patriots. In a single day Tye had captured eight militiamen, plundered their homes, and taken his captives to New York, moving in and out of Monmouth County with impunity despite martial law and the presence of several militias—all without any reported casualties. Although the notorious Tory John G. Simcoe, commander of the Queen's Rangers, was present, Tye received credit for the raid in newspapers.

Throughout the summer of 1780, Tye led his "motley band" on raids into Monmouth County, burning barns and looting farms. On one such raid in late August, Tye and his men captured Hendrick and John Smock, brothers of Barnes, and sent them to join the latter in prison in New York City.[27] On September 1, 1780, Tye attempted his greatest feat. For years Loyalists had tried to capture Captain Josiah Huddy, famed for his leadership in raids on British positions in Staten Island and Sandy Hook and despised by Loyalists for his quick executions of captured Tories. Colonel Tye led a small army of blacks, refugees, and Queen's Rangers against Huddy's home in Tom's River. The Loyalists seem to have had both good intelligence and the advantage of surprise, for this night Huddy's home, normally the center of Patriot activity in the area, was occupied only by its owner and a female friend, Lucretia Emmons. But in the attack, Huddy proved a formidable foe. As Tye's men attacked, Huddy ran from room to room firing muskets, which Miss Emmons feverishly reloaded, creating an illusion that the house was flush with Patriots. Imagine the Loyalists' consternation when, after managing to set the structure ablaze two hours later, they flushed out only Huddy and his companion.

Meanwhile, the two hours of sporadic gunfire had been heard by area Patriots, and as Tye was conveying Huddy back to Refugeetown the state militia intercepted his party. During the ensuing skirmish, Huddy was placed in a longboat. While his captors plied the oars assiduously, he escaped by jumping overboard and swimming to his rescuers, shouting, "I am Huddy!"[28]

During the battle Colonel Tye received a bullet in the wrist.

Originally thought to be a minor wound, it soon proved fatal. Within days lockjaw set in, and lacking proper medical attention, Tye died. Though Tye's exploits were ended by this spoiled endeavor, this final chapter of his life was not closed until two years later, when Huddy, captured at last and interned aboard a British prison ship, was snatched by avenging Tories on a pretext and hanged on the shore of Monmouth County. A black man performed Huddy's execution. This rough and ready justice, occurring after Cornwallis's surrender at Yorktown and as peace negotiations were underway, caused an international furor that threatened to damage the tentative and tenuous peace. Locally, it aggravated animosities between Patriots and Tories. New Jersey Patriots gained a measure of revenge with their own surprise attack near Long Branch, during which they massacred an entire party of black Loyalists.[29]

The Black Revolution after Tye

Colonel Stephen Blucke of the Black Pioneers replaced Tye as the leader of black raiders in the New York area, but Tye's reputation lived on. Patriots remembered Tye's revolutionary activities with admiration in contrast to their hatred of white Tories. Even during the angry dispute over Huddy's execution, Americans recalled Tye as a "brave and courageous man whose generous actions placed him well above his white counterparts." Despite his opposition to the American side, Patriots admired his military skill and argued that had Tye been enlisted in the American forces, the war would have been won much sooner.[30]

As the war dragged on into the early 1780s, Blucke, his Black Pioneers, and the Black Brigade revived the fading hopes of local Tories, making frequent raids into Long Island and New Jersey even after Cornwallis's defeat made Patriot victory appear inevitable. On June 5, 1782, forty whites and forty blacks landed at Forked River, N.J., plundered Patriot homes, and burned a number of salt works to the great dismay of New Jersey's Patriots.[31] Such actions combined with growing numbers of escaped blacks indicate that, despite the British defeat at Yorktown, African Americans aided by white Tories continued their rebellion by any means possible.

One of the key areas of dispute between the American and English peace negotiators was the fate of the black Loyalists. George Washington, himself a slaveowner, argued that the fugitive slaves at least were American property and should be returned to the victors for distribution to their masters. British Commander General Guy Carleton, however, regarded the three thousand and more African Americans in New York City as faithful, valiant supporters of the Crown, who should not be deserted. To Washington's chagrin, Carleton declared that any blacks who answered proclamations made by English generals in 1775, 1776, and 1779 to join Crown forces were free and entitled to safe passage to Nova Scotia, the German principalities, England, or the West Indies. Carleton informed Washington in June 1783 that many blacks had already left New York, and, aware that the dispute would require many years of arbitration, agreed to enumerate African Americans leaving from New York.[32]

This list of three thousand men, women, and children is the single most valuable source for determining which African Americans chose to fight for freedom by picking up a musket for King George. It includes the names of at least twenty-four Monmouth County blacks, including three couples, three families, seven single men, and one single woman. The war clearly improved chances for black families to live together in freedom. One couple was composed of a free black man and an enslaved woman. Andy Loyal, thirty-six, was born free in Monmouth; his wife, Hagar, was a slave. Another family's escape removed the hardship of separate owners. Aaron Jones, forty-two, escaped from Hendrick Smock in 1777 along with his wife, Sarah, forty-two, and their son, Isaac, ten, both enslaved by Richard Stout of Monmouth.

Similarly, James Van Sayl, escaped from John Lloyd, joined his wife, Catherine, and their children, Mary and Peter, once enslaved by John Van Der Veer. Some blacks came to New York even if they were free in Monmouth, either seeking to remain with those who were part of their community or family. Peter Johnson, his brother Rob, his wife, Judith, and their daughter, Rachel, all came into New York. Monmouth County blacks formed relationships in New York City. Oliver Vinson, who escaped from James Furman in 1776, married Diana Vinson of Philadelphia. Peter Warner was from Monmouth County, his wife Effa from Princess Anne, Maryland.[33]

The elite Black Brigade stayed with the English until the final evacuation of New York City on November 25, 1783. Black Brigade members from Monmouth were Oliver and Diana Vinson, Aaron, Sarah, and Isaac Jones, and Thomas Drake, who left his master in Monmouth at the age of twelve to join the British forces. Other blacks from Monmouth served the British with distinction. Joseph Stewart, fifteen, formerly owned by Crawford of Middletown, served with the Black Pioneers; Samuel Smith, who escaped from Samuel Breese in 1778, worked for the wagonmaster general's department. Other Monmouth blacks, including Tom, Nero, and Vaughn Cowenhoven, were servants to British officers.

Summary

The Revolutionary War enabled some Monmouth County blacks to gain their freedom and offer inspiration to others. Colonel Tye, though he did not survive the war, turned Monmouth County society upside down with his brave deeds. Other members of the Black Brigade from Monmouth County had less spectacular but meaningful careers. They became beacons of freedom to their fellow blacks in Monmouth; their departure to Nova Scotia and, for a few, eventually to Sierra Leone, created a north star of hope for those left behind. Slavery did not end with the Revolution, but black actions during the conflict called its very existence into question. After the war, appeals to end slavery grew louder and stronger as blacks and sympathetic whites worked together to end bondage.

Notes

1. For visits to Corlies, see Shrewsbury Scrapbook, Haviland Record Center, New York, 47. For Meeting problems with Corlies over drinking and fighting, see "Shrewsbury Men's Monthly Meeting Minutes, 1757–1786" (microfilm MR-PH, Friends Library, Swarthmore), 6–11, 60, 145, 156, 163–64, 167. For decision to disown Corlies, see "Shrewsbury Minutes," 399–40, and discussion in Jean Soderlund, *Quakers & Slavery: A Divided Spirit* (Princeton, N.J., 1985), 124–26. For Corlies' wealth, see "Tax Ratables for Shrewsbury for 1779," Archives Section, Division of Archives and Records Management, Department of State, Trenton, N.J., (hereafter New Jersey State Archives); George Castor Martin, *The Shark River District: Monmouth County, New Jersey, and Genealogies of the Chambers, Corlies Families* (Asbury Park, N.J., 1914), 55–61; Land Conveyances, fol. 3, (341, 343) New Jersey State Archives; Stillwell Miscellaneous Papers, New-York Historical Society, Corlies's patriotism was very doubtful. He was suspected of spying for the British. See James Wilson to William Livingston, March 28, 1777, Governor's Papers, box 1, New Jersey State Archives (hereafter cited as Livingston Papers). Quakers canvassed Shrewsbury slaveholders in the 1760s. See Philips P. Moulton, *The Journal and Major Essays of John Woolman* (New York, 1971), 61–62, 117–20.

2. For text of Dunmore's proclamation, see Peter Force, *American Archives*, 4th ser., (Washington, 1840), 3:1185–87, and Francis L. Berkeley, Jr., *Dunmore's Proclamation of Emancipation* (Charlottesville, Va., 1941), frontispiece. For the best discussion of the proclamation and events leading up to it, see Benjamin Quarles, *The Negro in the American Revolution* (Chapel Hill, N.C., 1961), 18–31. See also Percy Burdelle Caley, "Dunmore: Colonial Governor of New York and Virginia, 1770–1782" (Ph.D. diss., University of Pittsburgh, 1939), 629–30; Gerald W. Mullin, *Flight and Rebellion: Slave Resistance in Eighteenth-Century Virginia* (New York, 1972), 130–36; Ronald

Hoffman, "The 'Disaffected' in the Revolutionary South," in *The American Revolution: Explorations in the History of American Radicalism*, ed. Alfred F. Young (DeKalb, Ill., 1976), 281–82.

3. For Titus's escape from Corlies, see *Pennsylvania Packet* (Philadelphia), November 8, 1775.

4. At the same time, for example, Shrewsbury Quakers John Hartshorne and Richard Lawrence freed their twenty-one-year-old male slaves. See Shrewsbury Scrapbook, 5, 7.

5. For discussion of northern blacks' quick response to Dunmore, see Gary B. Nash, *Forging Freedom: The Formation of Philadelphia's Black Community, 1720–1840* (Cambridge, Mass., 1988), 45. Nash estimates that word of Dunmore's proclamation reached Philadelphia in less than a week. Rumors of Dunmore's actions and the recruitment of slaves to fight the Patriots recurred throughout 1775. For Titus's association with Dunmore, see Quarles, *Negro in the American Revolution*, 21–24.

6. For the most recent work on these petitions, see Thomas J. Davis, "Emancipation Rhetoric, Natural Rights, and Revolutionary New England: A Note on Four Black Petitions in Massachusetts, 1773–1777," *New England Quarterly* 57 (1989): 248–64.

7. See *King by George Van Nest* v. *his own Negro Tom*, August 22, 1771; *King* v. *Korstore, negro of Jacobus Quick*, April 9, 1770 (for stealing cocks); *King* v. *James*, April 15, 1770 (for horse stealing and insulting a white man); *Garret Roseboom* v. *his Negro Jack*, July 17, 1770 (for insolence and disobedience); *King at the Request of Matthew Ten Eyck* v. *Tone*, May 17, 1771 (for stealing bacon and tobacco); *King* v. *Ben, Quamino, Seazor, Tom, Mary and Nance*, April 10, 1771 (for stealing three fowls and liquor). For all cases, see Dorothy A. Stratford, "Docket of Jacob Van Noorstrat, J. P., Somerset County," *Genealogical Magazine of New Jersey* 43 (1968): 65–67. For rumors of meetings, see New Jersey Provincial Congress to John Hancock (microfilm M247 R 82, National Archives), 169, 173. For colonization plans, see Eli Seifman, "A History of the New York State Colonization Society" (Ph.D. diss., New York University, 1965), 17.

8. See "The Petition of Sundrie of the Inhabitants Freeholders and Owners of Negroes in Shrewsbury," January 12 and February 2, 1774; "The Petition of Sundrie of the Inhabitants Freeholders and Owners of Negroes in Middletown," February 2, 1774, box 14, New Jersey State Archives, nos. 16, 17, 18. Over 100 Middlesex County

slaveholders sent a similar petition. See "The Humble Petition of the Inhabitants of the City of Perth Amboy," January 12, 1774, box 14, New Jersey State Archives, no. 16; printed in Clement A. Price, *Freedom Not Far Distant: A Documentary History of Afro-Americans in New Jersey* (Newark, N.J., 1980), 56.

9. See "Minutes of the Shrewsbury Committee of Safety, 1774–1776," in Larry R. Gerlach, *New Jersey in the American Revolution, 1763–1783: A Documentary History* (Trenton, N.J., 1975), 147–50.

10. *Ibid.*, 149–50; *Minutes of the Provincial Congress and Council of Safety of the State of New Jersey, 1775–1776*, ed. William S. Stryker (Trenton, N.J., 1879), 516–17. Patriots were not the only ones to have such problems. In Ulster County, N.Y., in February 1777, two Tories complained that during their confinement "their slaves absolutely refuse all obedience, taking advantage of the Petitioners Absence." *Calendar of Historical Manuscripts Relating to the War of Revolution in the Office of the Secretary of State*, 2 vols. (Albany, 1868), 1:643.

11. *Minutes of the Provincial Congress and Council of Safety of the State of New Jersey.*

12. This number is determined by analysis of the statements of origins and former masters made by blacks in the "Books of Negroes," book 1 ("Book of Negroes Registered and Certified after Being Inspected by the Commissioners Appointed for His Excellency Sir Guy Carleton, General and Commander-in-Chief on Board Sundry Vessels in Which They Were Embarked to the Time of the Sailing from the Port of New York between 23 April and 31 July 1783"); book 2 ("Book of Negroes Registered and Certified . . . by the Commissioners . . . between July 31 and 30 November 1783"); book 3 ("Negroes Inspected on the 30th November 1783 by Captain Gilfillan of Armstrong on Board the Fleet Laying Near Statten Island, in the Absence of the American Commissioners and Secretary, Which Numbers Have Since Been Regularly Registered and Certified by Said Two Captains") (Washington, D.C.: National Archives). I have edited these lists in *The Black Loyalist Directory: African Americans in Exile after the American Revolution.* (New York, 1996). Subsequent references are to this edition. Also used in obtaining the number of thirty-one blacks were runaway notices, Patriot damage claims, and Loyalist claims.

13. Charles L. Lundin, *Cockpit of the Revolution: The War for Independence in New Jersey* (Princeton, N.J., 1940), 109, 153–57, 159–64. For the British Navy, see David Syrett, *The Royal Navy in American*

Waters, 1775–1783 (Aldershot, Hants, England, 1989), 16, 25–42, 93–104.
The number fifty is based upon claims made by Patriots of slave losses
in the "Damages by the British in Essex . . . Bergen . . . Somerset and
Middlesex Counties, 1776–1782," New Jersey State Archives. Unfortunately, the Monmouth County claims are the only ones that do not
survive. There are, however, scattered claims in family papers at the
Monmouth County Historical Association, Freehold, N.J.

14. For the concept "wave of revolt," see Herbert Aptheker, *American Negro Slave Revolts*, rev. ed. (New York, 1969), 1, as quoted in
Peter H. Wood, "'The Dream Deferred': Black Freedom Struggles
on the Eve of White Independence," in *In Resistance: Studies in African, Caribbean, and Afro-American History*, ed. Gary Y. Okihiro
(Amherst, Mass, 1986), 166–88. For King quote, see Phyllis Blakeley, "Boston King: A Black Loyalist," in *Eleven Exiles: Accounts of Loyalists in the
American Revolution*, ed. Phyllis R. Blakeley (Toronto, 1982), 266.

15. For Van Sayls, see *The Black Loyalist Directory*, 81. For Navesink,
see Edward J. Rasen, "American Prisoners Taken at the Battle of
Navesink, 1777," *Genealogical Magazine of New Jersey* 45 (1970): 50.

16. *Minutes of the Council of Safety of the State of New Jersey* (Jersey City, N.J., 1872), 43, 52. For the Joneses, Vincent, and Drake, see
The Black Loyalist Directory, 209–11.

17. "American Loyalist Transcripts of the Manuscripts, Books, and
Papers of the Commissioners, Entering into the Losses and Services
of the American Loyalists Held under the Acts of Parliament 23, 25,
26, 28, 29 of George III, Preserved amongst the Audit Office Records
in the Public Records Office of England, 1783–1790, Transcribed for
the New York Public Library" 76 vols. (New York, 1898), 15:69, 77,
239, 255, 499–503 (Van Mater); 16:529; 39:103, 195, 283.

18. Colonel Asher Holmes Papers, 1778, Loyalist folder 1, Special
Collections, Alexander Library, Rutgers University; Lundin, *Cockpit
of the Revolution*, 400–406. For black Patriots, see most recently Ri-
chard S. Walling, *Men of Color at the Battle of Monmouth, June 28,
1778: The Role of African Americans and Native Americans at
Monmouth* (Hightstown, N.J., 1994). For servants, see Ira K. Morris,
*Recollections of Old Camp Vredenburg and an Incident of the Battle of
Monmouth: Southern Agents in Freehold and Margaret Rue* (Freehold,
N.J., 1905), 18–22. For teamsters, see [William S. Stryker], *Official
Register of the Officers and Men of New Jersey in the Revolutionary War*
(Trenton, 1872), 859–61, 863, 866, 869.

For Tye, see John E. Stillwell, *Historical and Genealogical Miscellany: Relating to the Settlement and Settlers of New York and New Jersey,* (New York, 1903), 5:290. For British custom of informally awarding titles, see Michael Craton, *Testing the Chains: Resistance to Slavery in the British West Indies* (Ithaca, N.Y., 1982), 52–99.

19. For Loyalist plots and anger, see Edward H. Tebbehoff, "The Associated Loyalists: An Aspect of Militant Loyalism," *New-York Historical Society Quarterly* 63 (1979): 115–44. See also *Royal Gazette* (New York), June 5 and 23, 1779.

20. For the July 15 raid, see *New Jersey Archives,* 2d ser., vol. 4 (1914): 504. For Moody's participation, see *Lieutenant James Moody's Narrative of His Exertions and Suffering in the Cause of Government since the Year 1776,* 2d ed. (London, 1783), 11–12; for fear of uprising in Elizabeth Town, see *Gaine's Weekly Mercury* (New York), June 23, 1780; Edward F. Hatfield, *History of Elizabeth Town, New Jersey* (New York, 1868), 476; Aptheker, *Negro Slave Revolts,* 89.

21. For weather and crops in New York City, see David Ramsay, *The History of the American Revolution,* 2 vols. (Philadelphia, 1789), 2:181–84, 191. For trading with the enemy, see "Summary of Actions against Those Trading with the Enemy," Revolutionary Manuscripts, State of New Jersey, County of Monmouth, New Jersey Historical Society, 2:61–63. One of those arrested was "Negro Joe, slave of Widow Stevens of Middletown."

22. For raids, see *Pennsylvania Evening Post* (Philadelphia), April 12, 1780.

23. For account of Murray's death, see Franklin Ellis, *The History of Monmouth County, New Jersey* (Philadelphia, 1885), 209.

24. For the attack on Smock, see *ibid.* For British attack, see *Pennsylvania Packet* (Philadelphia), June 13, 1780. For cannon, see *New Jersey Archives,* 2d ser., vol. 4 (1914): 434–35, and Ernest W. Mandeville, *The Story of Middletown: The Oldest Settlement in New Jersey* (Middletown, N.J., 1927), 63. For Smock's damage claims, see "An Account of Captain Barnes Smock for Loss of Arms," New Jersey State Archives, misc. mss. 1059, 1077, 1092. See also David Forman to William Livingston, June 9, 1780, *The Papers of William Livingston* 5 vols., ed. Carl E. Prince et al. (Trenton, N.J., 1979–1990) 3:423, and Asher Holmes to William Livingston, June 12, 1780, Holmes Family Papers, Monmouth County Historical Association, Freehold, N.J. For martial law, see "Acts of Assembly of the State of New Jersey" [October 29,

1779–July 19,1780] (Trenton, 1780), 243; and William Livingston to the Assembly, June 7, 1780 in *Livingston Papers,* 3:421; for a nice description of Tye's attack, see Sidney Kaplan, *The Black Presence in the Era of the American Revolution, 1770–1800* (Greenwich, Conn., 1973), 66–67.

25. For removal of blacks to interior regions, see *New Jersey Gazette* (Trenton), June 5, 1780. For mass exodus of blacks, see *New Jersey Journal* (Chatham), June 13, 1780, *Pennsylvania Post* (Philadelphia), June 23, 1780. For Loyalist confidence, see *Historical Memoirs of William Smith,* Ed. William H. W. Sabine 2 vols. (New York, 1956–58, reprint 199), 2:261, 286, 289, 314–17. For Livingston, see *Livingston Papers,* 3:427.

26. For the raid of June 22, see *Pennsylvania Evening Post* (Philadelphia), June 30, 1780.

27. For the August raid, see *New Jersey Archives,* 2d ser., vol. 4 (1914): 603.

28. For accounts of this famous battle, see Nathaniel Scudder to Joseph Scudder, September 11, 1780, New Jersey Historical Society; *Gaine's Weekly Mercury* (New York), September 25, 1780; *Pennsylvania Packet* (Philadelphia), October 3, 1780.

29. For first reports on Huddy's capture, see *New Jersey Gazette* (Trenton), April 24, 1782, in which Tye's death in 1780 is prominently mentioned. The article describes Tye as "justly to be more feared and respected than any of his brethren of a fairer complexion." For the Huddy-Asquill case, see Allan J. Donor, "The Melancholy Case of Captain Asquill," *American Heritage* 31 (February 1970): 81–92. For the surprise attack, see [Edward Wooley], "Reminiscences of the Negro Hill Massacre," Steen Papers, box 1, folder 13, Monmouth County Historical Association, Freehold, N.J.

30. For encomiums to Tye, see for example John H. Barber, *Historical Collections of New Jersey: Past and Present* (New Haven, Conn., 1865), 365; Ellis, *Monmouth County,* 88, 195–99; Edwin Salter, *A History of Monmouth and Ocean Counties* (Bayonne, N.J., 1890), 429–30.

31. For late actions by Loyalists, see *New Jersey Archives,* 2d. ser., vol. 5 (1915): 446.

32. The best single discussion of these negotiations remains Quarles, *The Negro in the American Revolution,* 158–82.

35. *Black Loyalist Directory,* 11, 40, 132, 189, 179, 209–11.

4

From Revolution to Emancipation 1783–1804

In the aftermath of the American Revolution, Monmouth County's white citizens were less concerned with black freedom than with rebuilding a society ravaged by eight years of jousting armies and incessant raids by Loyalists and Patriots. During the war slave owners in Monmouth had lost dozens of their chattel to the British Army. A few blacks had been killed in the conflict or recaptured during the British evacuation of New York City in 1783, but most had escaped to freedom in Nova Scotia. Despite these losses and the chaotic conditions of the Revolution, slavery remained entrenched in Monmouth County's rural economy.[1]

The war for self-determination had exacerbated the split between advocates and foes of slavery in New Jersey. In this discord slaveholders at first held several advantages: the political clout that wealth bestows, the sympathies of fellow Patriots, and the restraining influence of an uncertain economy. Opposition to slavery was further weakened by association with the British, who, although vanquished, had gained from it some tactical benefits as well as the moral high ground. Yet by 1804 slavery had begun a slow retreat from New Jersey, subdued less by numerical strength—southern slaveholders were also a minority—than by geographic circumstance.

This chapter traces the tortuous path to gradual emancipation as it unfolded on three fronts: first in the legislature and courts, the scenes of political arguments over and rulings on slavery and manumission; second, in Monmouth County's farms and homesteads, where African Americans persevered in their efforts to become free and independent; third, in the everyday life of blacks, who extended and cultivated the range and richness of their indigenous culture. The story is told chronologically, decade by decade; the events themselves unfolded continuously, of course, not in neat segments. Inevitably, legislative and judicial affairs take the story beyond the confines of Monmouth County. Yet if New Jersey law affected all of the state's citizens, it did not reduce them to an homogenous whole, erase their identification with their county, or check their propensity for spontaneous political action, typically in groups defined by locality.[2] To help ground statewide events in county occurrences, population and demographical figures are reintroduced; as in chapter 1, they count Monmouth lives and help define the parameters of local black experience.

The Promise of Revolution

The last quarter of the eighteenth century was not without political promise for New Jersey's blacks. Progressive state leaders wrote, and in 1776 adopted, a state constitution that permitted any inhabitant worth £50 and resident of a county for a year to vote for state officers. Its features were noteworthy in two ways. First, by requiring a year's residence within a given county, not merely within the state, the constitution mandated suffrage as a local privilege. This was no doubt a purely pragmatic recognition that records for individuals were local and that mobility was limited. Second, as in neighboring Pennsylvania, this loose construction opened suffrage to free black males and black and white women. Although opponents bitterly complained in close elections, there is evidence in local histories that blacks and white women voted in small numbers throughout the 1790s.

William Livingston, New Jersey's first governor (1776–90), was an early advocate of emancipation. Encouraged by Governor Livingston, David Cooper, a western New Jersey Quaker, joined with other Quakers to present in 1785 a bill to the legislature seeking abolition and an end to the commerce in slaves. The lawmakers passed on March 2, 1786 a ban on the foreign slave trade in the state. As bans go, this one was less than formidable. Africans brought illegally into the state remained slaves, fines on captains looked a good deal like tariffs, and punishments were slight. At the same time, the legislators took the opportunity to restrict the freedoms of emancipated blacks. The act ordained that any free black convicted of a crime above petty larceny would be banished from the state. Travel outside of a black's home county was prohibited without a certificate authenticating the bearer's freedom. Moreover, free blacks from outside of New Jersey were denied entry to the state. As for the abolition of slavery, initially the focus of the bill, lawmakers carefully excised all references to emancipation. Yet in a sort of *quid pro quo*, they made the significant concession of removing from law the requirement, imposed in 1714, that masters wishing to free a slave post a bond (originally £200) several times larger than that slave's market value to insure that the newly freed person would not become a ward of the colony or state; from 1786 slaves able to fend for themselves could be freed without a bond being posted—provided they were thirty-five or older. Finally, legislators acted to make forced labor "humane" by imposing penalties on owners who mistreated their slaves.[3]

The year 1786 was significant also for the founding of the New Jersey Society for the Abolition of Slavery by Joseph

Bloomfield, future New Jersey governor (1801–12), and Elias Boudinot, New Jersey representative to both the Continental and the U.S. Congress (1778, 1781–83; 1789–95). Bolstered by such prominent allies, Governor Livingston applied pressure and in 1788 secured an amendment to the ban on the slave trade that toughened penalties, imposing forfeiture of ships and larger fines on captains. To prevent the kidnapping of free blacks by slave catchers, the amendment prohibited the sale of blacks out of state without their consent—a requirement easily evaded, all the more so as slaveholders "emigrating" from the state were exempted. A third clause required owners to teach their slaves born after passage of the act to read. As early literacy could only help this new generation become functionally independent of their masters, this stipulation might have been intended to prepare the ground for eventual emancipation. If so, it proved ineffectual in Monmouth County, where literacy rates or evidence of schools for blacks are recorded only from 1817. In sum, the 1788 amendment was slightly more forthright than the 1786 law in redressing injustices but no more successful than the earlier act in marshaling either the means or the will to enforce its modest requirements. Its feebleness is reflected in the absence of prosecutions for slave trading in court records.[4]

Slavery in Postwar Society

Amidst troubling economic conditions, Monmouth's white citizens were deeply divided over the question of the abolition of slavery. Patriots generally were disinterested in freeing slaves. Determined to impose order, bitter Monmouth County Patriots formed an association, known as the Retaliators, dedicated to jailing Tories, confiscating their estates, and banishing all opposition to the new government. The efforts of this group, led by Daniel Forman, alarmed many residents. British sympa-

This 1798 receipt traces the sales history of an enslaved Monmouth County woman by the name of Amy. Courtesy of the Monmouth County Historical Association.

thizers fled the country in the aftermath of the war, taking massive amounts of property and cash with them.[5]

On the other side of the slavery issue, Anglicans and Quakers sought to correct the contradictions between the institution and republican democracy by supporting manumission from the pulpit. But in the eyes of many, the actions of both groups during the Revolution had rendered their protestations suspect. Since the time of William Penn, Friends had encouraged each other to spurn war and seek the light of God in every man and woman, friend or foe. This imperative led Friends to declare themselves neutral during the war, a position easily construed as treachery by those caught up in the conflict. When Quakers inveighed against slavery, there was deep suspicion of their motives. For their part, Anglicans were members of a sect whose nominal head was King George III and which had understandably supported the British. Little wonder, then, that they were distrusted when, as key members of the New Jersey Society for the Abolition of Slavery, they suggested that slave owners renounce their right to the income and comforts that chattel can provide.[6]

One sign of the strength of slavery's grip on Monmouth society was that manumission appeals had little effect on private sales of slaves. Late in the war, privateers captured a black Loyalist from a British ship and auctioned him to a Monmouth slave owner. Later, a female slave was sold for her third time in about twelve years. In May 1786 Thomas Seabrook sold a "Neagro Woman Named Amy" to Jeames Holmes and Jacob Tice, who then sold her to Rulef Van Mater in 1789; Van Mater in turn sold her to Daniel Covenhoven in 1793. The receipt documenting these transactions was written by Van Mater in 1798, suggesting that Covenhoven was preparing to sell Amy again and needed proof of her provenance.[7]

Economic incentive remained a major factor in the perpetuation of slavery. Even as their numbers gradually dwindled, slaveholders in Middletown, Upper Freehold, and Shrewsbury between 1784 and 1808 possessed more than five times the average amount of land, four times the number of cattle, and five times the number of horses as freeholders without bondspeople. Meanwhile, farmers without slaves in eastern New Jersey eked out only a subsistence living. Lack of cash meant that such farmers were unable to purchase confiscated Loyalist estates or to speculate in land or militia scrip—major benefits of the Revolution for moneyed slaveholders. Enslaved blacks, then, were the spe-

cies of property that best insured prosperity, maintained larger
farms, and provided the means of mobility. Moreover, their value
increased with the westward migration of white laborers and
the restriction and eventual abolition of the foreign slave trade
after 1808.[8]

The scarcity of young white male laborers in the county
enhanced opposition to black emancipation. The tax ratables
for 1784 in Freehold, for instance, list fifty-four single white men
aged sixteen to forty, the group from which free laborers could
be drawn. In contrast there were 104 enslaved people in the
township; whether male or female, most worked in the fields.
The majority of laborers in Freehold continued to be slaves until
after the enactment of gradual emancipation. In Upper Freehold and Middletown disparities were not as sharp, but free
white males rarely outnumbered slaves. Only in Quaker
Shrewsbury, already moving toward free labor, did single white
males predominate in the pool of potential hired workers.[9]

Of the young whites who stayed in Monmouth, many found
themselves unable to purchase land in established communities,
where slaveholders held the reins of economic power. By 1784
over 80 percent of available land was taxed as improved for agricultural use. Land prices soared; buyers were asked to put up
one-third of the full price as down payment, and mortgages had
to be paid off in only a few years. Under the best of conditions,
plans to purchase land meant saving all of the wages of a skilled
laborer for four years. Under such conditions, there was little
opportunity for aspiring freeholders, white or black.[10]

Pushed out of the old towns, whites settled in new ones.
Dover had emerged as an adjunct to Shrewsbury in 1767. Howell,
near Monmouth's southern border, developed similarly in 1801.
Stafford was incorporated in 1797. Dover, settled rapidly in the
decade after the Revolution, was a haven for middle-sized farmers. The tax ratables for 1789, for example, show that in com-

Table 4
African American Population, Monmouth County, New Jersey, 1784–1860

	POPULATION	TOTAL BLACK	FREE	SLAVE
1784	13,216	1,640 (12.4)	N.A.	1,640
1790	16,918	1,949 (11.5)	353	1,596
1800	19,872	2,101 (10.6)	468	1,633
1810	22,150	2,136 (9.6)	632	1,504
1820	25,038	2,230 (8.9)	982	1,248
1830	29,233	2,299 (7.9)	2,072	227
1840	32,909	2,265 (6.9)	2,180	85
1850	30,313	2,398 (7.9)	2,323	75
1860	39,346	2,658 (6.8)	2,658	—

Number in parentheses is the percent of African Americans in total population. Source: "An Estimate of the Ratables of the State of New Jersey, 1784," *New Jersey Gazette* (Trenton), December 6, 1784; Giles R. Wright, *Afro-Americans in New Jersey: A Short History* (Trenton, 1988), 81–86.

parison with Middletown, with its heavy reliance on slaves, Dover's farmers generally had fewer acres of developed land, fewer horses, and fewer cattle. All where there were neither slaves nor a black economy to attract free African Americans. What is particularly striking about these new towns is the virtual absence of any blacks. In a rehearsal of later white flight into the old Northwest, newly incorporated villages did their best to bar both slavery and black people.[11]

The effectiveness of such bars no doubt played a role in the extraordinarily limited growth of the county's black population after 1790, shown in Table 4. In contrast to the rapid increase of Monmouth's African Americans during the colonial period, the 1,640 blacks counted just after the American Revolution increased to only 2,658 by 1860. To put these numbers in perspective, they may be set against comparable figures for the North as a whole: in 1790 Monmouth was home to almost 3 percent of the North's approximately 60,435 blacks; in 1860 this figure had reduced by two-thirds to little more than 1 percent of the 226,152 African Americans living in the North.[12] During the same period the white populace tripled.

Clearly, Monmouth County was not the end of the road for many transient blacks, despite liberalizations in the slave code. Such growth as occurred may be attributed largely to the balance of genders and stable families within Monmouth's black community. For those in residence, the death of slavery was slow indeed. Free African Americans in Monmouth did not outnumber slaves until 1830. As late as 1850, seventy-five Monmouth blacks remained enslaved. Nor did emancipation, once obtained, guarantee economic independence. Not until the census of 1850 did independent black households exceed free dependents living in white households.

While Friends and reorganized Anglicans unquestionably contributed to abolitionism, much of the impetus for emancipation emanated from blacks themselves.[13] Those in Monmouth used a variety of methods to gain—or regain—their freedom. Some of the more enterprising turned to litigation. In 1789 the New Jersey Supreme Court compelled a slaveholder named Lyon of Shrewsbury to give up Margaret Reap, daughter of free blacks, Joseph and Flora Reap. Lyon held Margaret in bondage, contending there was no proof she was free. Testimony revealed that Flora Reap's former masters, the Eaton family of Shrewsbury, had freed her a number of years before, that she was known to be free, and that she had often worked for the widow Eaton and other residents. The court ruled that Margaret, her daughter, though lacking written proof, was free.[14]

Probate records, an important source of information, reveal that the Easton family was unusually magnanimous with Flora

Reap: years of faithful service rarely inspired grants of freedom. In the first years following the Revolution, Monmouth County slaveholders were especially reluctant to grant freedom. Only one Monmouth County will out of twenty-two probated between 1782 and 1784 provided freedom to enslaved African Americans. In that instance, Andrew Britton of Upper Freehold gave all of his slaves to his wife "until they reach the age of 25 year and no longer & then to be free," with the proviso that each of the affected bondspeople pay twenty shillings a year towards insurance of their upkeep. Britton had five slaves. The youngest, a six-year-old girl, would not be free until 1802. Even in this case, the slaveholder made sure he received some benefits from the enslaved's prime years.[15]

Blacks formerly enslaved by Loyalists sometimes sued for their freedom. Caesar Tite was a former slave of Grace Tite, who before the Revolution willed that he should be free at age twenty-one. Caesar "served his time" with Thomas Leonard, a Loyalist whose estate was confiscated and sold in 1778. Several Americans purchased Tite by turns, including David Forman and, finally, Lewis McKnight. Caesar Tite sued McKnight for his freedom in November 1782. Noting that the black was now twenty-four years of age, well above the customary age of emancipation, the court ordered him freed.[16]

Redress in the courts was not always available to African Americans. In most cases of owner versus chattel, the judicial system favored the owner. Moreover, the slow political process of postwar liberation seemed especially feeble—if not futile—to the individual bondsperson. Consequently, Monmouth County blacks continued to "steal themselves" after the American Revolution, as they had before, and to manifest other forms of defiance. In the two years following the arrival of peace, at least twelve Monmouth blacks escaped from their masters. Ben, a thirty-year-old man belonging to Hendrick Smock of Freehold, escaped in May 1784. Smock warned that Ben, who "spoke very well, . . . very likely will change his name and pass for a free man." Dressed in the garb of a house servant, Ben wore a browncloth homespun coat, a white coat, vest, corduroy breeches, blue mixed stockings, and a castor hat with a black ribbon around the crown. Like so many other escapees, Ben was identified by a "remarkable scar," this time on the face, "being shot with small shot about the size of duck or goose shot."[17]

Blacks could count their modest success stories, too. Rarely offered land or cash stipends for years of service, only a few free blacks could eke out bits of property. Nonetheless, a few examples of small groups of independent free blacks appear on the tax rolls beginning in 1784. Sixteen free blacks appear on the Middletown tax ratables for that year. Nine of the sixteen owned houses; three owned horses; five owned cattle. In Freehold an African American man named Bunn owned a one-hundred-acre farm in 1787, but no other free black owned land or any movable property beyond a cow or pig. In Shrewsbury seventeen free-black farmers appeared on the tax ratables for 1787. Tom Cavey and Ephraim Rawley owned seventy-five acres of land, while Samuel Lawrence owned 100 acres and five cows. The rest possessed a few cattle, horses, and hogs.[18] Because Monmouth's tax assessors appraised even the smallest amounts of property, this picture of black assets is likely complete. These free blacks with taxable property were but a fraction of emancipated African Americans in the county. The vast majority of free blacks, however, were too poor to be represented on the tax rolls and doubtless remained dependent on their former masters' farms.

A Cautious Approach to Abolition

In the face of sometimes daunting opposition, the work of antislavery advocates in New York and New Jersey continued unabated throughout the 1790s. Upper Freehold Quaker Richard Waln of Walnford worked assiduously to protect the rights of enslaved and free blacks. Waln wrote passionately to legislators pointing out abuses by unscrupulous masters and advocating the cause of emancipation. Yet as the century entered its last decade, many New Jersey legislators responded coolly, believing that the statues of 1786 and 1788 already removed the worst effects of colonial prohibitions against emancipation. A bill promoting gradual emancipation was easily defeated in 1790.[19] Two years later, given another opportunity to pass a gradual emancipation bill that freed newborn slaves after twenty-eight years, the legislators were content to forecast that "from the state of society among us . . . and progress of the principles of universal liberty there is little reason to think that there will be any slaves at all among us 28 years hence." This prophecy was off by half a century.[20] Another gradual emancipation bill was introduced in 1794; it too was voted down. Further attempts to end slavery in New Jersey met great opposition from legislators from Bergen, Somerset, and Monmouth counties. A further setback occurred in 1794 when the assembly passed a statute making it harder for blacks to sue for their freedom through the courts, curtailing the efforts which previously set enslaved blacks free.

Despite these legislative defeats, popular opinion and party newspapers cautiously shifted on the emancipation issue. Defying proslavery sentiments, a group of Monmouth citizens petitioned the legislature in 1794 to "lay a foundation for the gradual emancipation of slavery." Reflecting the hopes of many, the petitioners demanded an end to a system that doomed thousands in the state "to a lifetime of bondage." Signed by over 100 members of the Society of Friends, including the signature of Mingo, a free black associated with Quakers, the petition was evidence of a growing if still minority discontent with slavery in the county.[21] A bill of 1797, passed by a slender majority, hinted at gradual emancipation without unequivocally granting it. The act granted newborn slaves freedom after twenty-eight years of indentured service to their owner but further stipulated that all blacks, unless explicitly set free by their owner, were to be considered slaves for life. As with the statute of 1786, legislators gave with one hand and took away with the other. Employment without consent of the master was prohibited; travel after dark or on Sundays was forbidden to slaves, and minimum rewards were established for the return of violators; public whippings were mandated for minor slave offenses. The bill thus protected many aspects of slavery.[22]

Reconsideration of the bill was easily quashed that fall. In the next legislative session, however, abolitionists made legal headway through a comprehensive revision of the New Jersey slave code, enacted in 1798. The revised code allowed blacks to own real estate for the first time since 1713. It permitted free blacks from other states to enter New Jersey, provided they had a pass attesting to their freedom. And it removed from the books whipping penalties for unauthorized assembly by blacks. At the same time, another measure succeeded in raising the age of emancipation without bond from thirty-five to forty years, enabling owners to hold on to older slaves.[23]

A Groundswell for Emancipation

During the 1790s proslavery advocates used anti-Quaker sentiment to discredit emancipation. Some accused Quakers of harboring pro-British attitudes and were charged with "poisoning the minds of our slaves." Others argued that abolition was

Table 5
Disposition of Slaves by Will
Monmouth County, 1790–1809

Number of Wills Mentioning Slaves	97
Number of Slaves Mentioned in Wills	354
Bequeathals (total)	72
To Widow	43
To Son(s)	13
To Daughter(s)	10
Other Relatives	2
To Be Sold	4
Emancipations (total)	25
Unconditional	1
Gradual	20
Encumbered	4

Source: Monmouth County Wills and Inventories, Archives Section, Division of Archives and Records Management, Department of State, Trenton, N.J.

merely a Quaker plot to give more blacks the vote and control the state or revived old fears that free blacks would be unable to support themselves. Memories of the war caused other resentment of abolition proposals. Philip Freneau, poet, editor, political commentator, and resident of Mount Pleasant, near Middletown, summed up the attitudes of many Patriots when he observed that the British still owed the Americans two hundred dollars each for the three thousand slaves who left for Nova Scotia in 1783.[24] In such a political climate, bills calling for gradual emancipation rarely emerged from legislative committees.

Emancipation made greater headway among private citizens, where religious or ethical conviction could be expressed through grants of manumission. These occurred in unprecedented numbers during the 1790s. In all of New Jersey, 40 percent of wills mentioning slaves in that decade provided for emancipation. Most of these grants were by masters in Quaker-dominated western New Jersey. In Monmouth County the figure was closer to 26 percent. As Table 5 shows, between 1790 and 1809 twenty-five of ninety-seven slave owners' wills provided for emancipation. Most of these grants, however, were laden with conditions, and, significantly, only one will granted immediate emancipation.

As in the past, owners who died testate often drove hard bargains. But wills from the 1790s also reveal that as blacks and their white allies exposed the contradictions between Revolutionary rhetoric and slavery, masters grudgingly accepted the feasability—if not the desirablity—of free wage labor. As in the colonial era, most slave owners preferred to pass along slaves to their descendants, placing family wealth over humanitarian concerns. Those who caught the growing tenor of the times offered slaves a distant freedom. Moreover, heirs were not above strategems and subterfuge if these would help to maintain bondage. In a number of court cases from the early 1790s, blacks, aided by the New Jersey Society for the Abolition of Slavery, had to sue for the liberty they had been awarded in a master's bequest.

In one such case, Cornelius Wilson, his wife Hagar, and their children, Lydia and Anna, sued for freedom from Abraham Probasco. The Wilson family was from Morris County. They had been set free just before the American Revolution by their former master, William Winds, who had employed them as free people. Encouraged by Winds to save money as an indemnity against poverty, Cornelius Wilson and his family contracted with Abraham Probasco of Monmouth County to serve him for five years. Probasco asked for a bill of sale for five shillings, and he later used that deed to declare the Wilsons as his slaves. The family sued for their freedom in court and won.[25]

A 1790 court case reached back to a manumission nearly four decades old to affirm that freedom was now hereditary. In a will composed in 1752, Quaker Richard Horsfull of Freehold promised future freedom to his "Negro wench Nell" and ordered his son John to maintain her if she was incapable. John was also directed to pay Nell £10 annually for her support. In 1761 John Horsfull himself died. In his will he granted his slaves emancipation on terms more favorable than those his father had extended. Nell's husband, Spence, for example, was awarded freedom after three months indenture and given permission to use an acre of land, provided he and Nell vacated the Horsfull's premises. John Horsfull's testament also ordered that Spence and Nell's two daughters be sold for a term of fifteen years, after which they were to be free. Betty and Nelly, the young ladies, were indentured to John Couwenhoven of Freehold. During their fifteen years in service, Betty gave birth to a son, Silas. Couwenhoven claimed that as Betty was in bondage when Silas was born, Silas was born enslaved. Years later, Silas sued for his freedom. The State Supreme Court denied Couwenhoven's claim, arguing that Betty's term was limited, not perpetual, and as she had served her term, so her son's condition followed his mother's, insuring his liberty.[26]

Some blacks negotiated private contracts with their masters over the terms of their emancipation. Between 1790 and 1804 seventeen such agreements were recorded at the county courts; each took years to be effected. Eleanor Van Brunt freed Benjamin in 1797 by a contract made nine years earlier.[27] Lewis, a slave of Charles Axford, a Shrewsbury blacksmith, was sold to New Jersey Chief Justice David Brearley on April 28, 1780 with the contractual provision that "said Negro is to become free after thirteen years." When Brearley died eleven years later, his executors gave Lewis a pass stating that he had "two years and seven months to serve (as he is not wanted in the family) has the Liberty to travel for a few days Not exceeding thirty miles from

An Act

For the Gradual Abolition of Slavery.

—

Sec. 1. BE *it enacted by the Council and General Assembly of this State, and it is hereby enacted by the authority of the same,* That every child born of a slave within this state, after the fourth day of July next, shall be free ; but shall remain the servant of the owner of his or her mother, and the executors, administrators or assigns of such owner, in the same manner as if such child had been bound to service by the trustees or overseers of the poor, and shall continue in such service, if a male, until the age of twenty-five years, and if a female until the age of twenty-one years.

2. *And be it enacted,* That every person being an inhabitant of this state, who shall be entitled to the service of a child born as aforesaid, after the said fourth day of July next, shall within nine months after the birth of such child, cause to be delivered to the clerk of the county whereof such person shall be an inhabitant, a certificate in writing, containing the name and addition of such person, and the name, age, and sex of the child so born ; which certificate, whether the same be delivered before or after the said nine months, shall be by the said clerk recorded in a book to be by him provided for that purpose ; and such record thereof shall be good evidence of the age of such child ; and the clerk of such county shall receive from said person twelve cents for every child so registered : and if any person shall neglect to deliver such certificate to the said clerk within said nine months, such person shall forfeit and pay for every such offence, five dollars, and the further sum of one dollar for every month such person shall neglect to deliver the same, to be sued for and recovered by any person who will sue for the same, the one half to the use of such prosecutor, and the residue to the use of the poor of the township in which such delinquent shall reside.

3. *And be it enacted,* That the person entitled to the service of any child born as aforesaid, may, nevertheless within one year after the birth of such child, elect to abandon such right; in which case a notification of such abandonment, under the hand of such person, shall be filed with the clerk of the township, or where there may be a county poor-house established, then with the clerk of the board of trustees of said poor-house of the county in which such person shall reside ; but every child so abandoned shall be maintained by such person until such child arrives to the age of one year, and thereafter shall be considered as a pauper of such township or county, and liable to be bound out by the trustees or overseers of the poor in the same manner as other poor children are directed to be bound out, until, if a male, the age of twenty-five, and if a female, the age of twenty-one ; and such child, while such pauper, until it shall be bound out, shall be maintained by the trustees or overseers of the poor of such county or township, as the case may be, at the expence of this state; and for that purpose the director of the board of chosen freeholders of the county is hereby required, from time to time, to draw his warrant on the treasurer in favor of such trustees or overseers for the amount of such expence, not exceeding the rate of three dollars per month ; provided the accounts for the same be first certified and approved by such board of trustees, or the town committee of such township ; and every person who shall omit to notify such abandonment as aforesaid, shall be considered as having elected to retain the service of such child, and be liable for its maintenance until the period to which its servitude is limited as aforesaid.

A. Passed at Trenton, Feb. 15, 1804.

An Act for the Gradual Abolition of Slavery, 1804. Courtesy of the New Jersey Historical Society.

this Place to find a master of his own Choice." Lewis made an agreement with merchant Moore Furman of Trenton, who paid Brearley's executors 18 pounds, 15 shillings for the remainder of his time.[28]

By 1790, over 350 (or 18 percent) of Monmouth's 1,949 Af-

Table 6
Monmouth County Population by Township, 1790

	WHITES	FREE BLACKS	SLAVES	TOTAL
Middletown	1,672 (12)	62 (18)	491 (31)	3,225 (19)
Upper Freehold	3,084 (22)	108 (31)	250 (16)	3,442 (20)
Freehold	3,146 (23)	12 (3)	627 (39)	3,785 (22)
Shrewsbury	4,296 (31)	165 (47)	212 (13)	4,673 (28)
Stafford	881 (6)	—	2 (0)	883 (5)
Dover	890 (6)	6 (1.7)	14 (1)	910 (5)
Totals	13,969	353	1,596	16,918

Source: *Return of Whole Number of Persons within the Federal Districts of the United States for 1790* (Washington, D.C., 1802), 39. Numbers in parentheses are percents of total population.

rican Americans were free (see Table 6), the highest percentage in eastern New Jersey. Free blacks lived in those areas where Quakers, Anglicans, and Presbyterians made up a significant proportion of the population. Accordingly, Shrewsbury and Upper Freehold had the highest percentages of free blacks while the Dutch communities of Freehold and Middletown lagged far behind. For example, Shrewsbury in 1790 was home to 165 free blacks and 212 enslaved people; Freehold had 12 free and 627 enslaved. In the newly incorporated towns of Howell, Dover, and Stafford, scarcely any blacks lived, free or otherwise. By 1800 free blacks numbered 468, accounting for 22 percent of Monmouth County's 2,101 blacks and 10 percent its total population.[29]

In Shrewsbury, where 165 African Americans were free in 1790, only sixteen appeared on the tax rolls. Clearly, many free blacks were forced to remain as laborers for former owners.[30] By 1795, however, there were twenty-four free blacks living independently in Middletown.

As did their white counterparts, blacks without property toiled as free-wage workers. Theophile Cazenove, a Frenchman, who visited New Jersey in the 1790s, recorded that during the summer, wages for free black males were three pounds (ten dollars) per month or three shillings ($37\frac{1}{2}$ cents) per day. Black women worked for four shillings (fifty cents) per week. By contrast, white laborers, due to their allegedly superior skills, demanded and received five shillings per day at harvest time and three to four shillings per day in the spring. Annually, white farm hands earned thirty to forty pounds; they also demanded to be treated "politely."[31]

Although Cazenove sneered at their status and opined that free blacks were "worse off than when they were slaves," probate records indicate that free blacks slowly accumulated personal property during this era. Mingo, who died in 1802, owned a sizable estate worth over £685. His property possessions included wearing apparel worth seven pounds, "horses waggon & guns Saddle and bridle" worth twenty-five pounds, and grain, corn, rice, and "casks of cider in the cellar." Most of his estate consisted of £586 of "Notes and bonds against sundry people." Mingo's extension of credit was a common way for blacks in Monmouth, shunned by most white creditors, to borrow money.

A second, perhaps more typical free black was Caesar Abraham, who left small articles including axes, hoes, drawing knives, four chains, a tray, a hammer, a candle mold, a hat, and an assortment of lesser items. Abraham held four leases for small plots of land, none exceeding five acres in size, far below the amount necessary for subsistence. Whereas Mingo held little property but a clear position as a moneylender, Abraham, like most free blacks, had very little land and few avenues to improve his lot.[32]

The recently discovered papers of Sampson Adams, a free black from Trenton in nearby Mercer County, indicate how sym-

This 1790 deed was for a tract of land sold by Caesar Abraham, "a free negro," and Samuel Still, "a free negro," in Shrewsbury. Courtesy of the Moss Archives, Rumson, N.J.

pathetic Quakers, though unwilling to admit blacks to their meetings, occasionally helped local African Americans. Adams initially worked as a tenant farmer in the early 1780s. He slowly built up a small estate, purchasing "milch cows," and working as a day laborer for neighboring whites. His fortunes were uncertain. In 1786 he paid ten shillings for the poor tax; the following year, he had to petition for relief. In 1788 he somehow mustered up sufficient capital to buy a small amount of land, but lacked the cash to build a house. Again, throwing himself on the good will of whites, Adams was gratified when over thirty neighbors pitched in with labor and contributed such necessities as lumber and nails. In a pattern that became common, Adams worked his own land while hiring out to local white farmers as a day laborer. Upon his death in 1792, Adams had accumulated an estate, worth £84, that included numerous china dishes, clothing, farm tools, cows, and horses. He willed that his land be sold and the proceeds distributed to the county poor relief fund, to the Episcopal and Methodist churches, and to his sister, Violet. After the estate was sold, Violet received £44. Sampson Adams and Mingo were apparently esteemed by local whites, who gave time and energy to help them succeed.[33]

Most blacks in Monmouth County were less fortunate than Mingo and Sampson, and many were perhaps less resourceful in channeling ambition and deferring gratification. One outlet for frustration was petty crime, which occurred frequently throughout Monmouth and the rest of eastern New Jersey. Blacks, in concert with whites, stole items ranging from pieces of linen to horses and sheep, then sold these to receivers. Violators who were caught received thirty-nine lashes on the back. For unhappy slaves, the next escalation was burglary. Angrier slaves used arson; "Negro Jude" was arrested in 1792 for intent to burn the house of Roeloff Van der Veer of Freehold. The post-Revolutionary period also saw a spate of violent murders by slaves of masters and other whites in eastern New Jersey.[34]

Blacks sometimes turned on blacks at frolics. Unwilling or unable to understand how enforced docility could lead to violent eruptions, whites tended to view any activity that excited blacks as the potential cause of untoward acts. This was an age when extreme virtuosity or the ability to arouse audiences was often seen as a form of satanic power. A popular pamphlet promulgated that opinion when it indicated that New Jersey residents regarded black fiddlers as agents of the devil. Cart races, illegal in Monmouth County, also excited blacks and frequently turned into brawls. John S. Holmes wrote a neighbor in 1799 complaining about "such riots by negroes," which ought to be suppressed. He noted that "your man Jack has been with me and Shewd me his wound [that he received from] David Boone's Charles." It was at one such gathering that a minor theft escalated into murder. After stealing and selling several small items,

Tom, the slave of Barnes Smock of Monmouth (once a captive of Colonel Tye), got into a fight with Negro Sam of Bergen County and stabbed him to death.[35]

The case of Sambo, a bondsman in the Forman family of Mt. Pleasant, illustrates the controlled, even systematic brutality that Monmouth masters unleashed to enforce subservience, restrain boldness, and shatter recalcitrance. The Formans considered Sambo to be exemplary, a servant who "stayed close at home, was very submissive." These qualities, David Forman reported, "exalted our compassion," to "let him have a little liberty like all the rest of the Negroes in the county we permitted him to go out for an evening." Left to his own designs, Sambo immediately stole two geese and took them "to an Old Free Negroe here." Their compassion now abased, the Formans gave Sambo 100 lashes. After his back healed, Sambo built a pleasure sled to travel to frolics. After several such incidents combined with petty thefts, Forman shaved Sambo's head, gave him seventy lashes, and burned his sled. Sambo then ran away, was caught near Elizabethtown, and returned to Mt. Pleasant for trial. In a scene reminiscent of the 1690s, a court assembled "a little after sunrise." Sambo was convicted and sentenced to sixty lashes. Forman reported that "after several more beatings Sambo became more malleable."[36]

Abolition at Last

With the exception of New Jersey, every northern state passed an immediate or gradual emancipation act during the Federalist era: Vermont in 1777 as part of its state constitution, Massachusetts by 1783 through court rulings, Pennsylvania through its gradual emancipation act of 1780, which freed slaves at age 28. After New York's passage of its own gradual emancipation act in 1799 (freeing males at 28, females at 25), New Jersey remained the only state north of Delaware and Maryland to remain irresolute in setting a timetable for the extinction of slavery. Thomas Jefferson's election in 1800 ushered in a federal administration more circumspect than the Federalists about undoing the peculiar institution. In that election year New Jerseyans made ardent Jeffersonian Joseph Bloomfield their governor. Bloomfield was more than an advocate of emancipation; when elected he had been for fourteen years an antislavery activist. His father Moses Bloomfield had manumitted fourteen slaves in 1783 in compliance with the principles of the Declaration of Independence. During Joseph Bloomfield's governorship a legislative majority in New Jersey, comprising both Jeffersonian Democrats and Federalists, embraced antislavery.

In 1804 New Jersey's veteran advocates of gradual emancipation, seasoned by two decades of campaigning, offered a compromise to their Democratic Republican opponents. Slaves born before July 4, 1804, would remain enslaved for life; children of slaves born after that date would be free. The consequences ensuing from this compromise no doubt gave slaveholders serious cause for apprehension. If parents are properties, who should be responsible for the cost of raising their freeborn offspring? If the state, in violation of every prior law and precedent, appropriates slaveholders' valuable properties, who should reimburse them? If slaveholders choose to impregnate chattel they have purchased—possibly fed and housed since childhood—and if this results in the birth of a property both made and claimed by the slaveholder, what right has any state to intervene in the disposition of that property? These were ticklish questions, and legislators answered them by proposing what amounted to an extraordinarily generous bribe. First, owners would be allowed twenty-five years' use of any male offspring of a slave, twenty-one years' use of any female offspring of a slave. Second, owners would be encouraged to abandon these children of slaves to the care of the overseers of the poor, at the expense of the state. In practice this meant that owners would collect money from the state for the offsprings' maintenance while continuing to use their labor. As in New York, from which the measure was copied, this so-called abandonment clause virtually guaranteed passage of the act, and in the event, passage by the New Jersey legislature was nearly unanimous. By 1808 fully $12,000, or 30 percent, of the state's budget was expended annually for the abandonment measure.[37]

Slavery in the Era of Emancipation

The 1804 act revealed the limited commitment to emancipation that prevailed in New Jersey. A modified slavery replaced complete servitude. The 1804 act did not free any slave immediately, although it perhaps placed greater pressure on masters to arrange private emancipations. For any enslaved black born after that date, masters would have full control of their lives and labors for over two decades. Historian Arthur Zilversmit has argued that masters generally accepted abolitionist logic and ideology and freed their bondspeople. But evidence drawn from a book of emancipations maintained by Monmouth County officials indicates that masters there did not rush to free their chattel. Cuff, a slave of Kenneth Anderson of Freehold, was freed the day after the gradual emancipation act took effect; other slaves waited until their masters had extracted years of labor.[38]

Gradual emancipation insured that in rural societies such as Monmouth where slavery remained popular, blacks would exist in the shadow of servitude. Between 1800 and 1810 the number of slaves in the county dropped from 1,633 to 1,504, a decrease of less than 8 percent. New Jersey citizens circulated petitions seeking the repeal of the entire 1804 abolition law. Angry Bergen County slave owners charged that abolition was "unconstitutional, impolitic and unjustly severe," and would "endanger the community." Opponents of slavery withstood such arguments, however, and the law was sustained. In no small part, the very distance of the day of actual emancipation lessened the concern of whites.[39]

During this period of pending but merely imminent manumission, blacks sometimes took extraordinary risks to hasten their day of liberty. Some entered into private contracts that could return a free man to slavery. One such free black who risked his liberty for the freedom of his family was Adam Riley, who purchased the freedom of his wife, Caty, and their two children from the estate of William Williamson of Freehold. In so doing Riley had to also agree to insure a £1,000 bond for the maintenance of Amey, "an aged wench belonging to the estate now have become Infirm and under Necessity of tender care and Attention." If Riley failed to keep up Amey, his wife and children could be sold to provide money for her maintenance.[40]

Blacks often turned for solace to religion, now an integral and largely indigenous aspect of their life in Monmouth, an important spiritual, social, and political outlet. While Monmouth County blacks lacked the organized church movement that sprouted in New York and Philadelphia, they nevertheless left signs of religious organization and involvement. Occasionally, Protestant churches baptized blacks in the post-Revolutionary years. But these privileges were restricted to servants.[41] Most churches were reluctant to admit black members as equals. Even the Society of Friends, an ally in the fight for emancipation, retained colonial-era prejudices against black adherents. James Pemberton, a Philadelphia Friend, explained in a letter why Quaker churches in Pennsylvania and New Jersey rarely admitted African Americans. The Friends, he noted, had few black applicants, and those failed to convince the "Collective Capacity" to tender admission to the church. Behind this reason lay another: blacks, once accepted, "must become intitled to the privilege of intermarriage." Pemberton believed there were few Friends willing to "introduce such a union in their families."[42]

While in New York and Philadelphia, Anglican, Presbyterian, Methodist, and Dutch Reformed Churches began to offer membership to blacks during the early nineteenth century, there is no record that their Monmouth counterparts embraced such liberalism at this time. Full admission of blacks to Monmouth's white Protestant churches lay in the future. At the same time, African Americans had, as a group, always preferred their own style of worship and own religious institutions, and during this period many blacks in Monmouth County formed their own religious communities.

The private meditations of the colonial period doubtless continued after the Revolution because some rural slaveholders insisted that Africans have no souls. Particularly important for the development of black religious expression during the post-Revolutionary period was the emergence of itinerant black preachers. Nathan Hatch has argued that white evangelical religion "unwittingly enhanced the leadership potential of black preachers, both slave and free."[43]

In the 1790s self-appointed African American circuit preachers visited Monmouth. One was George White, born a slave in Virginia in 1754. Leaving home in 1790 after gaining his freedom, White spent three years working in New Jersey before settling in New York City. Initially Anglican, he became a Methodist after a memorable evening service at the Bowery Church in New York. Further sanctified in a trance, White received a message to "declare what you have seen!" But his desire to preach was frustrated by Methodist authorities. After the quarterly Methodist meeting refused to license White, he became an exhorter in Shrewsbury and Middletown, specializing in prayer meetings that "many of my African brethren, who were strangers to religion before, were now brought to close in the offers of mercy," through trances and shouts. White had a vision of "three forms, like doves, presenting themselves to me a dark room." His career, which lasted into the 1820s, combined Christian theology with African symbolism. His trances and shouts were important components of African religious tradition.[44]

John Jea, a second black minister, also preached in Monmouth during the 1790s. He conducted camp meetings in rural New Jersey at which hundreds of blacks stepped forward to salvation. These meetings were based loosely on Presbyterian and Methodist "love feasts," at which any person could speak of their experiences and be given a soothing reception. Jea's services were held "out of doors in the fields and woods, which we used to call our large chapel." Designed to accommodate the work schedules of slaves, services were held continually from eleven o'clock on Saturday night to the same time Sunday evening.

Monmouth's distribution of slave families among innumerable owners made camp meetings highly charged events. In his theology, Jea instructed the slaves to do no evil and to learn to do well, for "the end of all their troubles was near at hand." He warned them to be careful of the company they kept and not to desire any of the "dainties of the world." Jea promised the throngs that "God had promised to deliver them that call on him in time of trouble."

The efforts of preachers like White and Jea to reach out to the black Christians did not result immediately in a formal black church movement in Monmouth. Rather, they offered a religious experience outside of the mainstream white denominations.[45] So far as these can be known, itinerant efforts such as theirs constituted the primary religious experiences of Monmouth's blacks during the early years of the nineteenth century.

Summary

The period from the close of the American Revolution to the enactment of gradual emancipation in 1804 showed considerable progress as well as significant limitations for Monmouth County blacks. While the numbers of free blacks steadily rose, they were still a distinct minority of the African American population. Blacks lacked many key rights and owned little property. As the political controversy over slavery swirled in the legislature, little planning was made for improving the economic and social conditions of blacks. Despite the faulty apportionment of political and social rights, hopeful signs of black autonomy could be seen both in the assemblies of blacks worshiping God, which provided a basis for cohesive community, and in the growing numbers of free blacks.

Notes

1. For discussion of postwar years, see Richard P. McCormick, *Experiment in Independence: New Jersey in the Critical Period, 1781–1789* (New Brunswick, N.J., 1950), 18–26. For recapture, see *Independent Gazetteer* (Philadelphia), September 20, 1783, and *New-York Weekly Gazette*, January 26, 1786.

2. In 1787 sixty "inhabitants of the county of Monmouth" petitioned the New Jersey Assembly with a complaint that the justices of the Supreme Court had "set aside some of the laws as unconstitutional," most particularly the right to limit the size of juries in some criminal trials—an ominous statute for Monmouth blacks before the Supreme Court rescinded it. See Austin Scott, "*Holmes* vs. *Walton,* The New Jersey Precedent: A Chapter in the History of Judicial Power and Unconstitutional Legislation," *American Historical Review* 4 (1899): 459–60. See also references below to other petitions by groups from Monmouth County.

3. Act of March 2, 1786, in *Acts of the Tenth General Assembly of New Jersey . . . Second Sitting* (Trenton, 1786). For a report of the bill, see *New Jersey Gazette* (Trenton), March 6, 1786. The best summaries

of this are in Arthur Zilversmit, *The First Emancipation: The Abolition of Slavery in the North* (Chicago, 1967), 178–81, and Marion T. Wright, "New Jersey Laws and the Negro," *Journal of Negro History* 28 (1943): 174–75. See also Clement Price, comp. and ed., *Freedom Not Far Distant: A Documentary History of Afro-Americans in New Jersey* (Newark, 1980), 73–85; W. E. B. DuBois, *The Suppression of the African Slave Trade to the United States of America, 1638–1870* (1896; reprint, Baton Rouge, La., 1969), 227, 230–31, 240; Henry Scofield Cooley, *A Study of Slavery in New Jersey* (Baltimore, 1896), 18–19.

4. Act of November 25, 1788, in *New Jersey Acts* 13 (1788), 486–88. See Zilversmit, *The First Emancipation*, 161–62; Wright, "New Jersey Laws," 176; Cooley, *A Study of Slavery*, 19. For Livingston on slavery, see *The Papers of William Livingston*, 5 vols., ed. Carl E. Prince et al. (Trenton, N.J., 1979–90) 5:255, 357–59, 366–67.

5. McCormick, *Experiment in Independence*, 47–50.

6. This account of widespread disdain for Anglicans and Quakers in post-Revolutionary New Jersey contrasts sharply with recent historical treatment that regards the Quakers' ideological campaign as the most effective agent against slavery in the post-Revolutionary North.

7. For sale of the Black Loyalist, see Adam Hyler Papers, Special Collections, Alexander Library, Rutgers University. For receipt, see Rulef Van Mater to Daniel Covenhoven, July 3, 1798, Slavery File, Monmouth County Historical Association, Freehold, N.J. See also Jonathan W. Forman to James Baird, 1804, for Negro Robin, Slavery File, Monmouth County Historical Association, Freehold, N.J., and Indenture of James Mott to Obadiah Bostwick, June 2, 1802, Mott Papers, Cherry Hall Papers, box 12, folder 5, Monmouth County Historical Association, Freehold, N.J.; Sales of Pompey, 50, on January 16, 1802, and Rob, 28, on March 25, 1804, in Van Liew–Voorhees Family Papers, Special Collections, Alexander Library, Rutgers University; and John S. Holmes Papers, General Store Accounts and Inventory of Goods Sold at Sheriff's Sale, box A, folder 20, Holmes Family Papers, Special Collections, Alexander Library, Rutgers University. See also *New Jersey Gazette* (Trenton), December 16 and 23, 1783; January 6 and February 3 1784; January 23 1786; and *Brunswick Gazette* (New Brunswick), November 8 1791.

8. For a complete enumeration of property holdings of slave holders and non-slave holders in Monmouth Country, see Graham R.

Hodges, "African Americans in Monmouth Country, New Jersey, 1784–1860" (Lincroft, N.J., 1992), appendix 1. For opposition to abolition, see Jackson Turner Main, *Political Parties before the Constitution* (Chapel Hill, N.C., 1973), 142–43; Dennis P. Ryan, "Six Towns: Continuity and Change in Revolutionary New Jersey, 1770–1792" (Ph.D. diss., New York University, 1974), 261–76, 280–85, 290. For prices of New Jersey slaves, see Zilversmit, *The First Emancipation*, 238–39.

9. See Abstracts of Tax Ratables, Monmouth County, 1778–1804, box 114, Archives Section, Division of Archives and Records Management, Department of State, Trenton, N.J. (hereafter cited as New Jersey State Archives).

10. Peter O. Wacker and Paul G. E. Clemens, *Land Use in Early New Jersey: A Historical Geography* (Newark, 1995), 70, 97.

11. Compare tax ratables for Middletown and Dover in Abstracts of Tax Ratables, Monmouth County, 1789, box 114, New Jersey State Archives.

12. Figures for the North derived from Ira Berlin, *Slaves without Masters: The Free Negro in the Antebellum South* (New York, 1974), 46–47, 136–37.

13. For impetus to emancipation, see Leon Litwack, *North of Slavery: The Negro in the Free States, 1790–1860* (Chicago, 1961); Zilversmit, *The First Emancipation;* and Gary B. Nash, *Forging Freedom: The Formation of Philadelphia's Black Community, 1720–1840* (Cambridge, 1988). A more critical appraisal of Quakers' roles can be found in Jean Soderlund, *Quakers & Slavery: A Divided Spirit* (Princeton, N.J., 1985). For a discussion of the failure of abolitionism on a national level, see Gary B. Nash, *Race and Revolution* (Madison, Wis., 1990), 25–56.

14. Helen Catteral, *Judicial Cases Concerning American Slavery and the Negro*, 5 vols. (Washington, D.C., 1936), 4:321–22.

15. For Andrew Britton, see Monmouth County Wills, 4987–91, New Jersey State Archives. See also Zilversmit, *The First Emancipation*, 242.

16. For Caesar Tite, see *Cases Adjudged in the Supreme Court of New-Jersey Relative to the Manumission of Negroes* (Burlington, N.J., 1795), 10–12. "Leonard's Audit Office Claim" notes the loss of "a negro indented servt to have his freedom at the end of five years." See Loyalist Claims, Manuscript Collection, New York Public Library, 15:239.

17. For Ben escaped from Smollett, see *New Jersey Gazette* (Trenton), May 31, 1784. For other fugitives, see also *ibid.*, April 6, August

3 and 23, and December 20, 1784, March 12, July 4, and August 29, 1785, March 12, May 22, and November 13, 1786; *Political Intelligencer* (Elizabeth Town), June 22, 1785; *Trenton Mercury and The Weekly Advertiser*, October 2, 1787; *Jersey Chronicle* (Mount Pleasant), November 15, 1795; *Trenton Federalist*, July 4, 1803.

18. Tax Ratables for Middletown, 1784–1785 and Tax Ratables for 1787, Shrewsbury Township, New Jersey State Archives. See also *Monmouth County 1790 Freeholders List,* comps. Elaine De Met Anderson and Ellen Thorne Morris (Lincroft, N.J., 1985).

19. For the 1790 bill, see Paul Finkelman, "State Constitutional Protections of Liberty and the Antebellum New Jersey Supreme Court: Chief Justice Hornblower and the Fugitive Slave Law," *Rutgers Law Journal* 23 (1992): 763. For information on Waln, see, for example, Waln to Elias Boudinot, April 17, 1790 and Waln to Isaac Collins, January 14, 1793 in Waln Papers, Haverford College, Haverford, Pa.

20. Quoted in Zilversmit, *The First Emancipation*, 161.

21. The Memorial of the Subscribers, Inhabitants of the County of Monmouth to the Legislative Council and General Assembly of the State of New Jersey [c.1800], Legislative Manuscripts, box 13, item 16, New Jersey State Archives.

22. Zilversmit, *The First Emancipation*, 185–88.

23. *Ibid.,* 175–76, 187–89; Wright, "New Jersey Laws," 177; and Ruth Bogin, *Abraham Clark and the Quest for Equality in the Revolutionary Era, 1774–1794* (Rutherford, N.J., 1982), 115. For the text of the 1798 law, see *Laws of the State of New Jersey Revised and Published under the Authority of the Legislature by William Paterson* (Newark, N.J., 1800), 307–13.

24. For Freneau's comment, see the *Jersey Chronicle* (Mount Pleasant), 29 August 1795.

25. For the Wilsons, see *Cases Adjudged*, 29–30.

26. For Richard Horsfull, see Monmouth County Wills and Inventories, item 1897, New Jersey State Archives. For John Horsfull, see Monmouth County Wills and Inventories, item 2785 New Jersey State Archives. For Supreme Court decision, see *State* v. *Anderson,* in *Reports of Cases Argued and Determined in the Supreme Court of New-Jersey from April Term 1790, to November Term 1795, Both Inclusive,* 2d ed., ed. Richard S. Coxe (Jersey City, N.J., 1877), 1:41–43.

27. For 1790s emancipations, see Miscellaneous Book B (1791–

1815), 49–75, and Road Return Book B, 18, Monmouth County Archives, Manalapan, N.J. published as *Manumission Book of Monmouth County, New Jersey, 1791–1844* (Freehold, N.J., 1992).

28. Monmouth County Wills and Inventories, items 6283, 6409, 6675, 6929, New Jersey State Archives. For Lewis, see Cherry Hall Papers, box 3, folder 5, Monmouth County Historical Association, Freehold, N.J. Furman was elected Trenton's first mayor in 1792.

29. *Return of the Whole Persons within the Several Districts of the United States . . . for the Year 1790* (Washington, 1802), 39; *Return of the Whole Numbers of People within the Several Districts of the United States . . . for the Year 1800* (Washington, 1802), 45.

30. See Tax Ratables for Middletown, Freehold, Shrewsbury, and Upper Freehold, 1784–95, New Jersey State Archives.

31. Rayner Wickersham Kelsey, ed. *Cazenove Journal, 1794: A Record of the Journey of Theophile Cazenove through New Jersey and Pennsylvania* (Haverford, Pa., 1922), 3. See also James Tallman's Register, 1800-1801, Special Collections, Alexander Library, Rutgers University. For statewide wage rates, see Wacker and Clemens, *Land Use*, 102–5.

32. See Kelsey, *Cazenove Journal*, 8. For probate records, see Mingo, 8500 M, New Jersey State Archives; Caesar Abraham, 7609–7616 M, New Jersey State Archives.

33. Sampson Adams Papers, Manuscript collections, William L.Clements Library, University of Michigan.

34. For theft of horses and sheep, see *State* v. *Joseph Vunck and William Covert*, Court of General Sessions, December 1795, Monmouth County Archives, Manalapan, N.J. For whippings, see *State* v. *Negroes Ben Hall and Cornelius Cunningham*, 1788. See also *State* v. *Negro Prince*, November 1794; *State* v. *Harry Jackson*, October 1796; *State* v. *Negro Dago*, October 1799. For arson, see *State* v. *Negro Jude*, April 1792, all in Court of General Sessions, Monmouth County Archives, Manalapan, N.J. Arson was a weapon used in other counties as well. For Bergen County, see *State* v. *Negro Bet*, case 37,213 (1780), and *State* v. *Cuffe*, case 37,223 (1794), in New Jersey Supreme Court Records, New Jersey State Archives. These are but a sampling of the numerous slave crimes entered in the Supreme Court calendar. For a spectacular account of a murder of a master, see *A Short Acount of the Trial of Cyrus Emlay, a Black Man . . . with His Confession* (Burlington, N.J., 1801), private collection of Joseph Felcone.

35. For black fiddler as agent of the devil, see *The Devil; or, The New Jersey Dance* (n.p., n.d. [c1790]), private collection of Joseph Felcone. For riots, see Holmes Family Papers, 1799, Special Collections, Alexander Library, Rutgers University. For Tom, see New Jersey Supreme Court Records, case 37,214, New Jersey State Archives.

36. Diary from Mt. Pleasant, New Jersey, 1798–1799, Forman Family Papers, New-York Historical Society.

37. For political agreement on abolition, see Carl E. Prince, *New Jersey's Jeffersonian Republicans: The Genesis of an Early Party Machine, 1789–1817* (Chapel Hill, N.C., 1967), 116. On passage of law, see Zilversmit, *The First Emancipation*, 191–98; Wright, "New Jersey Laws," 177. For example of boarding, see John S. Holmes Papers, box A, folder 13, Special Collections, Alexander Library, Rutgers University.

38. Zilversmit, *The First Emancipation*, 194; *Manumission Book of Monmouth County*, 3.

39. For the text of the 1804 law, see Price, *Freedom Not Far Distant*, 79–81. For reaction, see Zilversmit, *The First Emancipation*, 195–96, and Wright, "New Jersey Laws," 177–78. For legislative reaction, see Prince, *New Jersey's Jeffersonian Republicans*, 151.

40. For Riley, see Craig Papers, box 1, folder 4, Monmouth County Historical Association, Freehold, N.J.

41. See, for example, the Old Tennent Church Records, 1730–1850, 1:80–81, 83–84, 87, 89, 93, 95, 105, Monmouth County Historical Association, Freehold, N.J.

42. James Pemberton to James Philips, November 18, 1784, Gilder-Lehrman Papers, Pierpont Morgan Library, New York.

43. Nathan O. Hatch, *The Democratization of American Christianity* (New Haven, Conn., 1989), 107; Albert J. Raboteau, "The Slave Church in the Era of the American Revolution," in Ira Berlin and Ronald Hoffman,eds. *Slavery and Freedom in the Age of the American Revolution* (Charlottesville, Va., 1983), 193–217. For masters' beliefs that slaves had no souls, see Graham Russell Hodges, ed., *Black Itinerants of the Gospel: The Narratives of John Jea & George White* (Madison, Wis., 1993), 91.

44. For the complete narratives of White and Jea, see *ibid.*

45. *Ibid.* For discussion of love feasts, see Jonathan Crowder, *A True and Complete Portraiture of Methodism; or, The History of the Wesleyan Methodists* (New York, 1813), 242–43.

5

Gradual
Emancipation
1804–1830

New Jersey's gradual emancipation act of 1804 guaranteed that, unless deaths and voluntary manumissions should outnumber births and importations, New Jersey's population of slaves would continue to grow until at least 1825, the earliest date for required manumission. In fact, six years after the act's passage, Monmouth County's census enumerated 1,504 enslaved blacks, a decline of 129 slaves, or roughly 8 percent of the slave population, since 1800. During the same period the population of free blacks increased from 164 to 632. Clearly, the act's projected timetable for emancipation was more conservative than the quickening pace of manumissions in Monmouth County.[1]

But this pace was by no means uniform across the county. Shrewsbury and Upper Freehold had the strongest free black presence. In those townships free blacks accounted for over 60 percent of the African American population. In contrast, the Dutch communities of Middletown and Freehold moved torpidly on the antislavery issue. In Middletown the enslaved group comprised 80 percent of the population, outnumbering free blacks

507 to 127; in Freehold the count was even more disproportionate, with only 15 free blacks as against 702 slaves. By comparison, free persons constituted 13.5 percent of the nation's blacks
in 1810, with state figures ranging from nearly 75 percent free in
New England to 3.9 percent free in the deep South. Only the
most repressive areas of Georgia and South Carolina matched
the 2.1 percent figure of free blacks in Freehold.[2]

In 1810, then, Monmouth County residents were of two
minds about slavery. In some communities the peculiar institution was dwindling, as the Founding Fathers had anticipated; in
others the system flourished, as slaveholders clung stubbornly
to their dependence on slave labor. For New Jersey African
Americans in the first decades of the nineteenth century, the
struggle for independence—on any level—required determination, resilience, and valor.

Gradual emancipation did nothing in the short term to ham-
per the property rights of Monmouth County slaveholders.
Hence, the business of enslavement proceeded nearly unabated.
The 1804 act did not prohibit intrastate sales, so masters were
free to sell the time of any chattel. Advertisements appeared
regularly in the newspapers. Private sales also continued. In
October 1806 James Baird purchased a "Negro Boy . . . at a
private sale" for 180 dollars. Two years later Jonathan Forman
sold a slave named Robin to Baird for $300. Except in the un-
likely case that the "Negro boy" was no older than four and
that Robin was no older than six, both transactions involved a
lifetime of enslavement. Eight years later Baird purchased Bett,
twenty-six years old, from D. W. Disborough of New Brunswick.
In the 1814 deed Bett could still be referred to as a "slave for
life" because she was unlucky enough to be born before 1804.
In 1822, nearly two decades after passage of the gradual emancipation act and three years before its mandated manumissions
would begin, a Conover farm of 400 acres in Freehold was advertised for sale along with "Two Negro men."[3] Unless these

"men" were 18 or younger, they too were being sold as slaves for life.

Since date of birth triggered the 1804 act, a way was needed to establish legally the true ages of slaves. To this end Monmouth County kept a "Black Birth Book" in which masters had to register the date of birth, sex, and name of each child along with their own names and dates of residence to help verify future claims of freedom. As the 1800 and 1810 census manuscripts are missing, this book represents the fullest and most official portrait of local slaveholding.[4]

In 1807 Congress banned the importation of slaves into the U.S., effective the following year. The new law invigorated the domestic slave trade in the South, and New Jersey's slaveholders were not unaware that their chattel were a commodity suddenly grown scarcer, and all the more valuable for it. Sales of slaves to Southern markets pointed up a deficiency in New Jersey's laws: a simple, legal act, sale of property, within New Jersey could result, if the buyer was from out of state, in a loss of the limited but well-defined human rights bestowed upon that property by the assembly. In 1812 the New Jersey legislature responded by enacting a statute that discouraged sales out of state without agreement by the bondsperson. The wonder, of course, is that legislators could imagine a typical enslaved person up for sale having either the wherewithal or the access to counsel needed to bring a master to court—though such cases were not unknown.

Although the 1812 law may have resolved some troubling legal technicalities, it could not overcome the effects of ignorance, duplicity, and bribery. Illiterate blacks lacked expertise and legal backing in the fine points of the gradual emancipation act—which was further complicated by supplementary acts of 1804, 1806, 1808, 1811, and 1820.[5] Duplicity frequently took this form: to gain the consent of a slave assured future freedom in New Jersey, an owner would promise short-term service in the

South, knowing full well that the transaction would trap the black permanently in a state where slavery was perpetuated without challenge. Sometimes New Jersey masters played on the strength of family feeling to dupe blacks into such agreements. Samuel Thompson of Monmouth, for example, convinced a black mother, aged twenty-five and a "slave for life," to go to Louisiana because there her sons, Philip, three, and Ralph, five, would be servants only until the age of twenty-five. Through this ruse he stole rather than gained the boys' eventual freedom. A more involved deception may have been practiced by John R. Schenck of Monmouth. Posing as their magnanimous benefactor, he freed three slave children, signed them to apprenticeships, then gained permission to remove them to Ohio, part of the Northwest Territory, where slavery was illegal but where enforcement was difficult, so that the children may well have remained his slaves.[6]

As for bribery, an English visitor to New Jersey noted that the judges who determined the legality of a sale out of state were "base enough . . . to attest that slaves consented to be removed, when in many instances they had never examined them." In 1818, similarly, investigators found that New Jersey slave traders conspired with Judge Jacob Van Winkle of Middlesex County to export to plantations in Louisiana young blacks destined to be freed under the 1804 law.

Despite such evidences of callous self-interest, these incidents do not support the claims of economists Robert Fogel and Stanley Engerman that masters took compensation for gradual emancipation by selling many slaves down South. Census data demonstrates that masters generally freed the very young and the aged while retaining the services of men and women between the ages of fourteen and forty-five.[7] Thus, most enslaved people were compelled to remain with owners who intended neither to sell them South nor to hasten their day of freedom.

An initial census of names in the Black Birth Book shows that patterns of slaveholding established in colonial times persisted in Monmouth County into the antebellum decades. The average number of slaves held in the county was still two or three per family farm. And as in the colonial era, a different picture emerges when the entries are divided by family name. Twenty-seven related families registered 454 slaves, averaging almost seventeen slaves for each family name. The five leading families were the Van Maters, with seventy-nine entries, the Schencks, with forty-eight, the Formans, with thirty-four, the Hendricksons, with thirty-two, and the Holmeses, with twenty-nine. Together these five families account for over one-third of the entries in the Black Birth Book. At least for the first two decades of gradual emancipation (when the bulk of the registrations were entered), family slaveholding remained a robust institution in Monmouth County.[8]

Probate records substantiate the evidence of the Black Birth Book by indicating how closely masters held their bondspeople to families as legacies of inheritance. Despite the impetus of gradual emancipation, few masters let ideas of liberty decide issues of freedom in their wills; economics and loyal service weighed far more heavily in masters' judgments. The will of Kenneth Hankinson of Monmouth is illustrative. In his last testament Hankinson granted to his son Peter "my Negro Boy Lewis as his slave for life." Hankinson also established a timetable for gradual emancipation of his other slaves. Abraham would be freed in seven years, at age twenty-five. The indentures of Cyrus, nine, and Humphrey, eight, were to be sold until they too reached twenty-five, after which they would be free. Likewise, the indentures of three female slaves were to be sold until each reached age twenty-five, the cash proceeds being bequeathed to his two daughters. Finally, Hankinson extended to his inheritors a claim on Dick, "who is now run away," establishing a fifty-dollar reward for his capture and perpetuating his slavery "for life if he is ever taken."[9]

Lives of Enslaved Blacks

Gabe, Patty, Jack, Lac, and Charles were slaves of James Tallman, a Monmouth County farmer whose enterprise required typically varied duties of its black hands. In August 1826 Tallman used Gabe, Patty, and Jack in the afternoon "getting in the clover in the barn in eight loads." A few days later Gabe plowed about two acres; then he and Lac sowed two acres of "white flint wheat" and plowed it. Afterwards Gabe carted the manure. On a rainy day when the fields were wet, Gabe, Patty, and Jack were sent to "cut down the wild parsnips in the apple tree." For the next week or two Gabe, Lac, and Charles cut corn, dug potatoes, husked corn for four days, then on some very rainy days worked in the barn. The following year saw much the same routine. Gabe and the others worked in the corn fields, planted clover, "planted sweet potatoes, then harvested the hay." These routines were doubtless followed on most farms in Monmouth. Masters on smaller farms often worked alongside their slaves or on larger plantations acted as foremen and used their slaves to perform farm labor.[10]

Farm hands frequently worked while in poor health, to judge from notices of runaway blacks during this period. James was "much troubled with the phthistic"(tuberculosis). George, who ran away from Barnes Smock in 1806, had "rotted teeth." Henry, who fled from John D. Polhemus in 1822, was "a little lame caused by the fever falling in his right ankle, has been lamed twice or more." Peter, fugitive from Israel Clarke in 1822, had "a remarkable dent or depression in his forehead near the edge of his hair," perhaps the result of a cruel blow.[11]

Other notices reveal that many of Monmouth County's slaveholders spent as little as possible to clothe their bondspeople.

Unlike their urban counterparts, whose dress became more stylish in this period, rural slaves typically remained drab. Thus the notice for Dick, who ran away from John I. Conover of Lower Freehold in 1814, states that he wore "two round-abouts, a pair of trowsers of a faded brown, nankeen trowsers, lace boots, a wool hat pretty much worn." Ben, seventeen, who escaped from William A. Craig of Freehold in 1814 wearing a "black fur hat, bottle free coattee, light vest and a pair of striped tan & linnen trowsers and 2 tow and linen shirts," seems to have been prepared for colder weather.[12]

Though owners were parsimonious in their allotment of basic provisions, they did allow slaves time enough to earn some money of their own. One farmer permitted his servants to cut firewood, to crab and fish, and then to take the produce to market in New York City. Other bondspeople were permitted to hire out on their time off or on holidays. One farmer noted that his servant Jack worked in the woods on Pinkster because "he don't keep the Holy Day on account of the coming [horse] races the 15th Inst.; at races Jack one of 10,000 to see *Eclipse*."[13]

But holidays were few for slaves. Those with distant spouses could, depending on good behavior, expect to visit them at least once a month. Christmas was a week-long vacation. Easter accounted for a long weekend. Pinkster, in decline in the early nineteenth century, was being supplanted by General Training Day as the most raucous holiday of the year. Widely celebrated in rural New Jersey, General Training Day was a militia muster, resplendent with colorfully dressed volunteers astride their best horses. Blacks were limited to observance, but they seized the time for frolics.

Much of the tone of frolics was set by slaves who took the opportunity to vent frustrations, tensions, and accumulated physical energies. Sylvia DuBois, of nearby Somerset County, recalled much drinking of homemade brandy, fighting, and dancing[14]—activities typical at militia or lumber camps, and any place where hard-working people form social groups away from their families. On New Jersey's rural farms, when slaves had families it was usually the men who were forcibly isolated from wives and children. And so it fell to women to divert their own frustrations, tensions, and accumulated physical energies from simple release into behaviors that would sustain and nurture the African American family.

Slave Families

Sometimes slaves went to extraordinary means to preserve their families. Hannah and her two children, Maria and James, fled "on the road to Philadelphia" from Peter Forman in 1820. Hannah was in her late thirties and, Forman believed, pregnant. From his description she had evidently been a trusted and favored domestic for she wore "a black silk bonnet full trimmed, her hair pretty long, so that she frequently wears a comb, sometimes a cap, and had on a mill dyed wollen gown, a dark shawl dyed red, an oldish gray cloak." Her baggage included gowns, "one black, and one tow gown, two pairs of shoes." Her daughter wore a "dark bonnet, a mill-dyed frock, or a blue gingham. James wore a "wool hat, a sailor jacket of a mill dyed color, and pantaloons of the same." She was obviously willing to risk much by striking out on her own.[15]

Hannah was bold. Living in Monmouth County, she had to be. As the number of free blacks there increased, women, including mothers, remained in bondage in disproportionate numbers. Of 640 listings in the Black Birth Book, 324 are male and 316 female, a ratio far more even than is found in censuses of blacks overall in the county, where there was a sizable male majority.[16] The close ratio in the Black Birth Book indicates that the value of females increased after the passage of the gradual emancipation act in 1804 and the close of the foreign slave trade in 1808.

Why did black women appear more valuable? Most decisively, because women could produce children who would, under the gradual emancipation act, enter the world obliged to serve the master for a quarter century. Another reason was that women, as slaveholders had discovered, could be used as easily as men for many routine farm chores—and 72 percent of the owners who listed their occupation in the Black Birth Book *were* farmers, including the largest family-holders. In contrast to urban areas, where female slaves generally worked as domestics, rural bondswomen performed both house- and fieldwork. As Lois Green Carr and Lorena S. Walsh have demonstrated for the Chesapeake states in the late eighteenth century, black women were increasingly forced to labor in the fields beside the men, especially at harvest time. In addition, women worked throughout the year as dairymaids and with poultry.[17] Meanwhile, gradual emancipation ensured that a burgeoning pool of male contract laborers would be available for the heaviest farm chores.

Evidence in the Black Birth Book confirms the powers that masters held over black efforts at family formation. Only twenty-seven of the 640 birth registrations list both parents; one couple, Charles and Mary Johnson, owned by Samuel Forman, accounted for seven of these children. The remaining entries list only the mother's name—or worse, in fifty-four cases, no parents' names at all.[18]

In this and other ways, small-scale slaveholding, particularly among white relatives, continued to exacerbate the incidental social hardships of blacks. One extended family of masters and mistresses deployed its seventeen slaves over a sizable geographic area. Smaller holdings meant black relatives were divided among several families. Either way, an owner's financial mischance increased the likelihood of separation through sale and thereby threatened the stability and emotional life of the African American family. Even without this threat, family relations were greatly encumbered. Husband and wife, for example, could see each other only upon permission, a limitation that affected virtually every family decision.[19] With husbands and children often on other farms, and children sometimes sold away forever, it is remarkable that family connections prevailed at all.[20]

Black families found some support from religious organizations. Churches such as the Middletown Old First Church received domestic slaves into membership, but only on rare occasions. In 1826 a Mrs. Taylor at the Holmdel Baptist Church founded a Sunday school attended by eighty to one hundred black children as well as a few adults. Such schools emphasized biblical literacy; to which end the young scholars learned reading and writing. One of Mrs. Taylor's unique demands was that students study in their bare feet. Whether this request was intended to eliminate any distinction of wealth or was made for some more peculiar reason, Mrs. Taylor's Sunday school is the first known educational institution in Monmouth for blacks.[21]

Adult blacks were more likely to listen to the exhortations of George White and other A. M. E. Zion itinerants, who continued to preach throughout the county.[22] But the allure of redemption was not enough to stop some blacks from turning to crime. For example, Prince, the slave of Job Throckmorton of Freehold, stole bank notes from his master and cash from other whites. Sometimes valuable horses were stolen. Livestock was sometimes destroyed, as when Sam, a slave of John Scott, killed a cow. Many of the prosecutions for thefts, however, were for pathetically small items and spoke to the issue of want among local blacks. Zoe, a free black woman, was arrested for stealing a chest worth a dollar. Phoebe Cristy of Shrewsbury stole a turkey, and two dung-hill fowls.[23]

If petty theft infuriated whites, so did servants who, sometimes emboldened by drink, expressed their resentments directly. Aaron, who escaped from Peter Bergen of Andersons Mills in

Monmouth in 1823, was "very fond of liquor and tobacco, and when intoxicated very forward and very saucy."[24] There were also more violent threats and bold, physical confrontations. One enslaved man was provoked to threaten the property and life of a slaveholder. Barnes Smock, the son of a Patriot captured by Colonel Tye, claimed in 1826 that his neighbor's enslaved man, Samuel, threatened "to burn his buildings" and kill him.[25]

Lives of Free Blacks

With so many intertwined forces of self-interest resisting freedom, the growth of Monmouth County's population of free blacks before 1825 was slow. As the keystone of Monmouth's seventeenth- and eighteenth-century rural economy, slavery affected many, in similar (though not, of course, identical) ways. This engendered a culture of slavery, habits of mind and heart that, as with any culture, tended to conserve community values—until their economic underpinning gave way. But America's history, as much as any nation's, has been shaped by small groups, people of conscience, and new ideas that played against the system, sometimes taking hold and becoming part of another generation's system and culture. That critical point had not yet arrived for slavery in Monmouth County. For this reason many acts of manumission before 1825 were hedged or postponed to another generation. Manumissions to be effected in the short term were by their very nature inventions requiring uncommon perspicuity and commitment. They were cases where individuals made a difference.

A few assertive African Americans were clever and fortunate enough to make the system work for them, as the slave Stephen Parker did when he instigated his own sale to good advantage. In 1816 he persuaded antislavery advocate Samuel G. Wright to buy him from the notorious slave dealer Joseph Van Mater.

Wright completed the purchase and freed Parker the following year. Parker then lived and worked on Wright's farm at Merino Hill near Upper Freehold until his death.

In 1818 Wright offered to purchase "Negro boy George" from Van Mater. As the two men haggled over the price, Van Mater complained that George was easily worth $300, but Wright only agreed to pay $225. Offering to settle for $250, Van Mater noted that "the boy has a desire to be where he is," suggesting that even Van Mater, a slave trader, listened to the wishes of bondsmen. There is, however, little record of other such arrangements.[26]

More blacks won their freedom though grants of emancipation. Between 1804 and 1830, Monmouth County masters registered the emancipations of 328 slaves, of whom 180 were male and 148 female. The average age of emancipation in the 133 known cases was 31.3 years for males and 28.7 for females. Sixteen of the women and thirty-one of the men were over the age of thirty-four, which meant that masters had kept them in bondage for much of their prime adulthood. In twelve instances masters did not free their slaves until they were at least thirty-nine, in the last year of eligibility.[27]

Such "emancipations" were less acts of benevolence than calculated responses to changing legal conditions. They left more than a few emancipated blacks with little time to prepare for a proper funeral. Life expectancy for male and female African Americans, who survived infancy, was thirty-three to thirty-four years, figures that match the low estimates for blacks in the South.

The census for 1820 shows how tightly Monmouth County masters held onto blacks during their most productive years. Although over 45 percent of Monmouth's African Americans were free by that year, only 31 percent of the 958 blacks between the ages of fourteen and forty-five were emancipated. Nor could the county's free people look toward a productive future. Only 13 percent of the black population was older than forty-five. For male slaves the percentage was just a little over 10 percent. Monmouth's white population had little reason to fear an aged, dependent black population. Years of work had simply worn blacks out.[28]

Here, too, different communities in Monmouth County prepared their futures in contrasting ways. In 1820 in the town of Shrewsbury the vast majority of slaves were males under fourteen years of age. By law they would be manumitted when they reached their majority. Ironically, blacks in Shrewsbury were more likely to be enslaved in 1820 than they had been in 1790, when more than half were free. In contrast, in Middletown over two-thirds of the *free* males were under fourteen. For some, perhaps, voluntarily manumitting a child was a way to avoid maintaining someone whom the law would soon free. In any event, free male children in Middletown were greatly outnumbered by enslaved blacks in the prime years between fourteen and forty-five.[29]

The Free Black Economy

The census for 1830 documents the continued skewed relationship between gender and location. In Upper Freehold, for example, where 70 percent of free females were under twenty-four years of age, free women greatly outnumbered men. In Middletown, to the contrary, males outnumbered females. These local gender imbalances prolonged problems of family formation for Monmouth County blacks, even in freedom.[30]

But the bigger news that emerges from the 1830 census, the first taken after emancipations mandated by the law of 1804 began to take effect, is the expected but nonetheless dramatic change in the demographics of Monmouth County's black population. The number of free blacks rose to 2,134, or 90 percent of the African American population. For most blacks freedom was finally at hand.

Table 7
African American Population of Monmouth County in 1820 by Age and Status

	Freehold	Upper Freehold	Middletown	Shrewsbury	Howell	Stafford	Dover	Total
FREE MALES								
under 14	31	83	150	15	11	2	3	295
14–26	2	20	23	19	1	1	2	68
26–45	10	30	27	3	1	1	—	72
Over 45	21	27	22	9	1	2	2	84
Total	64	160	222	46	14	6	7	519
FREE FEMALES								
under 14	14	76	98	9	4	2		203
14–26	12	25	27	16	2	3	1	86
26–45	14	31	22	8	—	2		77
Over 45	19	18	20	10	1	3	3	74
Total	59	150	167	43	7	10	4	440
MALE SLAVES								
under 14	10	—	—	221	—	—	—	231
14–26	95	29	82	26	1	—	—	233
26–45	45	6	33	21	4	—	—	109
Over 45	28	4	18	15	—	—	—	65
Total	178	39	133	283	5	0	—	638
FEMALE SLAVES								
under 14	120	—	—	9	—	—	—	129
14–26	74	24	69	11	1	1	—	180
26–45	61	10	41	18	3	—	—	133
Over 45	32	13	18	7	1	—	—	71
Total	287	47	128	45	5	1	0	513

Souce: Fourth Census of the United States of America for 1820 (Washington, D.C., 1822).

Yet the census also demonstrates the fragility of the free black economy and the tenacity of bondage relationships in the county. Nearly 1,000 free blacks lived with white farmers, working as laborers and domestics. In Middletown, for example, the number of dependent blacks outnumbered black householders by 339 to 251. In Shrewsbury and Upper Freehold, fully one-third of the free black population lived in white households. Children and young adults comprised the greatest number of free blacks in white households, which insured that masters retained their peak productive years of labor.[31]

A few blacks redefined themselves in freedom, at least part of the time, by becoming entrepreneurs. David Yorkshire, a free black, bought "sundry liquors and molasses" from Daniel Schenck of Monmouth County, purchases that suggest an investment in a still or tavern.[32] Most blacks able to break away from the master's farm participated in the economy by taking pay for what they had always done. Farmers typically hired free blacks on a seasonal basis, paying them an average of three to four dollars a month for six months labor, plus food and washing. Samuel Wright—the man who helped slaves Stephen Parker and George gain their freedom—was exceptionally liberal with blacks. Wright was uncommonly fair in paying both white and black laborers according to the degree of skill a job entailed rather than by their race. For example, a day of mowing paid $62\frac{1}{2}$ cents while a day of loading dung paid only $37\frac{1}{2}$ cents. Women were paid less, averaging only $37\frac{1}{2}$ cents a day.[33]

As in Pennsylvania, where slave owners used the apprenticeship system to retain the labor of their former slaves, Monmouth farmers created a *cottager* system, which coexisted with slavery, to exploit black labor.[34] In Monmouth's agricultural economy, where land had become expensive and difficult to obtain for newly freed blacks, this share-cropping status was often the only available way of life.

Table 8
African American Population of Monmouth County in 1830 by Age and Status

	Freehold	Upper Freehold	Middletown	Shrewsbury	Howell	Stafford	Dover	Total
FREE MALES								
under 10	108	68	116	74	4	3	9	382
10–24	96	75	125	71	7	3	4	381
24–36	17	28	34	27	2	5	7	120
36–55	26	33	29	32	3	0	4	127
55–100	20	14	15	25	0	0	2	76
Total	257	218	319	229	16	11	26	1,076
FREE FEMALES								
under 10	78	99	109	71	6	1	6	370
10–24	98	108	75	45	6	4	3	339
24–36	20	32	43	35	2	3	7	142
36–55	28	38	30	38	0	0	2	136
55–100	18	16	15	20	0	2	0	71
Total	242	293	272	209	14	10	18	1,058
MALE SLAVES								
under 10	0	0	0	0	0	0	0	0
10–24	0	0	0	0	0	0	0	0
24–36	21	2	22	3	2	0	0	50
36–55	9	3	12	8	1	0	0	33
55–100	11	0	9	2	0	0	0	22
Total	41	5	43	13	3	0	0	105
FEMALE SLAVES								
under 10	0	0	0	0	0	0	0	0
10–24	0	0	0	0	0	0	0	0
24–36	21	6	15	4	1	0	0	47
36–55	23	4	11	5	0	0	0	43
55–100	18	1	7	3	0	0	0	29
Total	62	11	33	12	1	0	0	119

Source: Manuscript Census of the State of New Jersey, 1830, Alexander Library, Rutgers University.

The hiring of Isaac Vincent of Middlesex County exemplifies the cottager relationship between a free black and a white farmer. It also illustrates a type not well enough known—a somewhat successful, enterprising African American. In 1810 Samuel Wright offered Vincent, a free black from Middlesex County, a regular job on his large sheep farm at Merino Hill near Upper Freehold. Wright had first employed Vincent in 1809, at fifty cents per day. Their relationship established, Vincent was hired for the growing season in 1810 at ten dollars a month. Along with other black day laborers, Vincent plowed and mowed grain, planted and harvested corn, and tended sheep. In October, Wright offered Vincent an annual contract starting the following March, which specified a salary of ninety dollars a year plus a house, a plot of land for planting and pasture for his cow, and the right to use Wright's horses to draw six cords of wood from his property. If he wished to live independently, Wright promised to pay Vincent 120 dollars annually. Wright also let Vincent charge meat, textiles, and cash against his account.

Vincent may have taken Wright's offer to help pay for his farm in East Windsor, Middlesex County. In 1810 county tax ratables listed Vincent as owner of a small lot, worth five dollars, on which he kept two horses and a cow. Vincent's family was large, numbering eleven males and females from three generations. Vincent does not appear on the tax rolls again until 1818, when his property was about the same. Wright's relationship with Isaac Vincent seems more in accord with local hiring practices than what David Brion Davis has called the Quaker "gift for assimilating utility and national interest to a humanitarian effort." Their relationship was an interim step in the development of a free wage economy. Vincent was an independent contractor, not a slave. Wright's best offer resembled more a "mild slavery" than the free choices of a nascent capitalism.[35]

Despite the odds against economic independence, more and more blacks were able to live on their own. This self-sufficiency was precarious, but in the quarter century after enactment of gradual emancipation 1,000 African Americans in Monmouth County had achieved autonomy.[36] Cuffe Minkerson's probate record and inventory indicates the range of worldly possessions for independent black farmers in Monmouth in this period. Minkerson, who died in Freehold in 1813, left his real estate to his wife, Esther. Although he did not list the size of his property, Minkerson felt confident that enough would be left over after payment of debts to support his wife. After her death, the land and personal estate would be sold, with two shares given to his sons, Cuffe and Jeremy, and one share each to daughters, Betty, Rose, and Cathy. Minkerson's personal property included many farm inplements, including wagons, plows, harrows, scythes, hatchets, lumber, and kitchenware as well as a cow and a calf. While his total estate was worth less than $120, the extent of his personal property was impressive. Like Mingo, Cuffe Minkerson also loaned money to members of the black community.[37]

Exemplary individuals like Minkerson showed free blacks that they could, despite endemic racism, take their liberty and make it work. African Americans also used storytelling to empower themselves for success in the land they had built. Their stories included a new kind of black hero quite different from the sly and clever spider or rabbit of plantation slave tales. Their heros were, to the contrary, rooted in the contemporary world and marked by an ability to perform everyday tasks extraordinarily well—so well, in fact, that one's sense of the possible is redefined As we share the hero's world, our own horizons of credible possibility are expanded.

Although some tales may have been purely mythic, the names of real African Ameicans were also attached to their heros. One such character was Jim Henry from Middletown. Henry was renowned for his skills with a flail, a threshing tool made of hickory and rawhide. Daily, Henry could thresh five to eight bushels more than his fellow workers.[38] Although Henry was

This rare hand-colored photograph is of James Henry Minkerson and his mother Jane Shemo Minkerson Taylor, Marlboro, N.J., c. 1890. Courtesy of Monmouth County Historical Association.

born in slavery, he owned a power in his labor that no master or overseer could enslave. Images like his could only prove inspiring to those awaiting an all-too-gradual legal emancipation. Stories about persons like Henry could also hearten free blacks, who would need empowering images by the bucketful to invest the coming generations of economic and political hardships with a measure of heroic spirit.

Summary

By 1830, a quarter century after the enactment of gradual emancipation, the vast majority of blacks were free in Monmouth County. They still encountered legal discriminations and economic limitations, but the number of free, independent blacks in the country clearly demonstrated that the extinction of slavery was at hand. Yet legal liberty was not met by political freedom, as no black could vote or hold office. In 1807 the New Jersey legislature restricted the suffrage to white males. Civil discrimination also occurred in the courts. If free blacks became paupers, they were returned from the town of origin and placed under control of their former master.[39] Economically, blacks advanced just beyond a state of bondage. Locked into a subsistence agricultural system, most found ownership of property an elusive goal. It would take the next few decades of struggle to achieve true freedom.

Notes

1. *Aggregate Amount of Each Description of Persons within the United States of America . . . According to Law, in the Year 1810* (Washington, D.C., 1814), 162–63.

2. For Monmouth County figures, see table 4. For national figures, see Peter Kolchin, *American Slavery, 1619–1877* (New York, 1993), 81.

3. For the farm, see *True American* (Trenton), February 22, 1822. For the Baird sales records, see Slavery File, Monmouth County Historical Association, Freehold, N.J. See also Miscellaneous Book C, 2, 24, 120. Monmouth probate records also indicate balanced values of males and females. See for example, two inventories with eight slaves or more: Cornelius Cowenhoven, 8669 M, and Chrinyeonce Van Mater, 8571 M, Archives Section, Division of Records and Archives Management, Department of State, Trenton, N.J. (hereafter cited as New Jersey State Archives). For other sales, see *Monmouth Star* (Freehold), March 18, 1820, and the *Fredonian* (New Brunswick), August 11, 1811 and January 20, 1814. For examples of families selling slaves years before freedom, see Ten Eyck Family Papers, box 3, folders 21 and 22, Special Collections, Alexander Library, Rutgers University. See also the very interesting reminder notice from Catherine Remsen to Cornelius G. Conover, July 23, 1813, asking him to pay for a female slave named Chris, sold to Conover's sister, Mrs. William Hendrickson. Conover Family Papers, box 13, folder 3, Monmouth County Historical Association, Free-

hold, N.J. For a useful discussion of slave sales following a master's death, see Andrew D. Mellick, Jr., *The Story of an Old Farm; or, Life in New Jersey in the Eighteenth Century* (Somerville, N.J., 1889), 610–13.

4. *Black Birth Book of Monmouth County, New Jersey, 1804–1848* (Freehold, N.J., 1989).

5. For an overview of the gradual emancipation act, see Paul Finkleman, "State Constitutional Protections of Liberty and the Antebellum New Jersey Supreme Court," *Rutgers Law Journal* 23 (1992): 753–87, especially 761–66.

6. Clement A. Price, *Freedom Not Far Distant: A Documentary History of Afro-Americans in New Jersey* (Newark, N.J., 1980), 85-86. For English visitor, see Arthur Zilversmit, *The First Emancipation: The Abolition of Slavery in the North* (Chicago, 1967), 216–17. For the removals out of state, see Slave and Manumissions File, 1771–1837, entries for May 16 and July 8, 1812 and for July 16, 1818, and Miscellaneous Book C, 9, Monmouth County Archives, Manalapan, N.J. For a fuller discussion of the scandal, see Frances D. Pingeon, "An Abominable Business: The New Jersey Slave Trade, 1818," *New Jersey History* 109 (1991): 15–37. For original documents, see Bureau of Archives and History, box 22, nos. 81–86, box 25, nos. 8–11, box 26, nos. 47–50, New Jersey State Archives. For a discussion of the scandal and the fates of these slaves in Louisiana, see Ann Patton Malone, *Sweet Chariot: Slave Family and Household Structure in Nineteenth-Century Louisiana* (Chapel Hill, N.C., 1992), 100–103.

7. Robert W. Fogel and Stanley L. Engerman, "Philanthropy at Bargain Prices: Notes on the Economics of Gradual Emancipation," *Journal of Legal History* 3 (1974): 377–401. For data, see Table 7.

8. Based on my analysis of the Black Birth Book, 49–64.

9. See Will and Inventory of Kenneth Hankinson, 8715 M, New Jersey State Archives. For Dick, see *True American* (Trenton), April 25, 1814.

10. James Tallman's Ledger from Monmouth County, 1800-1801, 6, 13, 20, Special Collections, Alexander Library, Rutgers University.

11. For James, see *True American* (Trenton), June 4, 1822. For George, see *Trenton Federalist*, July 14, 1806; for Henry, see *True American*, October 12, 1822; for Peter, see *ibid.*., July 8, 1822.

12. For Ben, see *True American* (Trenton), July 25, 1814. See also Silas in *ibid.*, August 16, 1814.

13. Farm Accounts of Robert Drummond, 1822–1856, Shrewsbury,

N.J., Special Collection, Alexander Library, Rutgers University. James Hawkhurst, Account Book and Journal, 1797–1851, Manuscripts Collection, New York Public Library; Unidentified Account Book, Brookhaven, Long Island, 1774–1814, Manuscripts Collection, New-York Historical Society; Day Book of Charles Nicoll, 1780–1781, Manuscripts Collection, New-York Historical Society; John Neilson Farm Diary, 1802–1832" Neilson Papers, box 1, Special Collections, Alexander Library, Rutgers University Library. For development of horse racing, see Wayne Caldwell Neely, *The Agricultural Fair* (New York, 1935), 190–92.

14. See C. W. Larison, M.D., *Sylvia DuBois: A Biografy of The Slav Who Whipt Her Mistress and Gand Her Fredom*, (Ringoes, N.J., 1883), 66–67. See also Mellick, *Story of an Old Farm*, 607.

15. For Hannah and children, see *True American* (Trenton), December 16, 1820. See also December 9, 1813, July 21, 1824, November 13, 1824; April 15, 1825, May 23, 1825, July 9, 1825, September 7, 1825; March 13 1826; *Spirit of Washington* (Freehold), August 1, 1814, and *Fredonian* (New Brunswick), January 30, 1814, for other Monmouth runaways.

16.The ratio of nonwhite males to females in Monmouth in 1830 was 107.5 males to 100 females. See Peter O. Wacker, *Land and People: A Cultural Geography of Preindustrial New Jersey: Origins and Settlement Patterns* (New Brunswick, N.J., 1975), 201.

17. For occupations, see Black Birth Book, 67. For the Chesapeake states, see Carr and Walsh, "Economic Diversification and Labor Organization in the Chesapeake, 1650-1820," in Stephen Innes, ed., *Work and Labor in Early America* (Chapel Hill, N.C., 1988), 144–189. For women's duties, see Joan M. Jensen, *Loosening the Bonds: Mid-Atlantic Farm Women 1750-1850* (New Haven, Conn., 1986), 39–41.

18. Black Birth Book, 29–30, 65–66.

19. On this point, see Michael Tadman, *Speculators and Slaves: Masters, Traders, and Slaves in the Old South* (Madison, Wis., 1989), 133–79, and Barbara Jeanne Fields, *Slavery and Freedom on the Middle Ground: Maryland during the Nineteenth Century* (New Haven, Conn., 1985), 26–27. For a local example, see Mellick, *Story of an Old Farm*, 611.

20. See entries in Black Birth Book for Mary Hendrickson, 54, Margaret and Sarah Probasco, 57.

21. The Church Book, Box 1, Middletown, New Jersey Old First Church Papers, Special Collections, Alexander Library, Rutgers University. The Old First Church accepted three blacks in the twenty year

period between 1813 and 1833. For schools, see Holmdel Sunday School Records, 1826–1836, Holmdel Baptist Church, Holmdel, N.J. I am grateful to Ellen Morris for sharing this source with me. For general study of Sunday schools, see Ann Boylan, *Sunday School: The Formation of an American Institution, 1790–1880* (New Haven, Conn., 1988).

22. For White, see Graham Russell Hodges, *Black Itinerants of the Gospel: The Narratives of John Jea & George White* (Madison, Wis., 1993), 27–31.

23. For Prince, see *State* v. *Prince,* Court of General Sessions, March and July, 1825. For horse stealing, see *State* v. *John Frazier, Black man,* Court of General Sessions, April, 1814, *State* v. *Mena,* Court of General Sessions, 1808, and *State* v. *Dick,* Court of General Sessions, April, 1823. For female thieves, see *State* v. *Zoo,* Court of General Sessions, 1804, and *State* v. *Phoebe Christy,* Court of General Sessions, April, 1814. For Sam, see Court of General Sessions, July, 1816. For other instances, all in Court of General Sessions, see *State* v. *Abraham Johnson* (for assault), May, 1806; *State* v. *Mary Brake,* August, 1813 (for theft of a cow); *State* v. *William Cromwell,* May, 1814 (for theft of a handkerchief); and *State* v. *Joseph Richardson,* August, 1817 (for petty larceny); all in Court of General Sessions, Monmouth County Archives, Manalapan, N.J.

24. For Aaron, see *True American* (Trenton), November 15, 1823.

25. For Samuel, see Affadavit of Barnes Smock, January 31, 1824, Courts of General Sessions, Monmouth County Archives, Manalapan, N.J.

26. See Legal Papers, 1816–1817, box B-6, Samuel G. Wright Papers, Hagley Library, Wilmington, Del.

27. I calculated these figures from the Slave and Manumission Files, 1771–1837, Manumissions, 1815–1850, and Miscellaneous Books B and C, all at the Monmouth County Archives, printed as *Manumission Book of Monmouth County, New Jersey, 1791–1844* (Freehold, N.J., 1992).

28. See Table 7. For average ages in the South, see Jack Ericson Eblen, "New Estimates of the Vital Rates of the United States Black Population during the Nineteenth Century," *Demography* 11 (1974), 301–19. For comments on masters working slaves to death before emancipation, see Fogel and Engerman, "Philanthropy at Bargain Prices."

29. For these conclusions, see Table 7. See also Middletown Township, Tax List for 1827, Special Collections, Alexander Library, Rutgers University.

30. For these conclusions, see Table 8.

31. *Ibid.*

32. Ledger of Daniel Schenck of Monmouth County, 1799–1801, 30, 58, 61–65, 77, Special Colections, Alexander Library, Rutgers University. See also Abraham Van Neste, Account Book, 1828, and Benjamin Corlies Family Papers, both in Rutgers University Library, and John Van Cleff DeHar, Ledger, 1815–1816, Yale University Archives.

33. See Farm Accounts, 1809–1811, box B-8, Samuel G. Wright Papers, Hagley Library, Wilmington, Del.

34. For discussion of the apprenticeship and cottager systems in Pennsylvania, see Paul G. E. Clemens and Lucy Simler, "Rural Labor and the Farm Household in Chester County, Pennsylvania, 1750–1820," in Stephen Innes, ed., *Work and Labor in Early America*, 106–44, and Gary B. Nash and Jean R. Soderlund, *Freedom by Degrees: Emancipation in Pennsylvania and Its Aftermath* (New York, 1991), 167–92.

35. See East Windsor Township, 1810–1821; Middlesex County, Tax Ratables, boxes 44 and 45, New Jersey State Archives. My thanks to Betty Epstein for her immense help with Vincent. For Quaker fusion of antislavery and free wage labor, see David Brion Davis, *The Problem of Slavery in the Age of Revolution, 1770–1823* (Ithaca, N.Y., 1975), 249–54. In saying this, I am not criticizing Davis for failure to recognize market choices, as Thomas Haskell has done, but rather noting that rural Quakers like Wright were more closely tied to local conditions and perhaps more conservative in their approach to free labor. For Haskell, see his essays in Thomas Bender, ed., *The Antislavery Debate: Capitalism and Abolitionism as a Problem in Historical Interpretation* (Berkeley, Calif., 1992). For agreement on mixed development, see Peter O. Wacker and Paul G. E. Clemens, *Land Use in Early New Jersey: A Historical Geography* (Newark, 1995), 3–28. For evidence of black trade, see "James Tallman's Ledger from Monmouth County, 1800-1801," 6, 13, 20, Special Collection, Alexander Library, Rutgers University. For examination of the transition from bonded to free wage labor, see Clemens and Simler, "Rural Labor," 10644. For patterns of farm work in New Jersey, see Carl R. Woodward, *Ploughs and Politics: Charles Read of New Jersey and His Notes on Agriculture, 1715–1774* (New Brunswick, N.J., 1941).

36. See Table 8. By 1830, 1,101 free blacks lived independently, while 1,033 lived on the property of whites.

37. Will of Cuffe Minkerson, 9047 M, New Jersey State Archives.

38. For Jim Henry, see *Red Bank Register*, February 13, 1895.

39. Price, *Freedom Not Far Distant*, 90.

6

The Creation of Freedom 1830–1865

On May 14, 1840 Daniel Conover, a Middletown farmer, advertised the flight of two young, enslaved brothers. Aaron, nineteen years old, wore a light brown coat, "gray mixed Satinett pantaloons and a Swindon Vest." Aaron's brother Abram, whose age was not given, was an "intelligent boy dressed in Southell Roundabout and Pantaloons and a Swindon Vest." Conover offered a fifty-dollar reward for their capture.[1] The advertisement, published thirty-six years after the enactment of gradual emancipation and fifteen years after the first mandated emancipations, serves as a grim reminder of the persistence of slavery in Monmouth County.

Aaron and Abram were exceptions. By 1840 the number of enslaved blacks in Monmouth County had dipped to eighty-five. Yet ten years later there were still seventy-five. Only in 1860 did slavery disappear from Monmouth County (though not from the state, which still claimed fourteen "apprentices for life"). During the antebellum years, New Jersey blacks whom the law left enslaved were the forgotten few. New Jersey's legislators, having passed gradual emancipation, now behaved as though their slave system did not exist. When taking notice of African Americans, they preferred to weigh in on national debates over the extension of slavery into the western frontier.[2]

This political impassivity also made it harder for free blacks to establish a viable economic base in Monmouth County. Whigs and Democrats alike were not merely unconcerned about the weak political and legal position of blacks: many were genuinely hostile to reform. Farmers, by far the largest group of legislators in both parties, had little interest in urging greater rights or opportunities for people who provided a cheap and reliable source of agricultural labor.[3] While the shadow of slavery darkened the aspirations of the county's African Americans, the free black community made impressive gains as it grew. By the Civil War, Monmouth boasted a society of black churches, schools, and numerous independent black property owners. Such achievements manifest the strength and effort of the black community itself, unsupported by the state.

Government was not, of course, the only agent of social change in the antebellum North. Social experiment in the form of utopian communities visited New Jersey as it did other states during this era. Monmouth County was, in fact, home to the North American Phalanx, largest and most successful of some twenty-eight communes founded in the United States in the 1840s and 1850s on principles expounded by the French businessman Charles Fourier. Like some other influential Europeans of the nineteenth century, Fourier approached social reform as a determinist, adducing the condition of the individual from environment and deducing the proper structure of society quite precisely from "historical imperatives" and similar general principles. If blacks looked to the Fourierists for a more just society, they did not look long. The Fourierist approach was quite different from that of reform-minded New Englanders, whose abolitionist tendencies were rooted in a strong sympathy for the individual. European Fourierists knew in advance the make-up

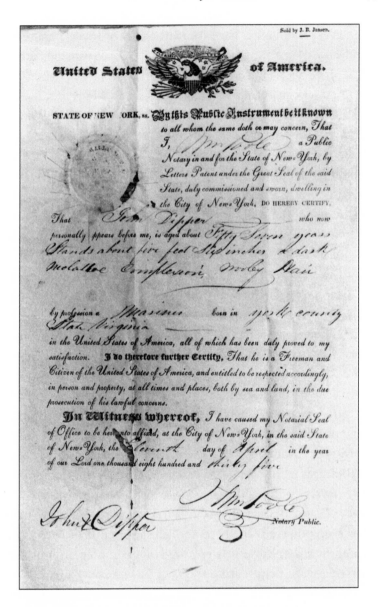

"Freedom papers" like this one for John Dipper were prized documents for African Americans. This one promises the bearer U.S. citizenship—thirty-three years before the Fourteenth Amendment did so. Courtesy of the New Jersey Historical Society.

(e.g., every woman to have four husbands or lovers) and even the ideal size (1,620) of the phalanxes that were to usher in 80,000 years of Perfect Harmony. Not surprisingly, then, when the North American Phalanx purchased the Van Mater estate near Red Bank for their *phalanstère* and found a number of freed blacks and their families living on the old plantation, they simply evicted them. No need to get utopia off to a bad start by alienating local whites.[4]

While northerners of both races were mounting a massive abolitionist effort to confront openly the horrors of Southern slavery, within their midst the institution remained. This irony was not lost on the state's more progressive residents, who renewed calls for reform in the 1830s. Reformers in the New Jersey Anti-Slavery Society waged a petition campaign for revisions of the slave code. Their efforts failed in the face of white political alignments across the region. New Jersey Democratic legislators were loath to jeopardize "the interest of their party at the South."[5] More petitions from blacks and whites landed on legislators' desks in 1842, including some demanding a return of the right to vote. They were bitterly disappointed, as the government refused to act.

In 1845 Alvan Stewart, a New York lawyer, argued the case for abolition before the New Jersey Supreme Court. In *State v. Post* Stewart contended that slavery was a violation of the Due Process Clause of the federal Constitution. He argued that Congress is empowered legally to abolish slavery everywhere in the United States because it is required to guarantee a republican form of government. Citing the 1844 New Jersey Constitution, which affirmed the natural rights of all persons to life and liberty, Stewart maintained that slavery was thereby automatically extinguished. Taking a position that anticipated by over a decade Chief Justice Roger Taney's infamous opinion in the *Dred Scott* case, opposing attorneys responded that such an affirmation was not intended to free slaves but was a rhetorical flourish and "not part of the Constitution." The majority of the court agreed, concluding that the federal Constitution could have abolished slavery but did not, and thus its authors could not have intended to decide such an important issue on "an indefinite political proposition."[6]

The following year the New Jersey legislature transformed the state's remaining enslaved people into "lifetime apprentices." As Giles Wright has observed, this 1846 revision of the statutes did not free any of the state's remaining 700 slaves, but it did ensure that their future children would be free. The law also obligated masters to continue supporting aged slaves. Notwithstanding this provision, the legislators, in refusing to end slavery once and for all (as New York State had done in 1827), affirmed that in New Jersey property rights took precedence over human rights.[7]

Thus protected, Monmouth County masters extracted any possible economic gain from the peculiar institution. Fifty-two slave registrations were made in the Black Birth Book after 1830, twenty-nine for people born after that date.[8] As late as 1848, D. Schenck of Holmdel lay claim to twenty-five years of a newborn's life by registering the birth of Alonzo, son of Susan Paterson. Schenck's registration disregarded the new 1846 law; he based his claim instead on the gradual emancipation act of 1804, which he believed entitled him to Paterson's forced labor for the next twenty-five years.[9] The absence of any further records suggest that Schenck was probably successful in retaining Alonzo's labor, at least until the Civil War.

Sales of slaves continued throughout the 1830s and 1840s. The proposed sale of one slave, Yaff, in 1835 mentioned the daunting information that he was presently confined in the county jail. In 1837 Peter Smock offered "a healthy black woman, 34–35 years old," who "is sound, and healthy and used to all sorts of domestic work." One slaveholder offered eight slaves for sale the same year. The youngest three, girls of eight, ten, and thir-

$10 Reward

---❖❖❖---

RUNAWAY from the Subscriber living in Monmouth county, near the Court-House, a black boy, of a lightish colour, named Elias; but since, it is said, has changed his name, and calls himself Bob. He is about 5 feet 9 inches high, rather slender built, a little round shouldered, about 19 years of age; on his under lip has a scar occasioned by the kick of a horse, and on the main joint of his little finger, on his right hand, has a scar, which he received by the cut of a scythe; one of his big toes has been split by the cut of an axe. He had on when he left home, a dark homespun drab cloth coatee, mixed sattinet pantaloons, and black hair cap. He took another suit with him, which he was seen dressed in at Hightstown, on Sunday evening last, white hat, striped roundabout, and tow trowsers. Whoever will take up said boy and return him to the subscriber, shall receive the above reward, with all reasonable charges.

WILLIAM VANDORN.

September 21st, 1830.

Runaway Slave Notice, 1830. Courtesy of Monmouth County Historical Association.

teen years, had to serve until they were twenty-one. An administrator of the estate of Daniel Brewer sold Lucy, a ten-week-old infant, "to hold under the term under the present law." In 1840 another eight-year-old girl was offered for sale in the newspaper. In his 1848 registration Schenk claimed the right to sell Alonzo Paterson at any time during his twenty-five years of bondage. The next year in Middletown the remaining six years of service of Jack were sold by Joseph Doty to Charles J. Hendrickson.[10]

Advertisements for "self-emancipated" blacks revealed their continued financial value. Notices for indentured servants normally offered rewards of six cents—sometimes as little as a penny—indicating how little value was placed on such servants. In contrast, Daniel Conover's offer of fifty dollars attests to his determination in recovering escaped chattel. In another instance,

William Van Dorn of Freehold published a broadside asking the return of Elias, who has "changed his name, and calls himself Bob." Van Dorn's broadside carefully described Bob's physical appearance, including a scar on his under lip "occasioned by the kick of a horse." Van Dorn warned that Bob had been seen Sunday night in nearby Hightstown wearing a white hat, striped roundabout, and tow trousers. At least fifteen such notices appeared in county newspapers during the 1830s. These notices not only illustrate the value of slaves, they afford us a view of the human condition of the black population. Bill Miller, who escaped from Peter S. Conover, had "a large scar over one of his eyes." Aaron, likewise, had a "large scar over one eye." Peter, who left Theodorus Conover on August 23, 1838, was described the same way.[11] These scars were visible signs of the slaves' hazardous life. Like many enslaved people in the South, the backs of these self-emancipated slaves were undoubtedly further testimony of human misery and brutality.

Surviving copies of Monmouth newspapers are scanty for the antebellum period, but five fugitive notices have been discovered from the 1840s. One was for Hannah, "aged between 50 and 60 years," who escaped from Gertrude Antonides—a mistress clearly fonder of authority and comfort than of her aged servant. Two notices appeared as late as September 26, 1857, when William Armstrong and John Golden advertised the flight of their indentured servants. Return of Armstrong's Charley carried a twenty-dollar reward, an amount far exceeding the normal gratuity of six cents offered for return of a white fugitive servant. That the notice appeared years after the furor sparked by the Fugitive Slave Act of 1850 is a measure of the stubborn power of servitude in Monmouth.[12]

Obtaining freedom legally was a frustrating process for Monmouth blacks throughout much of the antebellum era. Masters continued to limit manumissions to older men and women. Twenty-seven manumissions are recorded for Monmouth County after 1830, the latest being for Samuel Carney, a thirty-nine-year-old man freed in 1850 by James Throckmorton. Of seven manumitted males whose ages were given, the average was 33.7 years. Several manumissions involved blacks purchasing other blacks. Abraham Williams and Edward Shemo bought Amey Williams for five dollars from slave owner Teunis Schenck. Later, Lucy Riley, "a colored woman," purchased her children Jackson and Mary Jane from John H. Holmes of Middletown. These personal victories reveal what was no doubt a prolonged trauma for black families during the period of gradual emancipation: the split between free and enslaved family members.[13]

Enslaved blacks were still too valuable for many masters to release at time of death. Between 1816 and 1841 masters bequeathed 192 slaves to their relatives. A few of these were aged blacks, cared for by loyal masters. For example, Lydia Conover of Freehold listed her "coloured woman, Cate," for one dollar. Far more typical was Hendrick Hendrickson of Middletown, whose 1841 inventory listed Barziller, fourteen, Thomas, eleven, and George, eight. In all, ninety-five boys and seventy-one girls under the age of sixteen were inventoried in Monmouth wills between 1830 and 1855. If slavery was a moribund institution, this only made slave-owning families all the more determined to squeeze as much value as possible from its remnants.[14]

Amid these onerous social conditions, African Americans in Monmouth struggled to sustain independence and create community. One major obstacle was the county's reliance on poorly paid agricultural work. The tax lists for Upper Freehold in 1839 show a free black society struggling to survive economically. Of sixty-one names of "colored persons" on the list, all were at the minimum tax level. Robert Jobs of Shrewsbury owned an estate worth 168 dollars, while Hagar Smock's inventory from 1837 lists a total estate of less than forty dollars.[15] Blacks trying to make ends meet were caught in the Panic of 1837. Like millions

Isabella was photographed with her children John and Effie, August 12, 1889, outside the home of Mary Holmes Taylor, Middletown, N.J., where she was employed as a domestic. Courtesy of Robert and Mary Johnson.

of their white counterparts trapped in a credit crunch, blacks in Monmouth failed economically, some with debts of less than twelve dollars.[16]

The hardships of rural life for blacks are evident in coroner's reports for Monmouth County. Work conditions proved deadly. Mink was killed when he "fell to the barn floor from above." Charles Holland died when kicked by a horse. Charles Johnson was crushed in a granary. Sailors fell overboard their ships and drowned. Others died from exposure to harsh weather. For example, Edmond Truxton, a black boy, was found dead in William Conover's field. James, a "colored boy, age 13," froze to death while intoxicated in Freehold. Mothers expressed despair by infanticide. Deborah, an infant, was murdered by her mother. Other blacks, whose records are sealed, committed suicide.[17]

Outside of agriculture there was little work for Monmouth's blacks. Undertaker J. Sansbury of Eatontown occasionally hired blacks to dig graves at seventy-five cents per day. Many women found the opportunity to work as domestics. One advertisement called for a "Colored Woman to do the work of a small family." The successful applicant needed to be well recommended and skilled as a cook, able to do washing and drying and to be childless.[18]

During the first decade after gradual emancipation began to be effected, almost all of Shrewsbury's people of color were dependent farm laborers. Cottagers outnumbered independent householders 212 to 162 in the census of 1840. Dependency was especially high during the most productive years. By the census of 1850, however, the situation in Shrewsbury had improved greatly, with independent households increased to 303 and black dependents dwindling to 84. Countywide, the number of independent black households had increased to over 1,600. At the same time, farm work remained the principal occupation for the county's blacks. In 1850 over 80 percent of Monmouth blacks were listed as "laborer." Evidently, black farmers had to hire out as hands or tenant farmers to survive. Indicative of this arrangement is the hiring agreement made in 1851 between John S. Holmes and a black man named Jacob. Holmes agreed to pay Jacob 120 dollars per year, less house rent.[19] One reason so many Monmouth blacks lived as well as worked on others' lands was that they were young. More than 70 percent of the African Americans in the 1850 census were under forty. During an era of declining rural birth rates, black laborers in an agricultural economy like Monmouth's remained essential.[20]

Despite extraordinary external pressures, family life in Monmouth endured and expanded. Borrowing Ann Patton

Malone's taxonomy of slave households—single males and females (solitaires), nuclear families, extended families, and single
males and females with children [21]—to analyze data collected in
federal censuses between 1830 and 1860, hardships of family life
for Monmouth's African Americans are clearly revealed. In the
census of 1830, with slavery still viable, single males and females
and single adults with children predominated over nuclear families and extended families. After ten years, several of which were
marked by economic depression, solitaires again were the domi-
nant household formation, though free nuclear families rose
sharply over the decade. An alarming number of free women
were unmarried and without children; in the 1840 census they
totaled 246, or nearly 11 percent, of the county's free black population. Similar patterns were present ten years later, even though
slavery was by then virtually extinct: as in the 1830s, single blacks
made up the majority of the black households, while the number of nuclear families dropped sharply.

During the 1850s, despite a worsening climate for black civil
rights, the black family in Monmouth made a comeback. The
census of 1860 shows that while the numbers of nuclear families
did not increase greatly during the 1850s, the average size of
families grew to the highest point recorded during the antebellum era, with highs of over three children per family in Middletown and Manalapan.[22]

Monmouth's tiny black middle class continued to accumulate property. In Shrewsbury by 1860 black community wealth
amounted to $14,350, in Manalapan it topped over $10,000. In
Upper Freehold, Aaron Cole and Aaron Miller each owned over
$5,000 in property, reflecting individual gains by African Ameri-
cans. Tiny bits of evidence show emerging patterns of genteel
consumerism. Hagar Smock's inventory included several chests,
pictures, lamps, and books. When he died in 1837, Robert Jobs
owned several looking glasses, chairs, candlesticks, Windsor
chairs, and carpeting.[23]

Barred from official state and local politics, blacks found an outlet for their political instincts among the abolitionists. With the establishment of an antislavery society in Newark during the 1830s, New Jersey blacks were able to join the abolitionist movement. Quaker homes in Upper Freehold reportedly served as safe houses on the underground railroad.[24] In the 1840s the movement in New Jersey became more militant as black ministers and political figures concentrated on the lack of civil rights in the state. In 1849 New Jersey's first Negro Convention prompted free blacks in Monmouth, Mercer, Middlesex, and other counties to make unsuccessful appeals to the legislature for black suffrage.[25]

Black community continued to find collective manifestation through religion. A few white churches extended the hand of fellowship to blacks. The Marlboro Township Old Brick Church enrolled several black women as members in the late 1830s. The Holmdel Dutch Reformed Church sanctified black marriages in the 1850s.[26] Soon, however, even these small numbers of blacks began to move outside the white congregations.

Why did Protestant congregations hold so little appeal for the emerging black community in New Jersey generally and in Monmouth County specifically? First, black membership was primarily limited to live-in domestics rather than to independent freeholders. Second, New Jersey Protestants tended to be either sympathetic to slavery or, at least, nostalgic for an era of servitude and faithful servants. They also tended to support the American Colonization Society—New Jersey was a center of procolonization activity—with its plans to resettle free blacks in Liberia. Supporters of colonization condemned the foreign slave trade but not the institution of American slavery; they contended that free blacks were doomed to poverty in the United States yet as Christians were unwilling to challenge the racism that led Henry Clay to contend that free blacks "can never here enjoy the advantages, social and political, of freemen." In short, New

These photographs of an unidentified African American man and woman from the Red Bank area attest to the presence of a small but growing middle class in Monmouth in the 1850s. Courtesy of Moss Archives, Rumson, N.J.

Jersey Protestants were, as a group, unashamed racists. And that made it hard for most African Americans to feel unselfconscious with them when kneeling in prayer.[27]

The third difficulty for blacks was that white churches refused to promote potential and qualified black ministers. As a result, the black church movement took hold throughout Monmouth County during the 1830s. Most congregations developed within the African Methodist Episcopal Church. In 1833 the Red Bank A. M. E. Zion Church was established on Wharf Avenue. Two years later the Union A. M. E. Zion Church began congregating in Allentown. Within a few years additional churches formed in Freehold, Fair Haven, Manalapan, Navesink, Shrewsbury, and Long Branch. These churches were all part of the flourishing African Methodist movement.

It is noteworthy that Monmouth County blacks, like their counterparts elsewhere in the region, generally avoided denominations associated with slavery. Some individual blacks joined the Episcopalian, Dutch Reformed, and Presbyterian churches, but in Monmouth County there were no examples of black congregations that worshipped according to the tenets of those churches. One reason was that African Americans had already developed a taste for their own indigenous forms of worship.[28] A second reason is that the older, established Protestant sects kept blacks and their forms of worship at arms length.

This was true even when black congregations forged ties with parent white churches. Exhorter Edward Berry led the members of the Tinton Falls, or Macedonia, "class" of the white Old First Methodist Church for 1844. Berry's status reflected the historic refusal of the Methodist Church to grant blacks the status of licensed minister. Ten of the forty-eight members of the congregation were named Berry. Other prominent family names included Taylor, Rock, Holmes, Hankinson and Stillwell, all derived from important slaveholding families in the county. Twenty-five of the forty-eight members of the congregation were women.

A decade later these black Methodists sought recognition as Episcopalians. In response, George Washington Doane, Bishop of the Diocese of New Jersey, visited the all-black congregation at Macedonia. Doane was struck by the quiet beauty of the small chapel's lights, "which glimmered through the pines." He confirmed eight blacks and noted approvingly that Berry was now a candidate for the priesthood. Despite Doane's reassuring (if paternalist) remarks, the congregation was rejected by the Episcopal Church, perhaps over concern that blacks were reinventing white theologies for their own use and installing their own leaders.[29]

The African Methodist Union allowed blacks the independence and local autonomy they preferred. The creation of a black ministry in Monmouth County was shaped by the traditions such earlier itinerants as George White and John Jea and by Southern fugitives, who brought great intensity to their search for meaning in life through the ministry. As W. E. B. Du Bois

Saint James African Methodist Episcopal Zion Church in Matawan. Built 1851. Photo from *Matawan, 1686–1936* (Federal Writers' Project, 1936).

observed in *The Souls of Black Folk*, the preacher is "the most unique personality developed by the Negro on American soil." Du Bois described the preacher as a "leader, a politician, an orator, a 'boss,' an intriguer, an idealist . . . with a combination of adroitness and deep-seated earnestness."[30]

Monmouth's first indigenous clergymen included ministers such as H. C. Turner, pastor of the Freehold A. M. E., Deacon Lewis Conover, founder of the Woodville A. M. E. Zion in Manalapan, Reverend John Wooby of the Union A. M. E. Zion Church in Allentown, and Reverend John Boggs of Allentown. A second-generation black Monmouth minister of prominence was Reverend A. C. Garrison, born in 1846. Garrison moved to California early in his life, then returned to preach around New

York and New Jersey, eventually settling in Long Branch, where he organized the A. M. E. Zion Church. Few if any of these ministers could live on their meager pastoral earnings. Wooby, Conover, and Boggs all worked as farmers. At their deaths, Wooby and Berry owned little except small plots of land.[31]

Education always had a special meaning for rural blacks. It was equated with freedom and power. It also eluded blacks until the 1840s. Although education for blacks was mandated as far back as 1788, little had been done. In one of the first acts after its founding, the American Colonization Society established schools in Piscataway, N.J., in 1817 to help the process of black removal to Africa. As deepening racism influenced antebellum politics, public integrated schools became highly controversial. Blacks attempted to integrate a town school in Fair Haven, but the superintendent closed the school after complaints by white parents. A mysterious fire then destroyed the black school. After that, segregation characterized Monmouth schools. In Freehold, blacks attended a separate school from the 1840s onward. Each year the town superintendent of schools reported on the progress of black education. At the black school, students learned the alphabet, reading, and writing. The superintendent noted that the school was "tolerably convenient," but that it was "small, badly arranged and cannot be sufficiently warm in the winter." Nonetheless the number of students attending the school showed the deep interest of Monmouth's blacks in education. Starting from twenty-five in 1847, the number rose to sixty-one students in 1851. Overall, 196 blacks were attending schools in Monmouth in 1850. Enrollment then slipped to a few dozen, then rose to ninety-three by 1860. The superintendent described B. C. Spaulding, the principal during these years, and Adele V. Compton, his assistant, as "experienced and efficient teachers." Not relying completely on public institutions, Monmouth blacks also opened their own schools. In 1858 the Union A. M. E. Zion Church in Allentown established its own school for local children.[32]

A little understood aspect of Monmouth County black society was its relationship with its African past. Black attitudes toward Africa were mixed during the antebellum period. In the cities despair over worsening conditions in the United States prompted some black abolitionist intellectuals to downgrade African influences, preferring to think and act in accordance with Anglo-American mores. Thus, the term *African* was frequently replaced by *colored;* the title of the black New York City newspaper, *The Colored American*, exemplifies this point of view. At the same time, other intellectuals were rethinking their rejection of things African and perceiving in the home continent answers to African American problems.[33]

While African American urban intellectuals were probing such philosophical problems, rural blacks were spreading an African folk vernacular. Evidence of this may be seen in the traditional African cemetery adornments found in Bergen, Richmond, and Monmouth counties, where broken pottery and pipes link the interred spirit with the outer world. In contrast to recent arguments that antebellum African Americans stopped believing that their souls returned to Africa after death, the pipes and scattered pottery on graves suggest that rural blacks clung to traditional beliefs.[34]

African influences are also visible in Monmouth's folk art. Job, reputed to have been a Freehold carpenter, produced an extraordinary cigar store Indian around 1825. Much of the figure resembles similar wooden caricatures of the period. At the same time, the figure is marked by a masklike African face, long, tubular arms, and androgynous breasts. As a work of folk art it demonstrates how a thin crust of American acculturation covered African memories and motifs.[35]

As in West African societies, blacks in New Jersey were greatly concerned about their coffins, and the purchase of a coffin was typically one of their largest expenditures. J. Sansbury's account book in Eatontown lists innumerable purchases of coffins. Most

"Afro-American Cigar Store Indian" attributed to Job,
polychromed wood, ca.1800–1825, found in Freehold.
Courtesy of the New York State Historical Association.

were inexpensive, but Charles Juber paid eighty-five dollars for
"best quality Rose Wood." In times of need, churches gathered
together to purchase a decent burial for a member.[36]

The Civil War Years

As the United States became embroiled in the controversy
over slavery and prepared to split apart in 1860, New Jersey's
politicians offered little hope for black citizens. The state was
profoundly pro-Southern and openly hostile to talk of general

emancipation. In the election of 1860, New Jersey's voters favored Illinois Democrat Stephen Douglas, making it the only free state not awarding its electoral votes to Abraham Lincoln. Indeed, running closely behind Douglas and Lincoln was the candidate of the Southern Democrats, the proslavery John Breckinridge.[37] Within such a hostile environment, the accomplishments of the county's black citizens are remarkable.

The census of 1860 shows for the first time the full emergence of an economically independent black population in Monmouth. The number of free, independent blacks of both genders in Monmouth outnumbered dependent blacks by a ratio greater than four to one. Although census data on occupations shows blacks mired in low-paying or subsistence jobs—as laborers, day laborers, servants, or waiters—small but significant groups appeared in more independent occupations. Watermen, stage drivers, hostlers, blacksmiths, and oyster men eked out difficult but autonomous existences.[38]

Land ownership was the principal form of wealth for blacks in Monmouth County. As new towns emerged around the county, blacks sought opportunity through real estate in newer developed areas and in established towns in the east. Significant independent black populations developed in the newer towns of Ocean, Atlantic, Raritan, and Manalapan. Although the 1860 census records show many blacks with no land or with property worth less than $500, they also reveal twenty-four blacks in the county whose personal property exceeded $1,000 in value. The richest of these twenty-four was William Larebe of Upper Freehold, whose land was valued at $4,500. Significantly, Larebe's personal estate was worth only $50, less than a third of the average of $178 for black landowners with property worth over $1,000. The total worth of black real estate in Monmouth County in 1860 was $78,341, an average of about $302 for each listed property owner.[39]

How did Monmouth's black land-owning class compare with

similar groups? Few studies have analyzed the wealth of rural free blacks in the North. Joan Geismar's study of Skunk Hollow in Bergen County, N.J., uncovered a total property value of over $600, divided among but six property owners. Loren Schweninger offers fuller analysis of free blacks in the upper South in the antebellum era. By comparison, Monmouth County's average holdings are far smaller than those of free blacks in Kentucky, Maryland, Missouri, Virginia, North Carolina, and Tennessee, states in which, one would think, free blacks faced similar if not worse barriers to advancement than their northern counterparts.[40] The disparity may be partly explained by Monmouth County's high land values.

As Kathryn Grover has pointed out in her study of African Americans in Geneva, N.Y., property ownership offered blacks more than the usual psychological benefits in the mid-nineteenth century. In New York and New Jersey, no black without land could be a citizen until 1871. Although voting was still an elusive goal, land ownership seemed the best means to obtain the suffrage. Unlike bank savings or investments in stocks and bonds—still uncommon for poor whites or blacks—property ownership gave tangible wealth. Once acquired, land and a home offered succor from the world and a base for a subsistence income. Nor did a black freeholder have to beg a white landlord for a home.[41]

Probate records also reveal a tiny black middle class with its own supportive lending system. Monmouth County blacks did not invest heavily in personal property other than land and farm equipment. Lorenzo Schenck and Hagar Denise, two of the more prosperous, owned few possessions. Both left estates of which the larger portion comprised outstanding loans to other blacks. Denise owned only a few chairs and quilts, yet her estate inventory listed over $600 owed by two neighboring blacks. She also bequeathed $200 to her niece and another $100 to a nephew. Schenck's personal estate, including farm equipment,

Charles Williams and Julia Reevey, shown here in these charcoal re-touched photographs, purchased property in Fair Haven in 1855 and built a house that today is a local landmark. Courtesy of Winifred Robards and Harold Albert.

was worth about $350, but he was owed over $1,500. Blacks also began to act as executors of each others' estates. Less wealthy blacks were able to bequeath plots of land to their relatives. Peter Rock distributed four small parcels of land to his sons, as did Henry Cummings and Caesar Bennett. Bennett's estate was worth only $58, of which $18 were promissory notes.[42]

Although African Americans in 1860 could not be sanguine about political reverses of the previous decade, any one of them who cast a backward glance across the thirty-five years of man-dated manumissions must have been struck by how far free blacks had advanced their position in the course of a generation. Land ownership, organization of churches and schools, and the rise of a small middle class all heralded the arrival of a people of substance. These major strides had occurred despite living in a county where slavery was a very recent memory and for some still a reality, Monmouth blacks made major strides. Virtually all were former slaves or the children of such. They were deeply aware of the deprivations of their past, and they understood how far they had come.

As controversies over slavery and secession fractured the United States, New Jersey showed a grudging loyalty to the Union through a series of assembly resolutions that called for a peaceful settlement with the newly organized Confederate states. Among the extraordinary motions passed were recognition of Southern property rights over slaves, unqualified support for the repressive Fugitive Slave Act of 1850, and a series of laws attempting to hinder any movement of black freed people into the state. Throughout the Civil War, New Jersey politicians remained warm to the Southern cause, provoking President Lincoln to suspend the writ of habeas corpus in the state and to arrest a seditious newspaper editor. Early in the war Irish rioters battled police in an attempt to close the draft in Monmouth. Later, Southern agents dressed as women infiltrated Union troops at Camp Vredenburg in Monmouth, intending to recruit defectors. Confederate confidence in New Jersey's pro-Southern attitudes attests to the state's continuing proslavery sentiment.[43]

In 1863, the year the Emancipation Proclamation went into effect, New Jersey passed the infamous "Peace Resolutions," which denied Lincoln's ability to emancipate the slaves by proclamation and advocated, in the midst of war, that the Union seek a peaceable agreement with the Confederacy. New Jersey politicians worried about a massive slave insurrection in the aftermath of the proclamation. In 1864 New Jersey repeated its rejection of Lincoln by voting for his Democratic opponent, George B. McClellan, in the presidential election, the only northern state to do so.[44] (McClellan, a Philadelphia native and indecisive general, was later elected governor of New Jersey, serving 1878–81.)

Initially there was little that blacks in Monmouth could do to support the Union cause. Despite Frederick Douglass's pleas,

President Lincoln and his generals were reluctant to accept black volunteers. However, in the months after the Emancipation Proclamation was effected, on January 1, 1863, Monmouth's African Americans, like their brethren across the North, flocked into the Union Army and Navy. At least 156 blacks from Monmouth joined the Union forces between September 1863 and the close of the war in April 1865.

Most recruits were very young. Todd Allen, Adam Berry, James Conover, Thomas Frisby, James Logan, and Stephen Parry were only eighteen. But some black volunteers from Monmouth were much older. George Washington Elliott, James Forman, and Charles Handy were all forty-four, an advanced age for a recruit. Some whites earned money finding blacks willing to volunteer; others paid local blacks to substitute for them in the service.[45]

New recruits traveled to Freehold, the point of enlistment, for medical inspection, then to Philadelphia, where blacks reported to the general distribution center at Camp Penn. A few never made it past the center, deserting early in their military careers. Although a few recruits were sent singly to isolated regiments, most of Monmouth's black soldiers could be found in the 41st and 43d Regiments of the U.S. Colored Troops. Company C of the 43d Regiment had seventeen soldiers from Monmouth. These soldiers served as teamsters and pioneers (scouts) in the Virginia and Texas campaigns.[46] By 1864 Monmouth County officials had formed their own colored regiment to fulfill the county's militia quotas.

At least ten of these black soldiers died in combat. Others returned home with lifetime disabilities. Their pension applications cite wartime injuries that haunted them later. Silas Reeves suffered from chronic bronchitis and rheumatism contracted in rainy weather while on campaign in Virginia. James Morford contracted "ruptures" from exposure in the line of duty at Fort Barreas, West Florida. Cato Smith, who rose to the rank of sergeant in Company E of the 32d Regiment, came home with a broken constitution and died in 1871.[47]

Despite the contributions of these black veterans, New Jersey's white population remained hostile after the war to black rights. Movements to extend suffrage to blacks met with stony rejection. Federal proclamations and amendments passed in New Jersey through the back door. In 1863 Governor-elect Joel Parker, a native of Monmouth County, denounced the Emancipation Proclamation, while the state Democratic Party voted overwhelmingly to overturn it.[48] The Thirteenth Amendment, designed to end slavery, was initially defeated in New Jersey. So too were the Fourteenth Amendment, guaranteeing due process and citizenship, and the Fifteenth Amendment, insuring universal male suffrage.

New Jersey was not alone in denying full citizenship to blacks: referendums to enfranchise blacks were defeated in eight northern states between 1865 and 1869, including New York and Connecticut. New Jersey, together with Pennsylvania and Lincoln's Illinois did not even bring the issue before the voting public. Black males in New Jersey were not enfranchised until 1870, when the Fifteenth Amendment was ratified. (Black females, of course, had to wait, along with women of all colors, until the ratification of the Nineteenth Amendment in 1920.) The last legal vestige of slavery was removed in 1880, when the assembly abolished a law passed 150 years before permitting masters to bring troublesome slaves to the workhouse for whippings.[49]

In northern cities a resurgent black intellectual class abetted by white reformers and a nascent black middle class, offered a viable alternative to antebellum racism. But in rural Monmouth County, blacks remained isolated in a hostile and oppressive environment. Even so, Monmouth's African Americans made steady strides toward economic and personal freedom. At times their gains were slight and correspondingly fragile, yet together these rural black folk demonstrated a toughness, a tenacity, and a courage born out of generations of slavery. At the brink of the Civil War, Monmouth's black population owned land, operated churches and schools, and sustained a vibrant folk culture. To have achieved this measure of independence was a remarkable feat. By 1870 Monmouth's black males finally won full citizenship, a right many of them had earned in battle.

Notes

1. For Aaron and Abram escaped from Conover, see *Monmouth Democrat* (Freehold, N.J.), May 14, 1840.

2. Walter R. Fee, *The Transition from Aristocracy to Democracy in New Jersey, 1789–1829* (Somerville, N.J., 1933), 129–32.

3. For reviews of the politics of slavery in New Jersey during this period, see Charles Merriam Knapp, *New Jersey Politics during the Period of the Civil War and Reconstruction* (Geneva, N.Y., 1924), 5–23, and Herbert Ershkowitz, "New Jersey Politics in the Era of Andrew Jackson, 1820–1837" (Ph.D. diss., New York University, 1965). For leadership, see David Levine, "Party-in-the-Legislature: New Jersey, 1829–1844" (Ph.D. diss., Rutgers University, 1971), 61.

4. For the North American Phalanx, see Carl J. Guarneri, *The Utopian Alternative: Fourierism in Nineteenth-Century America* (Ithaca, N.Y., 1991), 257–58. For the contrast between the New England approach seen originally at Brook Farm and the approach of the Fourierists, see for example Octavius Brooks Frothingham, *Transcendentalism in New England: A History* (1876; reprint, Gloucester, Mass., 1965), 165–71. For a report of a Fourier community that differed "more in accidents than in essence from a [slave] plantation," see also Robert Southey, *A Journal of a Tour in Scotland in 1819*, ed. C. H. Herford (London, 1929), 261–65.

5. Arthur Zilversmit, *The First Emancipation: The Abolition of Slavery in the North* (Chicago, 1967), 217.

6. *Ibid.*, 219–20; Knapp, *New Jersey Politics*, 5–7; and Alvan Stewart, *A Legal Argument before the Supreme Court of the State of New Jersey at the May Term, 1845, at Trenton, for the Deliverance of 4,000 Persons*

from Bondage (New York, 1845). See also the Memorial of the New Jersey Anti-Slavery Society (Boonton), January 17, 1843, Archives Section, Division of Records and Archives Management, Separtment of State, Trenton, N.J. (hereafter cited as New Jersey State Archives).

7. For discussion of laws and court decisions of 1845–46, see Lee Caligaro, "The Negro's Legal Status in Pre-Civil War New Jersey," *New Jersey History* 85 (1967): 170–73. Giles R. Wright, *Afro-Americans in New Jersey: A Short History* (Trenton, N.J., 1988), 26. Zilversmit, *The First Emancipation*, 221–22.

8. *Black Birth Book of Monmouth County, New Jersey, 1804–1848* (Freehold, N.J., 1989), 15–16.

9. For Paterson, see Black Birth Book, 16.

10. For Yaff, see *Monmouth Democrat* (Freehold), March 5, 1835. For female slave of Peter Smock, see *ibid.*, November 8, 1837. For Lucy, see Sale of Betty and Lucy, October 16, 1837, see also "Sale of Candis," May 18, 1836. Monmouth County Historical Association, Freehold, N.J. For eight slaves, see *Monmouth Democrat*, October 5, 1837. For eight-year-old girl, see *Monmouth Democrat and Farmer and Workingman's Advocate* (Freehold), June 25, 1840. For Jack, see Deed of Sale between Joseph Doty and Charles J. Hendrickson, March 4, 1849, Monmouth County Historical Association, Freehold, N.J.

11. For notices, see "$10 Reward," Broadside Advertisement of September 21, 1830 for "Elias, also known as Bob," Monmouth County Historical Association, Freehold, N.J. For newspaper advertisments, see *Monmouth Democrat* (Freehold), March 12, 1835, July 7 and August 18, 1836, November 8, 1837, January 25, August 23, and September 6, 1838, May 14, 1840; *Monmouth Democrat and Farmer's and Workingmen's Advocate* (Freehold), June 25, 1840; *Monmouth Inquirer* (Freehold), May 21, June 2 and 9, and September 8 and 22, 1836.

12. For notices in the 1840s, see *Monmouth Inquirer* (Freehold), October 2, 1841, February 6, 1845 (Hannah), October 27, 1846, June 3, 1847, July 13, 1848, September 26, 1857 (Charley and Hekekiah Mulberry).

13. Slave and Manumissions File, 1771–1837 and Miscellaneous Book C, 128, 144, 147, Monmouth County Archives, Manalapan, N.J. The last recorded manumission was not in Monmouth. Paul Van Brunt of Bedminister Township, Somerset County, freed Harry on January 8, 1862. See Somerset County Manumissons, 1823–1862, reel 212, Somerset County Records, New Jersey State Archives. See also Carter G. Woodson, *Free Negro Owners of Slaves* (Washington, D.C., 1924), 23.

14. For Lydia Conover, see Item M10579; for Hendrick Hendrickson, Item M10518, in Monmouth County Wills, New Jersey State Archives.

15. Tax Lists for Upper Freehold Township, 1839, Monmouth County Historical Association, Freehold, N.J. For wills, see Robert Jobs, M10348; Hagar Smock, M10372, Monmouth County Wills, New Jersey State Archives. See also wills of Samuel Voorhees, M10489; Richard White, M10185; John Berry, M10191; and Silves Johnson, M10137, *ibid.*

16. For black insolvencies, see, for example, entries for Thomas Bowls, Samuel Braley, Moses Fields, Stephen Hendrickson, Lunn Higgins, Jonathan Riles, James Riley, Richard Schenck, Jr., John Senick, Cornelius Thompson, Ralph Van Brackle, Primus Vanderveer, Oliver Vincent and Thomas White, in Insolvent Debtors File, Monmouth County Archives, Manalapan, N.J. See also William Imlay, Justice of the Peace, Docket Book, 1828–1840, Special Collections, Alexander Library, Rutgers University, for Adam Congo's default of $12. For other indicators of poverty, see Commitments to the Poor House for Primus Belden, 1832 and Jeremiah Bowne, 1832, in Garret P. Conover Papers, Cherry Hall Papers, box 2, folder 8, Monmouth County Historical Association, Freehold, N.J.

17. See Monmouth County Coroner's Inquests, ser. 300, Monmouth County Archives, Manalapan, N.J.

18. For digging graves, see J. Sansbury, Day Book, Job Throckmorton Papers, Alexander Library, Rutgers University. For advertisement, see *Monmouth Inquirer* (Freehold), May 19, 1836.

19. For 1840 census enumeration of occupations anad dependence see Graham R. Hodges, "African Americans in Monmouth County, New Jersey, 1784–1860 (Lincroft, N.J., 1992), 69–74. For 1850 numbers see *Ibid.*, 77. Laborers constituted 434 of 534 listed occupations for free laborers in 1850. For contract, see Farm Accounts, 1851–1859, John S. Holmes Papers, Monmouth County Historical Association, Freehold, N.J.

20. See Hodges, "African Americans in Monmouth County," 75. County-wide, 921 of 1,129 males and 936 of 1,152 females were under forty years of age. Overall, 1,857 of 2,281 black residents of Monmouth were under forty years of age. For declining rural birth rates, see Lee A. Craig, *To Sow One Acre More: Childbearing and Farm Productivity in the Antebellum North* (Baltimore, 1993), 93–107.

21. Ann Patton Malone, *Sweet Chariot: Slave Family and Household Structure in Nineteenth-Century Louisiana* (Chapel Hill, N.C., 1992), 7–8.

22. The figures for 1840 and 1850 are derived from the Manuscript Census for New Jersey, Sixth Census, 1840 and Manuscript Census for New Jersey, Seventh Census, 1850, Special Collections, Alexander Library, Rutgers University.

23. For Cole and Miller see Manuscript Census for New Jersey, Seventh Census of the United States of America, 1850, Special Collections, Alexander Library, Rutgers University. For Hagar Smock, see inventory M10372, for Robert Jobs, see M10348, both in Monmouth County Wills, New Jersey State Archives. See also John Berry, M10191; Isaac Vincent, M11898; and Silves Johnson, M10137, *ibid*. For sales of looking glasses, see J. Sansbury, Day Book, 30, 193, *ibid*.

24. These reports reflect local traditions; however, two historians say that the underground railroad ran slightly east of Monmouth, from Trenton to New Brunswick. See Wilbur H. Siebert, *The Underground Railroad from Slavery to Freedom* (New York, 1898), 121–25, and William Still, *The Underground Rail Road* (Philadelphia, 1872). For traditions of underground railroad in Monmouth, see Elizabeth Wright-Miers to author, February 15, 1995, author's collection.

25. For coverage of these developments, see Clement A. Price, *Freedom Not Far Distant: A Documentary History of Afro-Americans in New Jersey* (Newark, 1980), 91, and Knapp, *New Jersey Politics*, 167–75.

26. For black marriages in white churches, see Holmdel Dutch Reformed Church Marriage Records, 188, 190, 192; Church Register for Old Brick Church, Marlboro Township, 1709–1851; and St. Peter's Church, Freehold, Church Records, 1837-1893, 18; all in Monmouth County Historical Association, Freehold, N.J.

27. Few of the state's blacks embraced the idea of colonization. At the same time, African American leaders in New York, New Jersey, and Pennsylvania labeled the colonization movement as an impediment to racial progress. For a survey of the rise of colonization movement and the black response in New Jersey, see Price, *Freedom Not Far Distant*, 89, 94–113. For Clay quote see James J. Hopkins, et. al *The Papers of Henry Clay*, 11 vols. (Lexington, Ky., 1959–1992), 2:384.

28. For histories of these churches, see Joseph Morgan, *Morgan's History of the New Jersey Conference of the A.M.E. Zion Church from*

1872–1887 and of Several Churches as Far as Possible, from the Date of Congregation with Biographical Sketches of the Members of the Conference (Camden, N.J., 1887), 57–71. For incorporation of black churches see entries for Free African Church of Shrewsbury (March 10, 1842); African Methodist Episcopal Church of Freehold (October 21, 1850); African Methodist Episcopal Church of Macedonia Zion Church (August, 1853); African Church of Allentown (June 18, 1853); African Methodist Episcopal Church of Fair Haven (March 30, 1861) all in Corporation Book for Monmouth County, 1667–1891, Monmouth County Archives, Manalpan, N.J. Lenora Walker McKay, *The Blacks of Monmouth County: A Bicentennial Tribute* (n.p., 1976), 45–54, and Timothy J. McMahon, *Historical Research on The Fisk Chapel* (Fair Haven, N.J., 1991). For early history of the A. M. E. Zion Church, see C. Eric Lincoln and Lawrence H. Mamiya, *The Black Church in the African American Experience* (Durham, N.C., 1990), 47–76.

29. Church Register, 1834–1856, of Old First Methodist Church at Long Branch Station, book A, 149, Monmouth County Historical Association, Freehold, N.J. For Doane's visit, see *The Episcopal Address to the Seventy-First Annual Convention in Grace Church, Newark, Wednesday, May 31, 1854 by the Rt. Rev. George Washington Doane, D.D. LL.D.* (Burlington, N.J., 1854), 13–14.

30. W[illiam] E[dward] B[urghardt] Du Bois, *The Souls of Black Folk* (1903; reprint, New York, 1969), 211.

31. Morgan, *Morgan's History*, 31–32, 59, 63, 72, 81; McKay, *Blacks of Monmouth County*, 62; Tax Lists for Upper Freehold Township, 1839. For a later Monmouth black minister, see Morgan, *Morgan's History*, 11, 18, 29, 38. For Wooby and Berry, see inventories M14446 and M14840, Monmouth County Wills, New Jersey State Archives.

32. For controversy and fire, see McKay, *Blacks of Monmouth County*, 31. McKay also reports on a school in Allentown. For Freehold, see Reports of the School Committee of Town Superintendent of Upper Freehold Monmouth County, New Jersey, 1846–1867, Monmouth County Historical Association, Freehold, N.J. For 1850, see *Statistics of the United States, Seventh Census of the United States of America* (Washington, D.C., 1851), 2:145.

33. For the classic discussion of naming and its political meaning, see Sterling A. Stuckey, *Slave Culture: Nationalist Theory and the Foundations of Black America* (New York, 1987), especially chapters 2–4.

34. For Bergen County, see Graham Hodges, *Black Resistance in Colonial and Revolutionary Bergen County, New Jersey* (River Edge, N.J., 1989), 10–12. For argument that blacks no longer believed their souls returned to Africa, see William D. Piersen, *Black Yankees: The Development of an Afro-American Subculture in Eighteenth-Century New England* (Amherst, Mass., 1988), 151. For argument about graves, see Margaret Washington Creel, *"A Peculiar People": Slave Religion and Community-Culture Among the Gullahs* (New York, 1988), 319–21.

35. Job's cigar store Indian is part of the permanent collection at the New York State Museum, Cooperstown. For informative commentary, see David S. Cohen, " In Search of Carolus Africanus Rex," *The Journal of the Afro-American Historical and Genealogical Society* 5 (1984): 149–63.

36. For coffin records, see "J. Sansbury, Day Book," 5, 14, 16, 30, 40, 44, 46, 47, 66, 71, 90, 97, 98, 101, 105, 114, 189, 191, 203, 245, 167 (Juber), 175, 221, 245 (for church).

37. Knapp, *New Jersey Politics,* 25–41, 78–90; William C. Wright, *The Secession Movement in the Middle Atlantic States* (Rutherford, N.J., 1973), 98–124.

38. See Manuscript Census for New Jersey, Eighth Census of the United States of America, 1860, Special Collections, Alexander Library, Rutgers University. For the career of one businessman, see Carl Lane and Rhoda Freeman, "John Dipper and the Experience of the Free Black Elite, 1816–1836," *Virginia Magazine of History and Biography* 100 (1992): 485–514.

39. See Manuscript Census for New Jersey, Eighth Census of the United States of America, 1860, Special Collections, Alexander Library, Rutgers University.

40. Joan H. Geismar, *The Archaeology of Social Disintegration in Skunk Hollow: A Nineteenth-Century Black Rural Community* (New York, 1982), 42–44; Loren Schweninger, *Black Property Owners in the South, 1790–1915* (Urbana, Ill., 1990), 76.

41. See Kathryn Grover, *Make a Way Somehow: African-American Life in a Northern Community, 1790–1965* (Syracuse, N.Y., 1994), 75–77.

42. For these conclusions, see Lorenzo Schenck, inventory 14188M; Hagar Denise, inventory 13084M; Peter Benham, inventory 11605M; Peter Rock, inventory 14534M; Henry Cummings, inventory 14479M;

Caesar Bennett, inventory 13069M; all in Monmouth County Wills, New Jersey State Archives. For executors, see Monmouth County Deeds, 1847, bk. A-5, 467–68; 1833, bk. C-3, 487; 1854, bk G-6, 413, Manuscripts Collection, New Jersey Historical Society.

43. See Knapp, *New Jersey Politics,* 40-78, and Larry A. Greene, "The Emancipation Proclamation in New Jersey and the Paranoid Style," *New Jersey History* 93 (1973): 108–23. For Confederate agents, see [Ira K. Morris], *Recollections of Old Camp Vredenburg and An Incident in Freehold of the Battle of Monmouth: Southern Agents and Margaret Rue* (Freehold, N.J., 1905). William Gillette has recently argued that New Jersey's reputation as a pro-Southern state is unwarranted. His contention concerning New Jersey's eventual allegiance to the Union is well taken, but in light of evidence presented in the last two chapters, there is little contradiction in portraying New Jersey politics and society as favoring the Union and abolition but against black rights, as was the case in neighboring New York. See William Gillette, *Jersey Blue: Civil War Politics in New Jersey, 1854–1865.* (New Brunswick, N.J., 1995), 1–8, 71, 184–85.

44. Greene, "The Emancipation Proclamation in New Jersey," 118, and Gillette, *Jersey Blue,* 202, 214.

45. For black recruits, see Colored Regiments, Civil War File, Monmouth County Archives, Manalapan, N.J. Within this large file are many payment vouchers for white recruiters or acknowledgments of substitutions. For payments of bounties, see Gillette, *Jersey Blue,* 257–58.

46. *Record of Officers and Men of New Jersey in the Civil War, 1861–1865,* 2 vols., comp. William S. Stryker (Trenton, 1876), 2:1496–573. For position, see Orderly Book, 43d Regiment and Muster Rolls, Company B, box 5440–41, Civil War (Colored Troops Collection), National Archives, Washington, D.C.

47. Pension Records for Silas Reeves, 1067416; James Morford, 16512; Cato Smith, 275458, Military Pensions (Civil War), National Archives, Washington, D.C. See also William R. Onquee, 456544; Daniel W. Frost, 2485931; Nimrod Warren, 925766, *ibid.*

48. Gillette, *Jersey Blue,* 214, 257, 302, 319.

49. Knapp, *New Jersey Politics,* 75–78; Greene, "The Emancipation Proclamation in New Jersey," 112. For vote, see Marion Thomp-

son Wright, "Negro Suffrage in New Jersey, 1776–1875," *Journal of Negro History* 33 (1948): 168–224. For abolition of workhouse law, see Alfred M. Heston, *Slavery and Servitude in New Jersey—Story of the Slave. Paper Read before the Monmouth County Historical Association on October 30, 1902.* (Camden, N.J., 1902), 13.

EPILOGUE

Legacies of Slavery and Freedom

During the Civil War, no northern state had been more reconciled to southern beliefs than New Jersey. Joel Parker, the governor-elect from Monmouth County, openly denounced the Emancipation Proclamation, while the state Democratic Party voted overwhelmingly to overturn it. However, the scores of rural blacks, young and old, who left their plows to take up swords knew at first hand what it was they fought. Family histories, personal experiences of oppression, which before had seemed a local concern, now were swept into the center of the nation's struggles and tribulations. Never again would Monmouth County be confined by the particularities of its geographic circumstances.

Yet neither could the county escape its common, local memories. Slavery in Monmouth had been no fad, easily forgotten, but a custom two centuries in the making. There no less than in the South did the institution leave its deeply ingrained heritage of social and economic racism. Like slaveholders elsewhere, whites in Monmouth County were fond of recalling their humane and paternalistic management of chattel and were quick to congratulate themselves on the mildness of slavery as they had practiced it. One aged black revealed his contempt for such attitudes in 1865, just after passage of the Thirteenth Amendment finally and forever doomed slavery in New Jersey. Adam Johnson, formerly claimed by the Forman family of Freehold, was in his cups when he took up a stout stick and, recalling a "trouncing" given him during servitude, pounded his old master's grave with a vengeance. For blacks the memory of servitude was often bitter and hard to erase. Even in death there were reminders: at the beginning of the twentieth century, obituaries of former slaves in Monmouth newspapers customarily identified local African Americans as former slaves and named their erstwhile masters.[1]

Some of those Monmouth masters had no doubt cultivated a paternalistic version of slavery, as they claimed. A slave isolated on a small farm had been treated, one way or another, as a social child within the clan. And when that slave had been a domestic, integrated into the routines of family life—particularly when they had acted as surrogate parent to a new generation of masters—bonds of affection were not unlikely to develop (however conflicted these might be). For their part, whites had cultivated the ideal of the kitchen family, of an economic support system enriched with the measure of stability and security family alone can provide.

Slaves in Monmouth were often considered part of the extended household and, according to whites, were taken care of as long as they "knew their place." But their place was still one devoid of rights and freedoms granted other Americans at the same time. Still, the master-slave relationship provided both parties with long established and well-defined social roles. Thus, as late as 1920 an African American mother "gave" her son and daughter to the Meirs, an old Huguenot family of Monmouth County. Like eighteenth-century black mothers, she believed that domestic servitude was her offspring's best hope for a secure life. Her children, Mary and William Wright, evidently believed their mother. Until their deaths in 1979 and 1984, the two worked on the Meirs's Monmouth farms without pay, Mary as a cook and skilled domestic at the ancestral home in Cream Ridge, Upper Freehold Township, William as manager of the household, garden, and farm of a sibling nearby. Each had separate living quarters within "their" family's farmhouse. Neither ever dined with the families, nor was literate, nor married, nor had families of their own. By middle age their indenture was a well-established secure way of life. The Thirteenth Amendment might foreclose the possibilty of legal slavery, but it could not force open horizons of possibility for those who would choose devoted bondage. And the complexity of slavery's legacy is such that in choosing symbiotic servitude over uncertain freedom, Mary and William honored their mother.[2]

Still by the late nineteenth century, the line dividing the races was distinctly black and white. Other reminders of the repressive, violent character of slavery were bound to surface. On March 5, 1886, at least five white residents of Eatontown in eastern Monmouth took part in the lynching of a black man named Samuel Jackson, also known as Mingo Jack, for the rape of Angelina Herbert, a young white woman. Jackson, formerly the slave of Samuel Laird of Colt's Neck, was between sixty-three and seventy years old, and since his emancipation some forty years earlier had worked as a farm laborer, butcher, and, most notably, as a jockey for a famous race-horse, Mingo Chief of Philadelphia. Jackson had an unruly reputation and reputedly had been previously charged with sexual assault. Although he did not fit Herbert's description of her attacker and denied any knowledge of the crime, Jackson was arrested and placed in the Eatontown jail. After the sheriff left for the night, a mob broke into the jail, seized Jackson, beat him, and then hanged him from a tree.

In the aftermath several whites were arrested for the crime.

At the ensuing inquest several local blacks testified on the eld-
erly Jackson's behalf, while the prosecutor received death threats
from angry whites. In the midst of this racially-charged atmo-
sphere the accused lynching party was acquitted. In the following months, other whites were briefly detained, then released.
The case continued to roil Monmouth's population as black
citizens pushed for further investigation. Nearly two years later,
a black man named Richard Carney, a notorious gang member
and sexual criminal, confessed to the crime and exonerated Jackson. In 1893, shortly after the death of Angelina Herbert, a Philadelphia reporter revealed yet another confession for Herbert's
rape. This one from a black sailor named John Miller. Jackson's
death was one of a very few lynchings in the nineteenth-century
North; its occurrence in Monmouth and the botched prosecu-
tion that followed demonstrated that true justice for African
Americans was still in the distant future.[3]

For a century after the Civil War, whenever African Americans worked for whites on isolated farms or otherwise beyond
the sphere of governmental reconnaissance, vestiges of the paternalistic cottager system were likely to tinge economic and
social relations. Happily, old patterns derived from slavery were
eclipsed by the legacy of freedom that Monmouth's blacks had
forged for themselves. Isaac Vincent, the Middlesex freeman
last seen in 1809 contracting to work for Samuel Wright, succeeded in establishing an economic foothold in the county. His
large family multiplied and thrived, at least one direct line establishing themselves not far from the Merino Hill estate on
which Isaac had worked. By the century's end the Vincents
owned several truck farms of eighty to a hundred acres in the
Upper Freehold area. On these they bred cattle and grew corn,
wheat, and potatoes for the markets in nearby Trenton. The
family tradition of industry and community involvement was
being carried on at the time of writing by Isaac Vincent's great-
grand daughter, Aida Louise Vincent Dorin, still employed as a

cook in her ninety-seventh year, still active and faithful as a member of the Allentown A. M. E. Church, her memory and faculties undimmed. In her one could find a living embodiment of the practicality, the economic tenacity, the faith, the good humor, and the dignity that enabled nineteenth-century African Americans in Monmouth County not only to endure but to progress and prosper. As they did so, they prepared Monmouth County, perhaps unknowingly, for the radically new circumstances of the late nineteenth and early twentieth centuries.[4]

With the end of Grant's presidency and the collapse of Reconstruction in 1877 came a national conservative backlash against the newly emancipated freedmen. As James Weldon Johnson put it, "The South lost the Civil War in 1865, but by 1900, in the fight waged on the Negro battle front, it had conquered the North; and all through the old free states there was a tendency to concede that the grand experiment was a failure."[5]

In increasing numbers blacks were again following the North Star. But now they traveled overground, as economic refugees—first singly, then in mounting numbers until it seemed a tide was rising from the South. Blacks arrived to find a North whose sympathies and ministrations were now largely reserved for new European immigrants, whose racism was now unleavened by abolitionists' ethical or moral suasions—indeed, was hardened by the pervasive perception of black failure. Amidst this the very real achievements of northern African American communities were of signal importance. In Monmouth County over 200 years, but especially from 1804 to 1865, the period of all too gradual emancipation, African Americans had continually tried to petition, purchase, or preempt their freedom. Manumission had been granted singly and only after being "earned" by each individual. Setting aside the rank injustice of this practice, liberty thus gained had a gravity, a dignity that whites might ignore but could not efface. Further, it was a liberty unburdened by the inflated and idealized expectations—and subsequent disenchantment—that attended the "gift of freedom" bestowed by a white federal government all at once upon southern blacks. Moreover, the successes of Monmouth's free black community had been achieved not by the brilliant intellectuals of the race—the Frederick Douglasses, the John Russworms, the Henry Highland Garnets—but by ordinary laborers, teamsters, and farm hands. It is not hard to imagine the social crises and depredations that would have ensued from the Great Migration had there not been in place in the North black infrastructures strong enough to survive economic discrimination, racial hostility, and cultural condesension.

At the Civil War's end, New Jersey was the northern state with the highest percentage of blacks per capita (3.2 percent); in Monmouth County the proportion of blacks was twice again as large. In succeeding decades keeping pace with the white population, the African American population of the county grew rapidly, from 2,910 in 1870 to 6,907 in 1900, then even more rapidly in the twentieth century, moving past 30,000 in 1950 to its present height of over 43,000, accounting for about a tenth of the county's population.

By the late nineteenth century, distinct African American communities had emerged in Red Bank, Asbury Park and other cities along the resort-dominated coastline. Whereas black New Jersey was generally urban—by 1910 almost 75 percent of the state's black residents lived in cities—Monmouth County remained primarily rural. Southern blacks moving into Monmouth County fit well into the farm economy and worked for established black residents as well as for whites.[6]

Among the new southern immigrants was the Heath family, who joined the black community in Middletown in 1885. As founding members of the Clinton A. M. E. Zion Church, they inculcated in young Bertha Heath the potent values of "church, family, and work," values that took her to an nursing degree in

1930, a B.S. from New York University in 1948, and an M.S. in public health from Columbia in 1958.[7] Through families like the Heaths and institutions like the Clinton A. M. E. Zion Church, Monmouth County African Americans had continuity even in the late twentieth century with the struggles and hard-earned attainments of their enslaved and free forebears, who knew success to be the sum of a hundred setbacks and who fashioned their institutions to be pillars of spiritual support, balms for the wounds of racism, tools for lasting achievements.

It was in another church, the Zion M. E. Church of Belmar, that parishioners gathered on August 31, 1913, to commemorate the fiftieth anniversary of Abraham Lincoln's Emancipation Proclamation. The issuance of the proclamation, on 22 September 1862, had been an extraordinary historical moment for all African Americans, signaling a fundamental shift in federal policy and presaging freedom for millions. It was a moment well worth commemoration. The proceedings that August day included songs from a guest soloist, a reading of the proclamation, and an address by George William Swain, a white minister from Brooklyn. In his emotional speech Swain argued that "the colored race owes everything to Lincoln for its freedom [and] the white race owes him much for teaching it true loving Christianity." The tone of Swain's rhetoric suited the lofty sentiments of the occasion; the content was, of course, purest invention, spun on the looms of white mythmaking.[8]

As this study has tried to document, Monmouth's African Americans gained liberty not through enlightened "charity" alone, but through their own insistence that freedom was due them, through their resistance to bondage in many ways, for many years, through their persistence in building a black community that included churches, land ownership, education, and memories of Africa. Though Monmouth County's black men and women still had far to go before gaining a modicum of genuine rights, they already came to the Emancipation Proclamation and the Thirteenth Amendment as partners, sleeves rolled up, ready to work.

Notes

1. For a good example of nostalgia for slavery, see Andrew D. Mellick, Jr., *The Story of an Old Farm; or, Life in New Jersey in the Eighteenth Century* (Somerville, N.J., 1889). For obituaries, see Elizabeth Johnson, *Red Bank Register*, April 12, 1922, and Charles Reeves, *Red Bank Register*, September 9, 1900. For Johnson's story, see *Freehold Transcript*, February 3, 1893. I thank Randall Gabrielan for information in this paragraph.

2. William R. Meirs, Jr., communication to author, February 17, 1995.

3. The case quickly attracted the attention of the national press. See *The New York Times*, March 7, 8, 9, 12, 16, 24, 31, April 2, 1886; February 26, June 5, 1888. I benefited from research done by Mauro Baldanza of Oceanport, N.J., using information in *The Shore Press* (Asbury Park, N.J.), March 5 and 11, 1886. I am grateful to Mr. Baldanza for sharing his research with me.

4. Aida Louise Vincent Dorin, interview with author, March 1995.

5. James Weldon Johnson, *Black Manhattan* (1930; reprint New York, 1991), 128.

6. For a survey of black farm owners, see *The Negro in New Jersey* (Newark, N.J., 1932), 84. For population summaries, see Giles R. Wright, *Afro-Americans in New Jersey: A Short History* (Trenton, 1988), 45, 87–98.

7. Dedication Statement for Heath Center, Monmouth County [ca. 1985].

8. [George William Swain], *Fiftieth Anniversary Celebration of the Proclamation Emancipation of Abraham Lincoln, Sunday, August 31, 1913* (Brooklyn, N.Y., 1913).

BIBLIOGRAPHY

Primary Sources

Unpublished Manuscripts

BODLEIAN LIBRARY, OXFORD UNIVERSITY

[Harrison, Francis]. "Observations Humbly Offered to His Grace the Duke of Chandos. Sharing the Advantages Which the Royal African Company May Receive by Settling an Agency at New York in Order to Supply that Province, the Colonies at East and West New Jersey, Connecticut, Rhode Island, Narragansett and the Southwest Parts of New England with Slaves." Ms. Gough Somersetshire 7 (S.C. 18217).

CLEMENTS LIBRARY, UNIVERSITY OF MICHIGAN, ANN ARBOR

Adams, Sampson. Papers.

DEPARTMENT OF STATE, RECORDS AND ARCHIVES, TRENTON, N.J.

"An Estimate of the Rateables in the State of New-Jersey, 25 November 1784."

"Damages by the British in Essex . . . Bergen . . . Somerset . . . and Middlesex Counties, 1776–1782."

Governor's Papers [William Livingston], box 1.

Inquisitions on the Dead, 1688–1798, 4 vols., Public Record Office, 1931.

Monmouth County Wills, 1680–1870.

Tax Rateables Series, Monmouth County, 1777–1831.

Unrecorded Wills, 12 vols., 1675–1800, New Jersey.

FRIENDS LIBRARY, SWARTHMORE COLLEGE, SWARTHMORE, PA.
Shrewsbury Men's Monthly Meeting. Minutes, 1757–86.

HAGLEY LIBRARY, WILMINGTON, DELAWARE
Wright, Samuel G. Papers.

HAVILAND RECORD CENTER, NEW YORK CITY.
Oblong (Pawling) Monthly Meeting. Minutes, 1757–81.
"Shrewsbury Scrapbook."

SECOND MIDDLETOWN BAPTIST CHURCH, HOLMDEL, N.J.
Holmdel Sunday School. Records, 1826–36.

MONMOUTH COUNTY HISTORICAL ASSOCIATION, FREEHOLD, N.J.
Colts Neck, Freehold, Holmdel, and Marlboro Township Dutch Re-
    formed Churches, Baptismal Records, 1709–90.
Craig Papers.
Christ Church. [Shrewsbury, N.J.]. Baptisms, 1751–75.
Holmes, Asher, to William Livingston, 12 June 1780. Slavery File.
Old First Methodist Church, Long Branch Station. Register, 1834–56.
Old Tennent Church, [Freehold, N. J.]. Records. 5 vols.
Reports to the School Committee of the Town Superintendent of
    Upper Freehold, Monmouth County, N.J., 1846–1867.
Holmes, Samuel. Book of Accounts. Box 4. Cherry Hall Papers.
"Slave Bills of Sale, 1700–1840."
Upper Freehold Township. Tax Lists for 1839.

MONMOUTH COUNTY ARCHIVES, MANALAPAN, N.J.
Coroner's Inquests, 1800–1940.
Court of General Sessions, 1727–1870.
Court of Oyer and Terminer, 1727–1850.
Insolvent Debtors Papers, 1800–1900.

PIERPONT MORGAN LIBRARY, NEW YORK CITY
Gilder-Lehrman Papers.

NATIONAL ARCHIVES, WASHINGTON, D.C.
Individual Pension Records, U.S. Colored Troops, Civil War Pension
    Records.
Regimental Records, 41st and 43rd. Regiments, U.S. Colored Troops.

"Book of Negroes Registered and Certified after Being Inspected by the Commissioners Appointed for His Excellency Sir Guy Carleton, General and Commander-in-Chief on board Sundry Vessels in which they were Embarked to the time of Sailing from the Port of New York between April 23 and July 31, 1783" (bk. 1); "Book of Negroes Registered and Certified after Being Inspected . . . between July 3 and November 30, 1783" (bk. 2). Washington, D.C.

"Book of Negroes Inspected on the 30th November 1783 by Captains Gilfillan and Armstrong on Board the Fleet Laying near Statten Island in the Absence of the American Commissioners and Secretary, which Numbers Have Since Been Regularly Registered and Certified by Said Two Captains" (bk. 3). Washington, D.C.

NEW JERSEY HISTORICAL SOCIETY, NEWARK.

Dipper, John. Papers.

"Memorial of the New Jersey Anti-Slavery Society (Boonton), January 17, 1843."

NEW-YORK HISTORICAL SOCIETY, NEW YORK CITY

Nicoll, Charles. Day Book, 1780–1781.

"Shrewsbury, New Jersey, Town Poor Book, 1743–1848."

"Unidentified Account Book, Brookhaven, Long Island, 1774–1814."

NEW YORK PUBLIC LIBRARY, NEW YORK CITY

"American Loyalist Transcripts of the Manuscripts Books and Papers of the Commissioners of Entering into the Losses and Services of the American Loyalists Held under the Acts of Parliament of 23, 25, 26, 28, 29 of George III, Preserved amongst Audit Records in the Public Records Office of England, 1783–1790." 76 Volumes. Transcribed for the New York Public Library, 1898, vols. 15–16.

Hawkhurst, James. Account Book and Journal, 1797–1851.

ALEXANDER LIBRARY, RUTGERS UNIVERSITY, NEW BRUNSWICK, N.J.

Hyler, Adam. Papers.

Holmes, Colonel Asher. Papers, 1778.

Drummond, Robert. Farm Accounts, 1822–56.

Hendrickson Family. Papers.

Holmes, John S. Papers.

Imlay, William, Justice of the Peace. Docket Book, 1828–40.

Neilson, John. Farm Diary, 1802–32. Neilson Papers, bk. 1.

"James Tallman's Ledger from Monmouth County, 1800–1801."

Ten Eyck Family Papers, 1740s–1840s, box 3, folders 21, 22.

Schenck, Daniel. Ledger, 1799–1801.

Census of the United States of America for 1830, Monmouth County. Manuscript.

Census of the United States of America for 1840, Monmouth County. Manuscript.

Census of the United States of America for 1850, Monmouth County. Manuscript.

Census of the United States of Ameica for 1860, Monmouth County. Manuscript.

Morris, Lewis. Papers.

Throckmorton, Job. Papers.

Van Liew-Voorhees Family. Papers.

YALE UNIVERSITY ARCHIVES, NEW HAVEN, CT.

DeHart, John Van Cleef. Ledger, 1815–16.

Watson, William. Papers.

Newspapers

Freehold Transcript

Gaine's Weekly Mercury (New York)

Monmouth Democrat (Freehold)

Monmouth Enquirer (Freehold)

Monmouth Star (Freehold)

New Jersey Journal (Chatham and Elizabeth Town)

New York Gazette

New York Journal or the Weekly Advertiser

New York Mercury

New York Times

New York Weekly Journal (Zenger)

New York Weekly Post-Boy

Pennsylvania Evening-Post (Philadelphia)

Pennsylvania Gazette (Philadelphia)

Pennsylvania Packet (Philadelphia)

Red Bank Register

Royal Gazette (New York)

Shore Press (Asbury Park)

Spirit of Washington (Freehold)

Trenton Federalist
True American (Trenton)

Published Books, Booklets, and Articles

Abstract of the Returns of the Fifth Census of the United States, 1830. Washington, D.C.: Printed by Duff Green, 1832.

Acts of the Tenth General Assembly of New Jersey . . . Second Sitting. Trenton: Printed by I. Collins, 1786.

Adams, Francis D. and Barry Sanders. eds. *Three Black Writers in Eighteenth Century England.* Belmont, Calif.: Wadsworth Publishers, 1971.

Aggregate Amount of Each Description of Persons within the United States of America . . . According to Law, in the Year 1810. Washington, D.C.: U.S. Treasury Department, 1814.

Acts of the General Assembly of the Province of New-Jersey from the Surrender of the Government to Queen Anne, on the 17th Day of April in the Year of Our Lord, 1702, to the 14th Day of January, 1776. Edited by Samuel Allinson. Burlington, N.J.: Printed by I. Collins, 1776. Evans Microcard 14911.

A Genuine Narrative of the Intended Conspiracy of Negroes at Antigua. Dublin: Printed by R. Reilly, 1737. Signed: T. V. and others.

Anecdotes and Memoirs of William Boen, A Coloured Man, Who Lived and Died near Mount Holley, New Jersey. Philadelphia: Richards, 1834.

Archives of the State of New Jersey. 48 vols. Newark: Printed for the State of New Jersey, 1880–1949. 2nd Ser. 4 (1914), vol. 5 (1915).

A Short Account of the Trial of Cyrus Emlay, A Black Man, Who Was Convicted of Robbery, Arson, and Murder, on Thursday, May 28, 1801—Received His Sentence on Friday, the 29th, and Was Executed, Agreeably to Said Sentence, on Friday, June 21, 1801. Aged about 35 with His Confession Taken from His Own Mouth a Short Time Before His Execution. Burlington, N.J.: Printed by S.C. Ustick, 1801.

"Baptisms and Marriages of the Lutheran Church from 1725." *New York Genealogical and Biographical Record* 97–99 (1966–68): 97: 95–105, 163–70, 223–32; 98: 17–23, 92–95, 150–53, 222–24; 99: 105–12; 134–40; 227–31.

Barber, John H., and Henry Howe. *Historical Collections of New Jersey: Past and Present.* New York: Published for the Authors by S. Tuttle, 1846.

Black Birth Book of Monmouth County, New Jersey, 1804–1848. Freehold, N.J.: Office of the Monmouth County Clerk, 1989.

A Brief Account of the Province of East: New: Jersey in America, Published by the Scots Proprietors. Edinburgh: Printed by John Reid, 1683.

Bridenbaugh, Carl, ed. *Gentleman's Progress: The Itinararium of Dr. Alexander Hamilton, 1744.* Chapel Hill, N.C.: University of North Carolina Press, 1948.

Carman, Harry J., ed. *American Husbandry.* . . . (original printing London, 1775.) New York: Columbia University Press, 1939.

Cases Adjudged in the Supreme Court of New Jersey Relative to the Manumission of Negroes and Others Holden in Bondage. Burlington, N.J.: Dennis, 1793.

Catteral, Helen. *Judicial Cases Concerning American Slavery and the Negro.* 5 vols. Washington, D.C.: Carnegie Institution of Washington, 1936.

Colonial Laws of New York from 1664 to the Revolution. 5 vols. Albany: James B. Lyon, State Printer, 1896.

Compendium of the Enumeration of the Inhabitants and Statistics of the United States . . . for 1840. Washington, D.C.: Printed by Duff Green, 1841.

Crowder, Jonathan. *A True and Complete Portraiture of Methodism; or, The History of the Wesleyan Methodists.* New York: James Eastburn, 1813.

The Devil; or, The New Jersey Dance. N.p., n.d. [c.1790].

de Warville, J. P. Brissot. *New Travels in the United States of America.* Cambridge, Mass.: Harvard University Press, 1964.

Doan, George Washington. *The Episcopal Address to the Seventy-First Annual Convention in Grace Church, Newark, Wednesday, May 31, 1854 by the Rt. Rev. George Washington Doane, D.D. LL.D.* Burlington: Printed at the Gazette Office, 1854.

Donnan, Elizabeth, ed. *Documents Illustrative of the History of the Slave Trade to America.* 5 vols. Washington, D.C.: Carnegie Institution of Washington, 1935.

"Dover Township, 1773 Rateables." Edited by David Fowler. *Genealogical Magazine of New Jersey* 59 (1984): 115–18.

Diary of William Dunlap. 3 vols. New York: Printed for the New-York Historical Society, 1930–32.

Dunlap, William. *A History of the Rise and Progress of the Arts of Design in the United States,* 3 vols. Boston: C. F. Goodspeed, 1918.

Edsall, Preston W., ed. *Journal of the Courts of Common Right and Chancery of East New Jersey, 1683–1702.* Philadelphia: American Legal History Society, 1937.

Everett, Henry Lawrence, ed. *The Old Middletown Town Book, 1667 to 1700; The Records of Quaker Marriages at Shrewsbury, 1667 to 1731; The Burying Grounds of Old Monmouth.* N.p., n.d.

[Swain, George William.] *Fiftieth Anniversary Celebration of the Emancipation Proclamation of Abraham Lincoln. Sunday, August Thirty-first, Nineteen Hundred Thirteen. At the Zion M. E. Church, Belmar, New Jersey.* Brooklyn, N.Y.: Brooklyn Eagle Press, 1913.

Force, Peter. *American Archives.* 4th ser. 5 vols. Washington, D.C.: Printed and Prepared under an Act of Congress, 1843–53.

Freiburg, Malcolm, ed. *The Journal of Madam Knight.* Boston: Godine Press, 1972.

[Grant, Anne.] *Memoirs of An American Lady, with Sketches of Manners and Scenery in America as They Existed Previous to the Revolution.* New York: Printed for Samuel Campbell by D. and G. Bruce, 1809.

Graydon, Alexander. *Memoirs of His Own Time with Reminiscences of the Men and Events of the Revolution.* Philadelphia: Lindsay and Blackston, 1846.

Gren, Charles F. *Pleasant Hills, New Jersey, Lake Nescochoque, A Place of Older Days, An Historical Sketch.* N.p., n.d.

[Hartshorne, Richard.] *A Further Account of New Jersey in an Abstract of Letters Lately Writ from Thence, by Several Inhabitants There Resident.* 1676; facsimile, A. A. Brant, n.d.

Hepburn. John. *The American Defence of the Christian Golden Rule; or, An Essay to Prove the Unlawfulness of Making Slaves of Men.* New York, 1715.

Hopkins, James J. et al. eds. *The Papers of Henry Clay,* 11 vols. Lexington, Ky., 1959–1992.

Journal and Votes of the House of Representatives of the Province of Nova Caesaria or New Jersey, in the First Sessions of Assembly, Began at Perth Amboy, the 10th Day of November, 1703. Jersey City, N.J.: Printed by John H. Lyon, 1872.

Journal of George Fox. 8th ed. 2 vols. London: Friends Tract Association, 1891.

Journal of the Procedure of the Governor and Council of the Province of East-Jersey, from and after the First Day of December Anno Domini–1682. Jersey City, N.J.: Printed by John H. Lyon, 1872.

Karlsen, Carol F., and Laurie Crumpacker, eds. *The Journal of Esther Edward Burr, 1754–1757.* New Haven, Ct.: Yale University Press, 1984.

Kelsey, Rayner Wickersham, ed. *Cazenove Journal, 1794: A Record of the Journey of Theophile Cazenove through New Jersey and Pennsyl-*

vania. Haverford College Studies, 13. Haverford, Pa.: Pennsylvania History Press, 1922.

Klepp, Susan E., and Billy G. Smith, eds. *The Infortunate: The Voyage and Adventures of William Moraley, an Indentured Servant*. University Park, Pa.: Penn State University Press, 1992.

Larison, C. W., M.D. *Sylvia DuBois: A Biografy of The Slav Who Whipt Her Mistress and Gand Her Fredom*. Ringoes, N.J.: Larison, 1883.

Laws of the State of New Jersey. Revised and Published under the Authority of the Legislature by William Paterson. Newark, 1800.

Lieutenant James Moody's Narrative of His Exertions and Suffering in the Cause of Government since the Year 1776. 2nd ed. London, 1783.

Livingston, Robert G., to Henry J. Livingston, 18 June 1752. In *Dutchess County Historical Society Annual* 6 (1921): 54–58.

Manumission Book of Monmouth County, New Jersey, 1791–1844. Freehold, N.J.: Office of the County Clerk, 1992.

Mellick, Andrew D., Jr. *The Story of an Old Farm; or, Life in New Jersey in the Eighteenth Century*. Somerville, N.J.: Unionist-Gazette, 1889.

Memorial of the Mount Holly Monthly Meeting of Friends Concerning William Boen, a Coloured Man, Received in the Yearly Meeting of Friends, Held in Philadelphia, 1829. Philadelphia: Representative Committee, 1831.

Minutes of the Board of Proprietors of the Eastern Division of New Jersey from 1685 to 1794. 4 vols. Perth Amboy: Board of Proprietors, 1949.

Minutes of the Council of Safety of the State of New Jersey. Jersey City, N.J.: J. H. Lyon, 1872.

Morgan, Rev. Joseph H. *Morgan's History of the New Jersey Conference of the A. M. E. Church*. Camden. N.J.: Printed for the Author, 1887.

Moulton, Philips P. *The Journal and Major Essays of John Woolman*. New York: Oxford University Press, 1971.

"Notes on the State of New Jersey, Written August, 1776, by John Rutherford." *Proceedings of the New Jersey Historical Society*, 2d ser., 1 (1867): 79–90.

Prince, Carl E. et al., eds. *The Papers of William Livingston*. 5 vols. Trenton: New Jersey Historical Commission, 1979–90.

Ramsay, David. *The History of the American Revolution*. 2 vols. Philadelphia: R. Aiken, 1789.

Return of the Whole Numbers of People within the Several Districts of the United States . . . for the Year 1800. Washington, D.C.: William Duane, 1802.

Return of the Whole Numbers of People Within the Several Districts of the United States . . . for the Year 1790. Washington, D.C.: William Duane, 1802.

Sheridan, Eugene R., ed. *The Papers of Lewis Morris.* 3 vols. Newark: New Jersey Historical Society, 1991.

Smith, William. *Historical Memoirs.* Edited and compiled by William H. S. Sabine. New York: New York Public Library, 1956–71.

Stanton, Daniel. *A Journal of the Life, Travels, and Gospel Labours of a Faithful Minister of Jesus Christ.* Philadelphia: Joseph Crukshank, 1772.

Statistics of the United States, Seventh Census of the United States of America. Washington, D.C.: A. O. Nicholson, 1854.

Stewart, Alvan. *A Legal Argument before the Supreme Court of the State of New Jersey, at the May Term, 1845, at Trenton, for the Deliverance of 4,000 Persons from Bondage.* New York: Finch and Weed, 1845.

Still, William. *The Underground Rail Road.* Philadelphia: Porter & Coates, 1872.

Stillwell, John E., ed. *Historical and Genealogical Miscellany: Data Relating to the Settlement and Settlers of New York and New Jersey.* 5 vols. New York: John Stillwell, 1903.

———. *Unrecorded Wills and Inventories, Monmouth County, New Jersey.* New Orleans, 1975.

Stryker, William S., ed. *Minutes of the Provincial Congress and Council of Safety of the State of New Jersey, 1775–1776.* Trenton: Naar, Day, and Naar, 1879.

Stryker, William S., comp. *Official Register of the Officers and Men of New Jersey in the Revolutionary War* Trenton: William T. Nicholson, 1872.

———. *Record of the Officers and Men of New Jersey in the Civil War, 1861–1865.* 2 vols. Trenton: John L. Murphy, 1876.

Stryker-Rodda, Kenn, ed. "Monmouth County Tax Rateables for 1778, 1779, 1780." *Genealogical Magazine of New Jersey* 49–50 (1974–1975): 49:75–88, 134–43, 50: 28–38, 81–94.

Tappert, Theodore, and John W. Doberstein. *The Journals of Henry Melchior Muhlenberg.* 3 vols. Philadelphia: Muhlenberg, 1942–58.

Thompson, Mary. *Sketches of the History, Character, and Dying Testimony of the Beneficiaries of the Colored Home, in the City of New York.* New York: J. F. Trow, 1851.

Thompson, Thomas. *An Account of Two Missionary Voyages by the Appointment of the Society for the Propagation of the Gospel in For-*

eign Parts. The One to New Jersey in North America, the Other from America to the Coast of Guinea. London: B. Dodd, 1758.

[Thompson, Thomas]. *A Letter from New Jersey in America, Giving Some Account and Description of that Province, by a Gentleman, Late of Christ's Church, Cambridge.* London: M. Cooper, 1746.

Trott, Nicholas, ed. *The Laws of the British Plantations in America, Relating to the Church, and the Clergy, Religion, and Learning.* London: Printed for B. Cowse, 1721.

Udemans, Godefridus Cornelisz, *'t Geestlijk roer van 't coopmans schip* (Dordrecht: F. Boels, 1638).

Van Horne, John C. *Religious Philanthropy and Colonial Slavery: The American Correspondence of the Associates of Dr. Bray, 1717–1777.* Urbana, Ill.: University of Illinois Press, 1985.

Whitefield, George. *Three Letters from Reverend G. Whitefield.* Philadelphia: B. Franklin, 1740.

Secondary Sources

Alleyne, Mervyn. *Roots of Jamaican Culture.* London: Pluto Press, 1988.

Anderson, Elaine De Met, and Ellen Thorne Morris. *Monmouth County 1790 Freeholders List.* Lincroft, N.J., 1985.

Aptheker, Herbert. *American Negro Slave Revolts.* New York: Columbia University Press, 1943.

Bailey, Rosalie Fellows. *Pre-revolutionary Dutch Houses in Northern New Jersey and Southern New York.* New York: William Morrow & Company, 1936.

Beattie, J. M. *Crime and the Courts in England, 1660–1800.* Princeton, N.J.: Princeton University Press, 1986.

Beckles, Hilary C. *Black Rebellion in Barbados: The Struggle Against Slavery, 1627–1838.* Bridgetown, Barbados: Antilles Publications, 1984.

———. *Natural Rebels: A Social History of Enslaved Black Women in Barbados.* New Brunswick, N.J.: Rutgers University Press, 1989.

———. *White Servitude and Black Slavery in Barbados, 1627–1715.* Knoxville, Tenn.: University of Tennessee Press, 1989.

Bender, Thomas, ed. *The Antislavery Debate: Capitalism and Abolitionism as a Problem in Historical Interpretation.* Berkeley: University of California Press, 1992.

Berkeley, Francis L., Jr. *Dunmore's Proclamation of Emancipation.* Charlottesville, Va.: University of Virginia Library, 1941.

Berlin, Ira and Philip D. Morgan, eds. *Cultivation and Culture: Labor and the Shaping of Slave Life in the Americas.* Charlottesville: University Press of Virginia, 1993.

Berlin, Ira et al. *The Wartime Genesis of Free Labor: The Upper South.* Ser. 1, vol. 2 of *Freedom: A Documentary History of Emancipation, 1861–1867.* New York: Cambridge University Press, 1993.

————. "The Structure of the Free Negro Caste in the Antebellum United States." *Journal of Social History* 9 (1976): 297–318.

————. "Time, Space, and the Transformation of Afro-American Society in the United States." In *Autre temps, autre espace: Études sur l'Amérique pré-industrial.* Edited by Elise Marientras and Barbara Karsky. Nancy: Presses Universitaires de Nancy, 1986. 131–46.

Bidwell, Percy Wells, and John I. Falconer. *History of Agriculture in the Northern States, 1620–1860.* Washington, D.C.: Carnegie Institution, 1925.

Blakeley, Phyllis R., ed. *Eleven Exiles: Accounts of Loyalists in the American Revolution.* Toronto: Dundurn Press, 1982.

Bogin, Ruth. *Abraham Clark and the Quest for Equality in the Revolutionary Era, 1774–1794.* Rutherford, N.J.: Fairleigh Dickinson University Press, 1982.

Bonomi, Patricia U. *Under the Cope of Heaven: Religion, Society, and Politics in Colonial America.* New York: Oxford University Press, 1986.

Boylan, Ann M. *Sunday School: The Formation of an American Institution, 1790–1880.* New Haven, Ct.: Yale University Press, 1988.

Burr, Nelson R. *The Anglican Church in New Jersey.* Philadelphia: Church Historical Society, 1954.

Bush, Barbara. *Slave Women in Caribbean Society, 1650–1838.* Bloomington, Ind.: Indiana University Press, 1990.

Butler, Jon. *Awash in a Sea of Faith: Christianizing the American People.* Cambridge, Mass.: Harvard University Press, 1990.

Caley, Percy Burdelle. "Dunmore: Colonial Governor of New York and Virginia, 1770–1782." Ph.D. diss., University of Pittsburgh, 1939.

Calligaro, Lee. "The Negro's Legal Status in Pre-Civil War New Jersey." *New Jersey History* 85 (1967): 168–80.

Carr, Lois Green, and Lorena S. Walsh. "Economic Diversification and Labor Organization in the Chesapeake, 1650–1820." In *Work and Labor in Early America.* Edited by Stephen Innes. Chapel Hill, N.C.: University of North Carolina Press, 1988.

Clemens, Paul G. E., and Lucy Simler. "Rural Labor and the Farm Household in Chester County, Pennsylvania, 1750–1820." In *Work and Labor in Early America*. Edited by Stephen Innes. Chapel Hill, N.C.: University of North Carolina Press, 1988.

Cohen, David Steven. *The Dutch-American Farm*. New York: New York University Press, 1992.

———. "In Search of Carolus Africanus Rex." *Journal of the Afro-American Historical and Genealogical Society* 5 (1984): 149–63.

Cooley, Henry Scofield. *A Study of Slavery in New Jersey*. Baltimore: Johns Hopkins University Press, 1896.

Craig, Lee A. *To Sow One Acre More: Childbearing and Farm Productivity in the Antebellum North*. Baltimore: Johns Hopkins University Press, 1993.

Craton, Michael. *Testing the Chains: Resistance to Slavery in the British West Indies*. Ithaca, N.Y.: Cornell University Press, 1982.

Creel, Margaret Washington. *"A Peculiar People": Slave Religion and Community-Culture Among the Gullahs*. New York: New York University Press, 1988.

Crow, Jeffrey J. *The Black Experience in Revolutionary North Carolina*. Raleigh, N.C.: Division of Archives and History, Department of Cultural Resources, 1977.

Davidson, Cathy. *Revolution and the Word: The Rise of the Novel in America*. New York: Oxford University Press, 1986.

Donor, Allan J. "The Melancholy Case of Captain Asquill." *American Heritage* 31 (1979): 81–92.

Du Bois, W[illiam] E[dward] B[urghardt]. *The Souls of Black Folk*. (1903); reprint, New York: Signet, 1969.

———. *The Suppression of the African Slave Trade to the United States of America, 1638–1870*. New York: Longmans, Green and Co., 1896.

Dunn, Richard C. "Servants and Slaves: The Recruitment and Employment of Labor." In *Colonial British America: Essays in the New History of the Early Modern Era*. Edited by Jack P. Greene and J. R. Pole. Baltimore: Johns Hopkins University Press, 1984.

Eblen, Jack Ericson. "New Estimates of the Vital Rates of the United States Black Population during the Nineteenth Century." *Demography* 51 (1974): 301–19.

Egmond, Florike. *Underworlds: Organized Crime in the Netherlands, 1650–1800*. Cambridge: Polity Press, 1993.

Ellis, Franklin. *The History of Monmouth County*. Philadelphia: Peck, 1885.

Ershkowitz, Herbert. "New Jersey Politics in the Era of Andrew Jackson, 1820–1837." Ph.D. diss., New York University, 1965.

Fee, Walter R. *The Transition from Aristocracy to Democracy in New Jersey, 1789–1829.* Somerville, N.J.: Somerset, 1933.

Fields, Barbara Jeanne. *Slavery and Freedom on the Middle Ground: Maryland during the Nineteenth Century.* New Haven, Ct.: Yale University Press, 1985.

Finkelman, Paul. ed. *The Law of Freedom and Bondage: A Casebook.* New York University School of Law Series in Legal History. New York: Oceana Publications, 1986.

———, ed. *Slavery & the Law.* Madison, Wis.: Madison House, 1997.

———. "State Constitutional Protections of Liberty and the Antebellum New Jersey Supreme Court," *Rutgers Law Journal* 23 (1992): 783–87.

Fischer, David Hackett. *Albion's Seed: Four British Folkways in America.* New York: Oxford University Press, 1989.

Fishman, George. "The Struggle for Freedom and Equality: African Americans in New Jersey, 1624–1849/1850." Ph.D. diss., Temple University, 1990.

Foucault, Michel. *Discipline and Punish: The Birth of the Prison.* Translated from the French by Alan Sheridan. New York: Pantheon Books, 1977.

Freiday, Dean. "Tinton Manor: The Iron Works." *Proceedings of the New Jersey Historical Society,* n.s., 74 (1952): 250–61.

Frey, Sylvia R. *Water from the Rock: Black Resistance in a Revolutionary Age.* Princeton, N.J.: Princeton University Press, 1991.

Gardner, D. H. "The Emancipation of Slaves in New Jersey." *Proceedings of the New Jersey Historical Society,* n.s., 9 (1924): 1–21.

Gaspar, David Barry. *Bondmen & Rebels: A Study of Master-Slave Relations in Antigua, with Implications for Colonial British America.* Baltimore: Johns Hopkins University Press, 1985.

Gates, Henry Louis Jr. *The Signifying Monkey: A Theory of African-American Literary Criticism.* New York: Oxford University Press, 1988.

Geismar, Joan H. *The Archaeology of Social Disintegration in Skunk Hollow: A Nineteenth-Century Rural Black Community.* New York: Academic Press, 1982.

Genovese, Eugene D. *Roll, Jordan, Roll: The World the Slaves Made.* New York: Pantheon Books, 1974.

Gerlach, Larry R. *New Jersey in the American Revolution, 1763–1783:*

A Documentary History. Trenton, N.J.: New Jersey Historical Commission, 1975.

————. *Prologue to Independence: New Jersey in the Coming of the American Revolution.* New Brunswick, N.J.: Rutgers University Press, 1976.

Gibson, George, and Florence Gibson. *Marriages of Monmouth County, New Jersey, 1795–1843.* Baltimore, Md.: Genealogical Pub., 1981.

Gillette, William. *Jersey Blue: Civil War Politics in New Jersey, 1854–1865.* New Brunswick, N.J.: Rutgers University Press, 1995.

Glatthaar, Joseph T. *Forged in Battle: The Civil War Alliance of Black Soldiers and White Officers.* New York: Free Press, 1990.

Gough, Robert J. "Black Men and the Early New Jersey Militia." *New Jersey History* 88 (1970): 227–38.

Greenberg, Douglas. *Crime and Law Enforcement in the Colony of New York, 1691–1776.* Ithaca, N.Y.: Cornell University Press, 1976.

Greene, Larry. "The Emancipation Proclamation in New Jersey and the Paranoid Style." *New Jersey History* 93 (1973): 108–24.

Grover, Kathryn. *Make a Way Somehow: African-American Life in a Northern Community, 1790–1965.* Syracuse, N.Y.: Syracuse University Press, 1994.

Guarneri, Carl J. *The Utopian Alternative: Fourierism in Nineteenth-Century America.* Ithaca, N.Y.: Cornell University Press, 1991.

Hatch, Nathan O. *The Democratization of American Christianity.* New Haven, Ct.: Yale University Press, 1989.

Hatfield, Edward F. *History of Elizabeth, New Jersey.* New York: Carleton and Lanahan, 1868.

Heston, Alfred M. *Slavery and Servitude in New Jersey: Story of the Slave: Paper Read before the Monmouth County Historical Association on October 30, 1902.* Camden, N.J.: Sinnickson Chew and Sons, 1902.

Hodges, Graham Russell, ed. *Black Itinerants of the Gospel: The Narratives of John Jea & George White.* Madison: Madison House, 1993.

————. *The Black Loyalist Directory: African Americans in Exile after the American Revolution.* New York: Garland, 1996.

————. *Black Resistance in Colonial and Revolutionary Bergen County, New Jersey.* River Edge, N.J.: Bergen County Historical Society, 1989.

————. "Black Revolt in New York and the Neutral Zone." In *New York in the Age of the Constitution, 1775–1800.* Edited by Paul A. Gilje and William Pencak. Cranbury, N.J.: Associated University Presses, 1993.

Hodges, Graham Russell, and Alan E. Brown, eds. *"Pretends to be Free":*

Runaway Slave Advertisements from Colonial and Revolutionary New York and New Jersey. New York: Garland Publishing, 1994.

Hoffman, Ronald. "The 'Disaffected' in the Revolutionary South." In *The American Revolution: Explorations in the History of American Radicalism.* Edited by Alfred F. Young. DeKalb, Ill.: Northern Illinois University Press, 1976.

Horton, James Oliver. *Free People of Color: Inside the African American Community.* Washington, D.C.: Smithsonian Institution Press, 1993.

Jensen, Joan M. *Loosening the Bonds: Mid-Atlantic Farm Women, 1750–1850.* New Haven, Ct.: Yale University Press, 1986.

Johnson, Whittington Bernard, *The Promising Years, 1750–1830: The Emergence of Black Labor and Business.* New York: Garland, 1993.

Jones, Alice Hanson. *Wealth of a Nation to Be: The American Colonies on the Eve of the Revolution.* New York: Columbia University Press, 1980.

Interpreter's Bible. 12 vols. Nashville: Abingdon Press, 1955.

Jordan, Winthrop D. *White Over Black: American Attitudes toward the Negro, 1550–1812.* Chapel Hill, N.C.: University of North Carolina Press, 1968.

Kaplan, Sidney. *The Black Presence in the Era of the American Revolution, 1770–1800,* [Greenwich, Ct.]: New York Graphic Society, 1973.

Knapp, Charles M. *New Jersey Politics during the Period of the Civil War and Reconstruction.* Geneva, N.Y.: W. F. Humphrey, 1924.

Kolchin, Peter. *American Slavery, 1619–1877.* New York: Hill and Wang, 1993.

Kulikoff, Allan. *Tobacco and Slaves: The Development of Southern Cultures in the Chesapeake, 1680–1800.* Chapel Hill, N.C.: University of North Carolina Press, 1986.

Landsman, Ned C. *Scotland and Its First American Colony, 1683–1765.* Princeton, N.J.: Princeton University Press, 1985.

Lane, Carl, and Rhoda Freeman. "John Dipper and the Experience of the Free Black Elite, 1816–1836," *Virginia Magazine of History and Biography* 100 (1992): 485–514.

Levine, David. "Party-in-the-Legislature: New Jersey, 1829–1844." Ph.D. diss., Rutgers University, 1971.

Leonard, Thomas Henry *From Indian Trail to Electric Trail: History of Atlantic Highlands.* Atlantic Highlands, N.J.: Atlantic Highlands Journal, 1923.

Levitt, James H. *For Want of Trade: Shipping and the New Jersey Ports, 1680–1783.* Collections of the New Jersey Historical Society, 17. Newark: The New Jersey Historical Society, 1981.

Lincoln, C. Eric and Lawrence H. Mamiya. *The Black Church in the African American Experience*. Durham, N.C.: Duke University Press, 1990.

Litwack, Leon F. *North of Slavery: The Negro in the Free States, 1790–1860*. Chicago: University of Chicago Press, 1961.

Lundin, Charles L. *Cockpit of the Revolution: The War for Independence in New Jersey*. Princeton, N.J.: Princeton University Press, 1940.

Lydon, James. "New York and the Slave Trade, 1700–1774." *William and Mary Quarterly*, 3d ser., 35 (1978): 375–95.

McAdoo, Harriet Pipes, ed. *Black Families*. Beverly Hills, Calif.: Sage Publications, 1981.

McCormick, Richard P. *Experiment in Independence: New Jersey in the Critical Period*. New Brunswick, N.J.: Rutgers University Press, 1950.

McKay, Lenora Walker. *The Blacks of Monmouth County: A Bicentennial Tribute*. N.p., 1976.

McLaughlin, William John. "Dutch Rural New York: Community, Economy and Family in Colonial Flatbush." Ph.D. diss., Columbia University, 1981.

McMahon, Timothy. *Historical Research on The Fisk Chapel*. Fair Haven, N.J., 1991. Typescript.

McManus, Edgar. *Black Bondage in the North*. Syracuse, N.Y.: Syracuse University Press, 1973.

Main, Jackson Turner. *Political Parties before the Constitution*. Chapel Hill, N.C.: University of North Carolina Press, 1973.

———. *The Social Structure of Revolutionary America*. Princeton, N.J.: Princeton University Press, 1965.

Malone, Ann Patton. *Sweet Chariot: Slave Family and Household Structure in Nineteenth-Century Louisiana*. Chapel Hill, N.C.: University of North Carolina Press, 1992.

Mandeville, Ernest W. *The Story of Middletown: The Oldest Settlement in New Jersey*. Middletown, N.J.: Christ Church, 1927.

Martin, George Castor. *The Shark River District: Monmouth County, New Jersey, and Genealogies of the Chambers, Corlies Families*. Asbury Park, N.J., 1914.

Mellick, Andrew D., Jr. *The Story of an Old Farm; or, Life in New Jersey in the Eighteenth Century*. Somerville, N.J.: Unionist-Gazette, 1889.

Menzies, Elizabeth G. C. *Millstone Valley*. New Brunswick, N.J.: Rutgers University Press, 1969.

Mintz, Sidney W. and Richard Price. *The Birth of African-American*

Culture: An Anthropological Perspective. Rev. Ed. Boston: Beacon Press, 1992.

Morrissey, Marietta. *Slave Women in the New World: Gender Stratification in the Caribbean*. Lawrence, Kans.: University Press of Kansas, 1989.

Morris, Ira K. *Recollections of Old Camp Vredenburg and an Incident of the Battle of Monmouth: Southern Agents in Freehold and Margaret Rue*. Freehold, N.J.: Monmouth Democrat Printer, 1905.

Moss, Richard Shannon. *Slavery on Long Island: A Study in Local Institutional and Early African-American Communal Life*. New York: Garland Publishing, 1993.

Moss, Simeon. "The Persistence of Slavery in a Free State." *Journal of Negro History* 35 (1950): 289–314.

Mullin, Gerald W. *Flight and Rebellion: Slave Resistance in Eighteenth-Century Virginia*. New York: Oxford University Press, 1972.

Narrett, David E. *Inheritance and Family Life in Colonial New York City*. Ithaca, N.Y.: Cornell University Press, 1992.

Nash, Gary B. *Forging Freedom: The Formation of Philadelphia's Black Community, 1720–1840*. Cambridge, Mass.: Harvard University Press, 1988.

———. *Race and Revolution*. Madison, Wis.: Madison House Publishers, 1990.

Nash, Gary B. and Jean Soderlund. *Freedom by Degrees: Emancipation in Pennsylvania and Its Aftermath*. New York: Oxford University Press, 1991.

Neely, Wayne Caldwell. *The Agricultural Fair*. New York: Columbia University Press, 1935.

Oliver, Paul. *Songsters and Saints: Vocal Traditions on Race Records*. New York: Cambridge University Press, 1984.

Parish, Peter J. *Slavery: History and Historians*. New York: Harper & Row, 1989.

Patterson, Orlando. *The Sociology of Slavery: An Analysis of the Origins, Development, and Structure of Negro Slave Society in Jamaica*. Rutherford, N.J.: Fairleigh Dickinson University Press, 1967.

Pennington, Edgar E. *Thomas Bray's Associates and Their Work among the Negroes*. Worcester, Mass.: American Antiquarian Association, 1939.

Pingeon, Francis D. *Blacks in the Revolutionary Era*. New Jersey's Revolutionary Experience, 14. Trenton, N.J.: New Jersey Historical Commission, 1975.

Pomfret, John E. *Colonial New Jersey: A History.* New York: Charles Scribner's Sons, 1973.

Potter, Jim. "The Growth of Population in America, 1700–1860." in *Population in History: Essays in Historical Demography.* Edited by D. V. Glass and D. E. C. Eversley. London: E. Arnold, 1965.

Price, Clement A. *Freedom Not Far Distant: A Documentary History of Afro-Americans in New Jersey.* Newark, N.J.: New Jersey Historical Society, 1980.

Prince, Carl E. *New Jersey's Jeffersonian Republicans: The Genesis of an Early Party Machine.* Chapel Hill, N.C.: University of North Carolina Press, 1967.

Quarles, Benjamin. *The Negro in the Civil War.* Boston: Little, Brown, 1953.

———. *The Negro in the American Revolution.* Chapel Hill, N.C.: University of North Carolina Press, 1961.

Raboteau, Albert J. "The Slave Church in the Era of the American Revolution." In *Slavery and Freedom in the Age of the American Revolution.* Edited by Ira Berlin and Ronald Hoffman. Charlottesville, Va.: University Press of Virginia, 1983.

Rasen, Edward J. "American Prisoners Taken at the Battle of Navesink, 1777. *Genealogical Magazine of New Jersey* 45 (1970): 93–104.

Rawley, James A. *The Transatlantic Slave Trade: A History.* New York: W. W. Norton, 1981.

Rediker, Marcus. *Between the Devil and the Deep Blue Sea: Merchant Seamen, Pirates, and the Anglo-American Maritime World, 1700–1750.* New York: Cambridge University Press, 1987.

Reed, Henry Clay. "Chapters in a History of Crime and Punishment in New Jersey." Ph.D. diss., Princeton University, 1939.

Reynolds, Helen Wilkinson. *Dutch Houses in the Hudson Valley before 1776.* New York: Dover, 1965, reprint of 1929 edition.

Rutman, Darrett. "Community Study." *Historical Methods* 13 (1980): 29–41.

Ryan, Dennis C. "Six Towns: Continuity and Change in Revolutionary New Jersey, 1770–1792." Ph.D. diss., New York University, 1974.

Salinger, Sharon V. *"To Serve Well and Faithfully": Labor and Indentured Servants in Pennsylvania, 1682–1800.* New York: Cambridge University Press, 1987.

Salmon, Marylynn. *Women and the Law of Property in Early America.* Chapel Hill, N.C.: University of North Carolina Press, 1986.

Salter, Edwin. *A History of Monmouth and Ocean Counties.* Bayonne, N.J.: E. Gardner and Sons, 1890.

Schmidt, Hubert. *Rural Hunterdon: An Agricultural History.* New Brunswick, N.J.: Rutgers University Press, 1945.

Schweninger, Loren. *Black Property Owners in the South, 1790–1915.* Urbana, Ill.: University of Illinois Press, 1990.

Sheridan, Richard B. *Sugar and Slavery: An Economic History of the British West Indies, 1623–1775.* Baltimore: Johns Hopkins University Press, 1973.

Siebert, Wilbur H. *The Underground Railroad from Slavery to Freedom.* New York: Macmillan, 1898.

Smith, Billy G. *The "Lower Sort": Philadelphia's Laboring People, 1750–1800.* Ithaca, N.Y.: Cornell University Press, 1990.

Soderlund, Jean. *Quakers & Slavery: A Divided Spirit.* Princeton, N.J.: Princeton University Press, 1985.

Spirenburg, Pieter. *The Spectacle of Suffering: Executions, and the Evolution of Repression: From a Preindustrial Metropolis to the European Experience.* New York: Cambridge University Press, 1984.

Steinfeld, Robert J. *The Invention of Free Labor: The Employment Relation in English and American Law and Culture, 1350–1870.* Chapel Hill, N.C.: University of North Carolina Press, 1991.

Stillwell, John E. *Historical and Genealogical Miscellany: Data Relating to the Settlement and Settlers of New York and New Jersey.* 4 vols. 1903; reprint, Baltimore: Genealogical Publishing Company, 1970.

Strassburger, John Robert. "The Origins and Establishment of the Morris Family in the Society and Politics of New York and New Jersey, 1630–1746." Ph.D. diss., Princeton University, 1976.

Stuckey, Sterling A. *Slave Culture: Nationalist Theory and the Foundations of Black America.* New York: Oxford University Press, 1987.

Sutherland, Stella. *Population Distribution in Colonial America.* New York: Columbia University Press, 1936.

Syrett, David. *The Royal Navy in American Waters, 1775–1783.* Aldershot, Hants, England: Scolar Press, 1989.

Tadman, Michael. *Speculators and Slaves: Masters, Traders, and Slaves in the Old South.* Madison, Wis.: University of Wisconsin Press, 1989.

Tebbenhoff, Edward H. "The Associated Loyalists: An Aspect of Militant Loyalism." *New York Historical Society Quarterly* 63 (1979): 115–44.

Thompson, Robert Farris. "An Aesthetic of the Cool: West African

Dance." In *The Theater of Black Americans, A Collection of Critical Essays*. Edited by Errol Hill. New York: Applause Books, 1987.

Van Der Merwe, Peter. *Origins of the Popular Style: The Antecedents of Twentieth-Century Popular Music*. Oxford: Oxford University Press, 1989.

Wacker, Peter O. *Land and People: A Cultural Geography of Pre-industrial New Jersey: Origins and Settlement Patterns*. New Brunswick, N.J.: Rutgers University Press, 1975.

Wacher, Peter O., and Paul G. E. Clemens. *Land Use in Early New Jersey: A Historical Georgraphy*. Newark, N.J.: New Jersey Historical Society, 1995.

Walling, Richard S. *Men of Color at the Battle of Monmouth, June 28, 1778: The Role of African Americans and Native Americans at Monmouth*. Hightstown, N.J.: Longstreet House, 1994.

Wax, Darold D. "The Negro Slave Trade in Colonial Pennsylvania." Ph.D. diss., University of Washington, 1962.

Wells, Robert V. *The Population of the British Colonies in America before 1776: A Survey of Census Data*. Princeton, N.J.: Princeton University Press, 1975.

White, Shane. *Somewhat More Independent: The End of Slavery in New York City, 1770–1810*. Athens, Ga.: University of Georgia Press, 1991.

Woodson, Carter G., comp. and ed. *Free Negro Owners of Slaves in the United States in 1830. . . .* Washington, D. C.: The Association for the Study of Negro Life and History, 1924.

Woodward, Carl R. *Ploughs and Politics: Charles Read of New Jersey and His Notes on Agriculture, 1715–1774*. New Brunswick, N.J.: Rutgers University Press, 1941.

Wright, Giles R. *Afro-Americans in New Jersey: A Short History*. Trenton, N.J.: New Jersey Historical Commission, 1988.

Wright, Marion Thompson. "New Jersey Laws and the Negro." *Journal of Negro History* 28 (1943).

———. "Negro Suffrage in New Jersey, 1776–1875." *Journal of Negro History* 33 (1948): 168–225.

Wright, William C. *The Secession Movement in the Middle Atlantic States*. Rutherford, N.J.: Fairleigh Dickinson University Press, 1973.

Yamin, Rebecca. "The Raritan Landing Traders: Local Trade in Pre-Revolutionary New Jersey." Ph.D. diss., New York University, 1988.

Zilversmit, Arthur. *The First Emancipation: The Abolition of Slavery in the North*. Chicago: University of Chicago Press, 1967.

INDEX

Officially Withdrawn